Thanks,
Frank!
MAY 2016

peace guerilla

unarmed and in harm's way,
my obsession with ending violence

Ben Hoffman

Published by CIIAN

Peace Guerilla
unarmed and in harm's way,
my obsession with ending violence

ISBN 978-0-986490705

Published by
The Canadian International Institute of Applied Negotiation
320 Laurier Avenue East
Ottawa, Ontario, Canada
K1N 6P6
Website: www.ciian.org

First published November 2009

Cover design: Kevin Hoffman
Text design: Gavin Ward Design Associates

Table of Contents

Acknowledgements   v

Main Characters   vii

Key Terms   xi

Maps of Africa, Sudan and Guinea-Bissau   xii

Preface   xiii

CHAPTER 1
Epiphany in Mostar   1

CHAPTER 2
Waging Peace with Jimmy Carter   13

CHAPTER 3
A Strategy to End War   21

CHAPTER 4
No Kony No Progress   27

CHAPTER 5
Clearing A Path For Peace With The LRA   45

CHAPTER 6
A Growing Sense Of Flim-Flam   55

CHAPTER 7
A Thumb Screw For Joseph Kony   71

CHAPTER 8
Flying Blind   95

CHAPTER 9
Checkmate   105

CHAPTER 10
All Roads Lead To Washington   131

CHAPTER 11
9/11   143

CHAPTER 12
Operation Iron Fist   155

CHAPTER 13
Endgame   165

CHAPTER 14
The Work Of Sisyphus   179

CHAPTER 15
Transformation   185

Epilogue   205

Acknowledgements

There is no greater honour to me than to enjoy the trust and confidence of another human being. As a professional mediator my service to others would not be possible unless I give and receive respect. And in being able to work as a trusted third party between warring sides, I am privileged to information that comes uniquely with the role I play. I am told things, in private and confidentially, that others are not to know. Yet, as I was sharing the experiences recorded here with colleagues at The Carter Center and others who take an interest in my work, I was repeatedly encouraged to "write a book" about this. They urged me to write about President Carter, the notorious Joseph Kony and his Lord's Resistance Army, about foreign and unknown Sudan – about the professional and personal challenges associated with trying to end war and establish peace, and then to prevent war in the first instance.

So I have done that. And to do it, I have had to reveal some things that if left unsaid, would make this true story a rather dry, technical account. I wanted the reader to see what goes on in the real world of peacemaking; and I wanted to reveal more of my own personal perspective than I typically convey. For, over thirty years now I have developed a professional mask, the mask of the clinician-mediator. This comes in part precisely because mediators do not take sides, and any inflections are easily interpreted by those in dispute as a potential bias. It comes in part because, like so many other professionals who encounter large amounts of human suffering and trauma, we must shield ourselves from the raw pain.

The story told here is entirely my version. When I have quoted people, I have drawn on my quickly scribbled field notes and on memory. And of course I have left strictly confidential things untold. It is my sincere hope that I have not taken unnecessary liberties that offend any of the people or the institutions that had a role to play in this story. Hopefully, this account will shed some new light on what is involved in peace work of this sort, and perhaps add to the base of knowledge upon which this work may be better undertaken.

And beyond acknowledging this feature of a book based on real people and circumstances which in some cases continue to be active today, I wish to acknowledge the help of the following people. For reviewing drafts of the text and providing helpful suggestions: Stan Suter, Alex Little, Milt Lauenstein, David Lord, Lou Kriesberg, Lisa Ibscher, Evan Hoffman and Warren Hoffman. For providing editorial assistance, Madelaine Drohan. And for much help on technical matters and the great boost she gave me in insisting that this was a story that I must write, my wife, Ann.

Main Characters

Archard, Mr. Douglas
Senior Country Representative, The Carter Center
Key member of Ben Hoffman's team, a career diplomat with previous experience in Sudan.

Babiker, Dr. Yahia
Deputy Director External Security, Government of Sudan
The main representative for the Government of Sudan, a senior negotiator and powerful leader in the Sudanese intelligence community, having responsibility for Sudanese relations with Joseph Kony and the Lord's Resistance Army.

Bashir, Al
President of Sudan
President of Sudan, a head of state with whom President Carter had strong, mutually respectful relations. A signatory to the Sudan Comprehensive Peace Agreement.

Burke, Mr. Chris
Field Representative, The Carter Center
Initially, a Carter Center intern who was invited by Ben to accompany him to Khartoum for a ten day assignment and who remained in the region, working in Sudan and Uganda for three years as a key member of Hoffman's team.

Bush, George W.
President of the USA
A new president whose support from the religious right in the USA had to be addressed to gain his approval for the USA to engage the Islamist Government of Sudan and to adopt a policy of peace in the war between the Sudanese government, based in the north, and the Sudan People's Liberation Movement/Army, based in the south.

Carter, Mr. Jimmy
former President of the USA; Chairman, The Carter Center
Mediator of the Nairobi Agreement signed by Uganda and Sudan in December, 1999; actively engaged in leading an institutional drive to help end the nineteen-year-old civil war in Sudan.

Crick, Mr. Tom
Senior Political Analyst, The Carter Center
An experienced employee of The Carter Center, recruited to play a second-in-command role on Hoffman's team, providing political and diplomatic strategic advice and taking on special assignments in Washington, DC, and in the field.

Garang, Dr. John
Leader, Sudan People's Liberation Movement/Army
A USA-educated PhD, a member of the Dinka tribe in southern Sudan, leader of the rebel forces, the Sudan People's Liberation Movement/Army. Died in a helicopter accident shortly after signing the Sudan Comprehensive Peace Agreement.

Ismail, Dr. Mustafa
Foreign Minister, Government of Sudan
A medical doctor who, as foreign minister, become increasingly engaged in talks to implement the Nairobi Agreement; highly influential in the policies adopted by the Sudanese government toward peace talks with the Sudan People's Liberation Movement/Army and in Sudanese relations with the Lord's Resistance Army.

Kony, Joseph
Leader, Lord's Resistance Army (LRA), Uganda
An enigmatic member of the Acholi tribe in northern Uganda, reputed to be a spiritualist and visionary; leader and commander-in-chief of the LRA in its northern insurgency against the Government of Uganda.

Lauenstein, Mr. Milton
Private US Citizen
Convened a group of conflict resolution experts to challenge them on whether and how violence can be reduced; privately financed a political violence prevention demonstration case in Guinea-Bissau.

Lord, Mr. David
Conflict Resolution Consultant, The Carter Center
Formerly, co-founder of Conciliation Resources, a nongovernmental conflict resolution organization; recruited by Ben Hoffman to take leadership in the north of Uganda in maintaining Carter Center relations with the Government of Uganda, the local community, including religious leaders, traditional Acholi leaders, and LRA contacts.

Mapendere, Mr. Jeffery
Senior Associate, The Carter Center
Formerly a freedom fighter in Zimbabwe, then member of the Zimbabwean Armed Forces, recruited to The Carter Center from studies in Canada to be a security expert on Hoffman's team.

Mbabazi, Amama
Minister of Defence, Uganda
A skilled lawyer-negotiator and senior politician in President Museveni's government, a known hardliner on relations with Sudan and in Uganda's policy and tactics with the Lord's Resistance Army.

Musevini, Yoweri
President, Uganda
The charismatic leader of Uganda who came to power by overthrowing Idi Amin's regime and whose attitude towards the Government of Sudan was hostile; a known supporter of the Sudan People's Liberation Army in its fight against the Government of Sudan, and a tough adversary of Joseph Kony and the Lord's Resistance Army.

Ndinyenka, Mr. Busho
Deputy Director General of External Security, Uganda
A career public servant in Uganda, responsible for a number of security assignments and the main representative for the Government in its issues with the Government of Sudan related to the Lord's Resistance Army.

Rugunda, Dr. Ruhakana
Minister of State, Government of Uganda
A senior member of Museveni's cabinet, a pediatrician educated in the USA, head of the Ugandan delegation in Ministerial talks with Sudan regarding implementation of the Nairobi Agreement.

Snyder, Mr. Charlie R.

Principal Deputy Assistant Secretary, Bureau of African Affairs, Department of State, Government of USA

A former senior officer in the US military, a policy advisor to Secretary of State Colin Powell and a key US official leading US efforts to bring an end to the civil war in Sudan.

Wai, General Tagme

Head of the Armed Forces, Guinea-Bissau

A member of the Balanta Tribe who assumed the key security position in Guinea-Bissau after General Seabra was assassinated in October 2004; and who was himself assassinated in March 2009.

Key Terms

Lord's Resistance Army

LRA is used throughout the text to mean both the name of the armed insurgency in northern Uganda, conducted by the Lord's Resistance Army, led by Joseph Kony, and the Lord's Resistance Movement, the political wing of the rebellion, also under the leadership of Kony.

Nairobi Agreement

The Nairobi Agreement was signed in Nairobi, Kenya, by President Museveni of Uganda, and President Al Bashir of Sudan in December, 1999. The Agreement was mediated by President Jimmy Carter and witnessed by Kenyan President Moi. The agreement outlined steps, that if successfully undertaken by both sides, with assistance from The Carter Center and UNICEF, would result in a restoration of diplomatic relations between these two hostile neighbours.

Sudan People's Liberation Army

SPLA is used throughout the text to mean the name of the armed rebellion in southern Sudan, conducted by the Sudan People's Liberation Army, led by Dr. John Garang.

Sudan People's Liberation Movement

The SPLM is the political wing of the rebel forces in southern Sudan, also under the leadership of Garang; a signatory to the Sudan Comprehensive Peace Agreement.

Sudan Peace Process

The Sudan Peace Process is the term used throughout the text to refer to a process intended to bring peace to a longstanding civil war between the Government of Sudan in Khartoum and the SPLA in the south of Sudan. The Sudan Peace Process based in Nairobi, Kenya was being conducted under the auspices of the Intergovernmental Authority on Development, an intergovernmental regional body of states in the Horn of Africa.

Maps of Africa,
Sudan (insert) and Guinea-Bissau (insert)

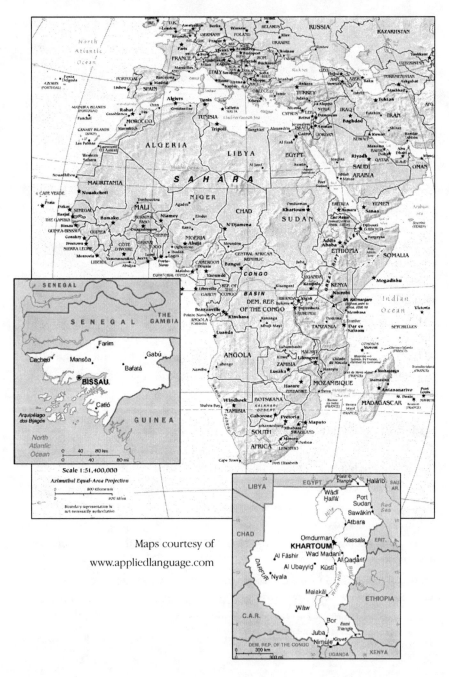

Maps courtesy of
www.appliedlanguage.com

Preface

This time I did not leave a sealed letter for my wife, Ann, in case I don't come back alive. She knows this is a dangerous assignment. She knows I'm here, alone, deep in the weeds in West Africa, to meet just two key people. They are supposed to be the good guys. Not the war lords. I will not be meeting another Joseph Kony this time.

But I'm not certain any more.

I don't know if they really are the good guys. Even if they are, and the bad guys find out I'm meeting with them, then the bad guys will be after me. If they come after me I hope they don't kill me. More likely they will send me a message. They'll mess up my room, or maybe rough me up.

Am I afraid? Yes, at times. But I have been here before and I am resolved to do my job. Once, when a man on my team had his life threatened, I had to pull him out of the country. Another had his leg broken when a man on a motorcycle deliberately drove into him as he was walking on a Ugandan street. We had to medevac him out of the country for surgery.

My experience has shown that when you get too close to the power, when you become a threat to those who live by violence, you can expect resistance.

It has taken me three years to get this close to the power. I don't know what there is about 'three years', but it is a recurrent number. It took three years to get a healing and reconciliation agreement for the boys who were abused by members of the Roman Catholic Church. It took three years after President Carter gave me the assignment to line things up so that there were peace talks to end the war in Sudan. And it has taken me three years to get here in my efforts to prevent war in Guinea-Bissau.

I'm a long way from those early days when I dreamed of having special healing powers. I wanted to pick up where my father had left off in his mystic endeavours, where he in turn had taken over from his mother and she had learned from my great grandfather. Instead, in thirty years, I've been all over the world working for peace, against violence. I have no special healing power. In fact, I have very little power at all.

It doesn't seem like I have accomplished much. Peace, I see, is a work in progress. It is something needed wherever and whenever people use power to abuse other people. And it takes everything you've got. Since I have limited resources and only so much knowledge and skill, I have to target my effort, be light on my feet and quick to move if need be. I am always targeting violence, pushing for the transformation of power from abusive to liberating forms.

Doing this inevitably takes you to the leaders – the war lords and the peace lords.

This time, I am hoping that the peace lords are the Prime Minister and the Head of the Armed Forces. They are holding this little African country together, trying to keep it from collapse. Just as the country crawled up from a trough of corruption and political infighting, from assassinations and coups d'états, now they have the drug lords to contend with. Those drug lords who exploit their country's fragility. They use Guinea-Bissau as a safe haven for cocaine moving from South America to continental Europe. And they use it with impunity.

Everyone is hungry here. Most of the political elite are on the take.

Maybe the Prime Minster and the Head of the Armed Forces are clean. Maybe they are the good guys. If they are, they will need all the help I can muster. Of course the UN and other big peace organizations are doing their part. But they are desperately slow.

The drug lords have to be put out of business. If the PM really tries to do this, his life is at risk. If he doesn't act, his country is compromised. The drug lords will own it.

You would think that by now, after thirty years, I would know who's who and what's what. Sure, I have years of experience stemming violence, and building peace. I have good instincts and in cases like this I also have good sources. And I check my sources. I've come to know this little country more than many foreigners ever will. Those who fly in, stay a while, fly out in another career move.

But until I push the right button enough, I am never certain. It's been a long hard road to get here. All I know now is that I am very close and if this story gets out, then I guess I got through OK. I played a role in preventing mass violence.

1

Epiphany in Mostar

The settlement was on the outskirts of Simferopol, the provincial capital of the Crimea. Some of the 200,000 Tatar returnees were struggling to make their new home here. They had come from all parts of the former Soviet Union, from their long banishment after Stalin had cleansed the Crimea of Tatars in 1944. Forty thousand of them had died that first winter. The rest were distributed throughout the Union, families broken up, use of their language forbidden, their cultural traditions destroyed. They were subjected to a never-ending attempt to Sovietize them.

This was 1994 and I was here at the request of a Canadian agency that worked mostly in Eastern Europe. It was worried that the Crimea might be a tinder box of ethnic conflict, and become another Yugoslavia.

"We can nearly see the town from here," she said, "and some of us have seen our grandfather's farm, but everything is in the hands of Russians now."

She was a beautiful Tatar woman in her early forties. Striking rich black hair, dark brown eyes, and high cheekbones. Intellectually and naturally charming. She was a school teacher in this tragic settlement.

We walked from uncompleted house to house, the whole place an arrested dream. Cement mixers sat idle, building materials lay strewn about. Not a home was finished. The owners had now settled into the first story. There was no running water, no electricity. It was bleak.

They were stuck in a limbo land. The Russian ruble had collapsed and their savings were worth nothing. They had given up their former citizenships to come home after fifty years of exile, and now they didn't have the 100 US dollars needed to buy Ukrainian citizenship.

She showed me a small handmade book. It was a few pages of flimsy paper tied together with a string. This was to be the text book she would use in her make-shift schoolroom. She had been interviewing the few remaining old people to record the cultural history of the Crimean Tatars, before the old ones died. For there were no books, no art or cultural artifacts left. Stalin had burned everything; the schools, mosques and cultural centres. Not a trace of the Tatars had been left.

She showed me a primitive drawing on one of the pages of the book. It was a Tatar woman in traditional costume; blue, yellow and red crayon the only lively colours to be found that dull grey day. Brokenhearted, but I tried not to show it, I left her standing alone in the muddy field amidst the half-completed homes.

As I walked away I wondered why these people would not take up guns against the ethnic Russians who now occupied grandpa's farm and their flats in the city. For surely the Tatars were living in a state of violence. Everywhere they turned the door was closed. Access denied. Their condition deteriorating.

But their leader, Mustafa Jemelev, who was wearing an old trench coat and a shabby suit underneath, was in his fifties and looked 70, had assured me that they were a moderate people. They did not want violence. I knew he had been imprisoned by the Russian authorities and subjected to 'special programs'. It was no wonder he looked twenty years older than he was. Now he was home. But, access denied. And even so, he did not want violence.

I could report back to the people in Canada who had sent me that I did not think the Crimea would become another 'Yugoslavia'.

But what did the Tatars need? And what did I have to offer?

What could I do about citizenship rights, access to property and economic opportunity, and cultural dignity?

How does a mediator deal with that kind of violence? When it is atmospheric, when the whole system is a form of violation?

Johann Galtung, a Norwegian and a grandfather of peace studies, gave it a name. He called it 'structural violence'. So now I had a word for it. I could name what it was I was witnessing in the Crimea. While there might not be open violence, the Tatars were suffering under structural violence.

And on my long trip back home to Canada, I struggled with my inability to help Mustafa and his people. My problem was that I was still thinking in terms of conflict and its resolution. I had not turned my attention to violence itself. But soon I would have to.

January, 1996, Bosnia-Herzegovina. The ink was still drying on the Dayton Peace Accord. The Americans had twisted a lot of arms and probably made a lot of promises to extract a deal from deeply bitter enemies, the Croatians, Serbians and Bosnians.

Five months earlier I had begun a process at the grassroots level which was intended to restore relationships in the still much-divided city of Mostar. Now I was in the city of Dubrovnik, one of the architectural wonders of the world. I was getting ready to make the trip inland to Mostar to begin a new peacebuilding project there. I was to begin a process that would lead to a meeting between four moderate Bosnians and four moderate Croatians, former neighbours who were now enemies. If things went well, they would become 'seeds of peace' in Mostar.

Dubrovnik itself was empty. From my hotel at the city's edge I found my way through the narrow stone streets leading to the big promenade around the main square that had once teemed with people. But there was not a soul around. Except for a few ghostlike elderly people, grandparents, holding the tiny upstretched hands of their grandchildren. They walked unspeaking, resolutely, as through fog.

Several historic buildings and monuments had been bombed, the red roof tiles torn off, leaving gaping holes in the buildings. The monuments were now wrapped in dull burlap, some crated up to guard against further bombing. These statues looked like Egyptian mummies that had wandered here during the war. Lost. It was a dead zone.

I spent the afternoon strolling about, aimlessly, sadly. The few listless merchants, who had survived nearly five years of war, idling away in their stores, saddened me more. I bought a few things here and there, things I didn't need but to spread around the little money I had.

Early Monday morning a young man picked me up at the hotel. About 30 years old, he was the driver of the vehicle that had been provided by the European authorities who were now acting as de facto administrators of Mostar. They were struggling to keep the ethnically divided city from descending into more violence. For the people of Mostar, Dayton Ohio was a long way off. The Accord was just a piece of paper. Tit-for-tat rifle fire had resumed in Mostar, across the great ravine created by the Neretva River that runs through the city.

The highway from Dubrovnik worked its way to Mostar through the mountains on the Dalmatian coast, past the foothills I had climbed the day before. As we drove along I could see a farm house here and there off in the distance. Strangely, one farm looked occupied and productive, cattle and crops in the fields. Another, next door, looked abandoned. Hard economic times, I thought.

At the roadside, every so often, old women sold oranges and other food stuffs. Their provisions looked sparse; a few root crops, eggs, and a chicken. Another worrying sign.

Occasionally we were stopped at security check-points. The young soldiers manning the barriers were dressed in drab, worn uniforms. They paid little attention to us after a quick glance at me in the back and a perfunctory look at my driver's papers.

We passed on. More farms. Some active, some abandoned but little movement anywhere.

The driver announced that we had to stop for petrol and he pulled quickly into a garage at the edge of the next village. He got out and went to buy cigarettes while I remained in the back, surveying the scene.

As the gas pump started and our tank was being filled by the station attendant, I looked behind me. The house right next door was destroyed by fire. It was charred and mangled looking, a few furnishings thrown about the front yard.

But this was just meters from where we stood; from where the gasoline was being pumped. How could there be such a fire so nearby and not a mark on the gas station? Surely the gas pumps might have blown up too?

Then it hit me. Ethnic cleansing!

The abandoned farms; one flourishing, the next one destroyed. This house, someone's home, looted, and surgically blown up yet the gas station was working fine.

This was a war between former neighbours, former friends and even former relatives. It was not a conventional war with professionally trained soldiers doing the fighting. The war-fighting was not like World War Two fighting that we had seen on TV and in movies. In that scenario professional armies planned an offensive, they attacked, were maybe rebuffed and then underwent a back and forth struggle to obtain and hold territory. This was men and women, ordinary citizens mobilized by fear and prejudice into militias, setting out to cleanse their neighbourhood of the alien 'other'. That the alien other was an old friend, that more than 60% of the marriages were inter-ethnic, did not matter. Depending on your ethnic identity, Serbs, Croats, and Bosnians were bad. They were despicable and should be routed out. The women and children and men were rounded up outside their homes. The women were raped and the men taken off in trucks. The house was looted, stripped of anything that could be used by the predators. The building was bombed.

Many people I knew remarked how strange it was. Europeans doing this to one another. In Africa, yes. But here? When Sarajevo had not that long ago hosted the world to Olympic Games. Not here where civilization was advanced, and where people were cultured.

We resumed our journey. Now I saw the remains of war without a tourist's veil.

I asked the driver, "How do you manage to get along with everyone?" He knew exactly what I meant.

"They all trust me. I know them. I am no threat."

"So some people can move across the lines?"

"Yes some."

"How bad is it in Mostar?" I asked.

"You will see." he said.

We came upon the city from the south. The skyline that I could make out was a zigzag of rooftops rising intermittently from the horizon. Closer up, I could see that only walls remained on most of the buildings, the roofs had been blown off. And the walls were broken, half walls, some with gaping holes ripped through the heavy stonework. We followed one of the few arteries that had been cleared of rubble. Not a soul was on the street. The destroyed buildings, once beautiful, were abandoned, their steel girders exposed like raw bones sticking out of torn flesh. Bare and twisted. The guts of the buildings protruded or lay in tangled heaps. Electrical wires, phone lines, plumbing conduits.

At street level someone – who? – had collected piles of scrap. Little fires burned here and there. But I saw no one.

Avoiding open places where we might attract gun fire, we drove at a crawl along further, toward the river, on the Croatian side.

Movement!

A platoon of peacekeepers, accompanied by a ground-hugging armoured vehicle turned a corner and came steadily, deliberately toward us. They marched like robocops; left, right, left, right – mechanically. They were heavily armed, dark and low.

Now far beyond them I caught a glimpse of something. I noticed a blanket hanging from a staircase landing, some four feet off the ground. The stairs itself ended about ten steps up, torn out in the bombing. And from behind that blanket, which was slowly pulled back, a little child stared out at me, and then darted back inside the make-shift shelter. The blanket remained still. There was no other sign of life.

When we reached the river we turned left and stopped at a building where I was to meet the man in charge of Mostar – the surrogate mayor.

A portly Spaniard, he reached his fleshy hand out to welcome me, warmly. He and his assistant, a keen East Indian from the UK, seemed truly excited to meet me. They gave me a quick tour of their spartan offices and I was impressed with how much at home they seemed here, in the middle of this.

He suggested we take a walk to the bridge before sunset so that I could see the new swinging bridge they had installed where the Stari Most once stood. The Stari Most, he explained, had been a cultural monument dating back to antiquity. It was a beautiful stone structure that spanned the Neretva River, joining both sides of Mostar in unity. After the Croatians and the Bosnians has beaten off the Serbs, they had turned on one another. They had blown up their lovely bridge.

Now a suspended steel contraption served as the walkway. I was told not to go out too far on it. Snipers were in the hills and there had been shooting.

We turned a corner a few blocks from where we had left the administrative office. He paused beside a blown up building, and leaned on the wall. He stepped out a few paces onto the bridge and darted back. "Be brief," he said, "just a quick look."

There was a part of me that simply did not want to step out there. But it seemed mandatory; something that must be done.

He could sense my reluctance. So he took the lead once again, with his assistant in tow. They stepped out rather boldly now, their shoulders back and heads held high. I got the clear sense that they knew the snipers with their high-powered rifles could see them through their scopes. And they were not going to be intimidated. They would be defiant in the face of violence. They were the peacemakers.

I followed. About five paces out, they stopped, paused and surveyed the landscape, taking what nevertheless seemed to me to be far too long. Then turning confidently, they led me off without a word.

As we walked silently back to the office I reflected on the view from the bridge. It really was a deep ravine. The river looked clean and clear as it broke over the large boulders below and the old rocks that had one time been part of a beautiful bridge that symbolized unity.

We talked about my assignment. He understood my goal was to open up the line of communication between a few Bosnians and Croatians in order to restore their relationship so that they could eventually weaken and convert the hardliners to peace. Of course there was a lot that needed to be done to make this possible. I knew that the four moderates whom we had found on both sides ran the risk of being killed by hardliners. I knew we had to create enough safety for this daring initiative to get started, and to continue successfully. I knew we were talking about months of work and that progress would be slow. He agreed to my plan. Now it was time to check into my hotel and get ready for dinner.

The Ero had been a fine hotel one day. Now it was the only hotel operating in Mostar. It looked tired, worn down by the war. Yet it was the only oasis of calm and civility in this destroyed urban landscape.

On check-in I was informed that a number of floors were out-of-bounds. The rooms there were filled with internally displaced people who simply had nowhere else to live. But I could use the bar and the restaurant which were open to the public. As I collected my bags and made for the elevator I glanced into the bar. It was like looking into a bar on the TV show, Star Trek. A bar on a space station. A place where alien creatures from all parts of the galaxy meet. Here, in Mostar, the crowded bar was filled with a mix of diplomats in blue striped suits, soldiers, red and yellow-haired hippy-looking young people who were working for humanitarian organizations, journalists in field clothes, and a documentary crew with their cameras and equipment piled in the corner. They all mingled in the dull light.

It was surreal. But it was nothing compared to the restaurant-cum-nightclub my host and I would visit later that evening.

At the curb outside the Ero, the sun was setting on the lifeless street as I waited for my contact to pick me up. We were going to one of two restaurants that still operated on the outskirts of the city. As I waited a black Mercedes pulled slowly to a full stop in front of me, just feet away. The driver and his male companion in the front looked directly ahead, paying me no heed. But I got a good long look inside the car as it paused at the intersection. The two men in the front, in their mid-forties were dressed in expensive looking suits, their gold watches and rings glinted as the rays from the sinking sun came in through the windshield. Their black hair was slicked back, their faces cleanly shaven, strong and confident. Two beautiful blonde women sat elegantly in the back, dressed to the nines, dripping with jewelry and they looked unconcerned about anyone or anything.

The car pulled away ever so slowly, none of the passengers having been distracted by my obvious curiosity as I stood alone on the curb, a solitary human figure in the shadowy horizon. The car moved off and disappeared as incongruously as it had appeared. I watched the empty space behind it long after, trying to make some sense of this.

Inside the Ero the bar was teaming with ex patriots from all walks of life and professions, the drinks going down hard and heavy. Here, just outside the Ero's front door, a silent, mangled urban landscape was severed by a black Mercedes with wealthy passengers oblivious to the world around them.

Where had these characters come from? These people who looked liked Chicago gangsters from the 1930s? How they made their money I could only imagine.

When I was finally picked up and we found our way to the restaurant, I could see that it was really a night club. Eating was a poor excuse for being there.

But it was 'the place' for the nouveau riche in Mostar. And it was hopping. Even this early in the evening it was a struggle to make our way through the crowd to a table at the rear, far from the dance floor with the large globe of disco lights hanging over it. As the evening wore on I got a sense of growing frenzy. The energy was raw, sexual. The large room, now packed, reeked of murder and corruption. Who was victim and who was offender? Perhaps there was blood on everyone's hands. The booze flowed. The music got cranked real loud. The bodies gyrated and undulated on the dance floor under shafts of red, green, blue, and yellow light.

I was happy when my host suggested that we leave. I was more than ready for bed.

Later that night I awoke in a cold sweat. It was pitch dark. Black. I could not move. I was gripped with terror. My heart was pounding. My eyes failed. There was not a sound.

Where was I? Where was the light? Had someone really banged at my door earlier, crying?

I fumbled around at my bedside and found a light switch. I turned it on. A dim light barely showed the outlines of furniture; a chair, a coffee table, my suitcase on the floor.

On automatic pilot I virtually crawled to the small table, found my briefcase propped up against it, fumbled inside for a pen and paper.

I drew a diagram spontaneously. It depicted two axes, like a cross, the horizontal one which I labeled, in big print, OUTCOME; the vertical one, JUSTICE. I sat there, vacant, staring at this. Suddenly I shivered with fear again and quickly glanced toward the door. Then at the window; nothing, no one.

I looked down again at the drawing, feeling removed from it; the product of automatic writing. Beside the word OUTCOME, I wrote the word 'voluntary', on the far right hand side of the horizontal line. At the far left of that line I wrote, 'imposed'.

I stared more at the diagram, focusing on the vertical axis, the one labeled JUSTICE. And I wrote at the top, beside the word JUSTICE, 'restorative'; and at the bottom, 'retributive'.

I paused, studying this.

In the upper right hand quadrant, bounded by the axis marked 'restorative JUSTICE', and the horizontal one marked 'voluntary OUTCOME', I scribbled the words, 'where I want to go'.

I just sat there, slowly coming to my senses; staring at the diagram. Then, in the lower left quadrant, bounded by the words 'retributive' (justice) and 'imposed' (outcome) I scribbled 'raw violence'. I stared at this for a while. Then, beside the words 'raw violence' I wrote MOSTAR. And I drew a big circle around the word Mostar. Then I turned off the lamp and crept along the floor and crawled back into bed.

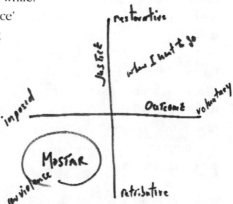

The next morning, feeling hung over from such a disturbed night, I went immediately back to the diagram. I knew something was missing but I could not put my finger on it. I knew as well that my conflict resolution skills, the 'tool kit' of techniques I had for helping others to resolve their conflicts, was inadequate in Mostar. My Harvard-based skills of negotiation and mediation were key elements in non-violent conflict resolution. But they pre-supposed some things about the people in conflict and the nature of the conflict that simply did not apply in Mostar. There the people had been, and some were still, willing to kill others who were vermin as far as they were concerned. In Mostar, justice was a case of reward and punishment, not one of reparations for harm done and the restoration of relationships. Outcomes were imposed in Mostar. They were not the product of voluntary acts. The moderates who were going to help me ran the risk of being killed, just for reaching out to the other side. Good faith negotiation was an empty term.

Weeks later, back in Ottawa, I showed this crude diagram to some of my colleagues. I tried to explain it, trying to make it meaningful to them. Then it hit me!

What was missing from my conflict resolution repertoire was a clear recognition that power is a central element in cases of war. So I redrew the diagram. I drew another axis running right through the centre of where the JUSTICE and OUTCOME axes inter-sected, on a diagonal from the lower left quadrant to the upper right quadrant. In big bold letters I labeled that axis, POWER. And in the upper right quadrant, the domain of voluntary outcomes and restorative justice, I inserted a concept that I had come across years before, 'power with' – that is, the power that comes from joining with others to create something new, a constructive use of power. And in the lower left quadrant I labeled the power found there as 'power over' – that is, imposed and abusive power.

As discouraged as I had been in Mostar, I realized that my epiphany there was that violence is the abusive use of power but that there must be other nonviolating forms and expressions of power. And unless there is some way to move people and societies that use power abusively 'up' the power axis, then real sustainable peace is not possible. In Mostar, and other cases of war, it is power that needs to be transformed. It is not conflict that needs to be resolved. In Mostar, we were way beyond conflict and its resolution. We were at a much deeper level of human relations. I knew that night in Mostar that new tools are needed to function there, to stop the violence and build sustainable peace.

This realization changed my practice as a mediator and it forced me to write a confession. I confessed to breaking all the rules of mediation. The rules, as mediation is taught in Canada and the US, are that mediators should be neutral; mediators should be non-directive with the people with whom they work; mediators should not negotiate with the parties in dispute; mediators shouldn't offer solutions to the people they are trying to help; and mediators should be impartial with respect to the outcome of the mediation.

I disagreed totally.

I had realized right there and then in Mostar that I am partial. I am partial to peace. That is my goal. And I realized that I care about the quality and nature of any agreement that people might arrive at with my assistance. I realized that I do direct the people with whom I mediate, making sure that each and every one gets enough air time so that their issues are brought forward. I realized as well that I negotiate with the people I am trying to help. I encourage them to put realistic proposals on the table, to give a little here to get something there. And I realized that I offer solutions. I don't impose my ideas and solutions on anyone but I certainly try to help them by offering creative ideas. I put practical proposals forward that will move things along and become part of an agreement that they will own and honour.

I knew that if peace is to come about in Mostar and in other cases of war, the peacemaker must 'wage' peace. This means the peacemaker must be active, assertive, vigilant and tireless in his or her efforts to have the killing stop and to build sustainable peace.

My confession was published and a few people wrote me to say 'thank you for finally telling it as it is – as it needs to be'.

In Mostar, the security situation continued to deteriorate and my plans of working with the moderates who were now at great risk were put on hold. Meanwhile, I led efforts in the Crimea to reduce inter-ethnic prejudice and to remove some of the obstacles to a dignified inclusion of the Tatars in their homeland. And I was also working in Romania to reduce tensions between the Hungarian ethnic minority in Transylvania and the Romanian majority.

Then I received an unexpected phone call on behalf of President Jimmy Carter. The Carter Center had heard about me from someone in Europe. Was I interested in becoming the Director of the Conflict Resolution Program at The Carter Center?

A hockey fan, I likened The Carter Center to the best team in the world league of peacebuilding. Taking this job I knew would be my opportunity to put all of the elements of my peacebuilding experience together. In the past I had been constrained by working almost exclusively with people at the grassroots level in war zones. Now I would have access to and be mediating with leaders, presidents, foreign ministers and rebel war lords. Whereas I had been constrained by limited resources, in some cases financing my own peacebuilding work, now I would have a team of world class practitioners working with me, and money to get the job done. And whereas in the past I had often worked without any official status and the lack of protection that comes with that, now I would have the cover provided by my association with a former President of the United States.

What I didn't know was just exactly what awaited me in Atlanta and how much it would take out of my hide. I was about to assume leadership on an assignment to end a 19-year-old civil war. I did not stop for three and a half years that took me deep into the abyss of human violence where I contended with the world's most notorious rebel, spies, high-placed leaders and would-be peace lords. That is 24/7 for three and a half years.

2

Waging Peace with Jimmy Carter

Everyone rose as President Carter entered the room, and so did I. A Canadian, I was used to a certain amount of majesty – British pomp and ceremony – but I had not expected that this was how The Carter Center's senior management team would greet its CEO. President Carter carried himself in a strangely modest yet strong manner. Behind him, Mrs. Carter looked graceful and elegant. It was a presidential moment, complete with stern-looking secret service officers, ear pieces and all. Rounding out the scene were my new colleagues – some of the world's best in their respective disciplines.

Of course, there was an agenda for the meeting and The Conflict Resolution Program's major initiative, the Sudan-Uganda Nairobi Agreement was on it. The Nairobi Agreement, mediated by President Carter just a few months ago, was intended as a building block for peace in war-ravaged Sudan. The Agreement was complicated and as the new Conflict Resolution Program Director, in addition to managing a number of other peace efforts, I had my work cut out for me to see that it was implemented. But things were not going well. Both countries had done the easy things required of them, but full implementation of the peace agreement was a long way off. I prepared myself to brief President Carter. I had been told by colleagues that he could be quite tough. He could centre you out.

What I hadn't realized was that President Carter reads everything, including the minutes of a senior staff meeting we had just had two days earlier. That was the meeting at which I had declared that my Program was overwhelmed with requests – an urgent plea for help from Haiti, the coup d'état in Ecuador, and a call for assistance in Spain's Basque Country. I needed to come to grips soon, with my priorities, resources, and the bold declaration that at The Carter Center we 'wage peace'. I had no underestimation in my mind what that might mean. But I wasn't sure then that the institution shared my view. And I needed to know how serious we were about Sudan, and the Nairobi Agreement, the Lord's Resistance Army and the children it had abducted.

All of these questions of mine Carter had known before he had entered the Zaban Room. Now seated, President Carter set the written agenda aside, raised his right arm and pointed his index finger directly at me.

"Ben," he said, "I want you to know that when I say we are committed to 'waging peace' in Sudan, I mean it. I want you and everyone here to know that you are responsible for Sudan. From now on I want everything relating to peace in Sudan to go to Ben. I met yesterday with Vice President Gore, and the other day with President Clinton. We had good meetings. I spoke about Sudan. The war in Sudan, which has cost millions of lives, could have been settled over six or seven years ago if the US government had wanted peace. I expect that we will be going to Washington soon, to meet with Secretary of State Madeleine Albright and Susan Rice. Ben, you are coming too."

In no uncertain terms I had been given my assignment. I was to lead an all-out, intensive effort to end the war in Sudan. But back in the privacy of my new office I wondered whether I had really understood Carter correctly. Was I really to take total leadership to, in effect, bring about the end of a war? A couple of my colleagues who knew the ropes told me that was exactly what I had been asked to do. But what did I have to guide me? Clearly, this would take more than a mediator's standard repertoire. I would have to draw on all of my strengths.

How would we proceed? I quickly researched and found that the current phase of Sudan's civil war had been going on for eighteen years. Eighteen years! Bordering nine neighbours and as large as the USA east of the Mississippi, two million people had been killed, another four million displaced! The war pitted forces loyal to the Government in the north, in Khartoum, against rebel forces in the south. The major rebel group in the south was called the Sudan People's Liberation Movement/Army. It was led by a USA-educated PhD, Dr. John Garang, a member of the Dinka tribe. The

Sudan People's Liberation Army was depicted in the United States as a friendly force waging a war of religious and political freedom on behalf of black African Christians in Sudan's south. Sudan was black-listed as a terrorist nation by the USA. It had been a home for some time to the notorious terrorist, the Jackal, and to Osama Bin Laden. It had economic sanctions imposed on it by the UN. It was characterized in the West, generally, as a slave-trading, human rights abusing, fundamentalist Islamist nation that had sided with Saddam Hussein in the 1990 Gulf War.

It is in the south of Sudan where the rich oil fields are found. And that was where the Government, based in Khartoum, was accused of a 'scorched earth policy'. Government forces and militias employed by the government, supported by helicopter gunships, were alleged to be gunning down and driving innocent black villagers and farmers from their homes, burning all that was left; and thus de-populating the oil fields. That too was where international oil companies, including Canadian-owned Talisman, were said to be consorting with the Government. Oil revenues from the south flowed to Khartoum in the north and this oil money fueled Khartoum's war machine.

Water was also a factor in the war. Nile River water. As good as gold in this parched desert region, the White Nile flows from its source in Uganda, northward, through the rebel-held southern region, to Khartoum. There it joins the Blue Nile, whose source is in Ethiopia. Then it flows further north to Egypt. Egypt desperately needs water and was on record as being opposed to the north and south separation of Sudan. For how could Egypt be certain that an independent sovereign southern Sudan would ensure its water supply?

It was a nasty, complicated war by any measure. And my job was to help end it.

Meanwhile, we had the Nairobi Agreement signed by Sudan and Uganda on our hands, and my job was to ensure that it was implemented. That was a tall order in its own right.

The first Carter Center document in the Nairobi Agreement file showed the path leading to the Nairobi Agreement was a request from Uganda's President Museveni to President Carter. Museveni wanted Carter's help to end an insurgency in northern Uganda. That is where the Acholi tribe lives. There, on the southern border of Sudan, Joseph Kony, an Acholi and leader of the Lord's Resistance Army, was fighting a brutal war against Museveni and the Government of Uganda. While I would come to learn first hand just how horrible this forgotten war was – for who had heard of the Lord's Resistance Army – the history, like so many of these situations, was twisted and disturbing.

Reading the file, I recalled that as a young person thirty years ago I had watched, horrified at television images of Idi Amin, then President of Uganda, slaughtering his own people. The bulk of his forces were members of the Acholi tribe from the north. At that time, Uganda certainly seemed primitive, and savage. Who could forget the face of terror that was Amin's?

Driven from the country by present-day Ugandan President Museveni, Amin's regime collapsed. The Acholi forces loyal to Amin were pushed back to their northern homeland, and they had scattered. Afterwards, the Acholi people were neglected by Museveni's government.

As recently as 1986 an Acholi medicine woman who was frustrated at being marginalized, Alice Lakwena, had led a rebellion against Museveni's National Resistance Army. She had convinced her followers that bullets could not hurt them and that the stones they threw were grenades! Lakwena and the Acholi had given Museveni a good fight. She and her fierce warriors had come within striking distance of Kampala. Defeated in the end, and exiled to Kenya, Alice had left a legacy of rebellion to her young cousin, Joseph Kony, who was waiting in the wings.

Kony called his group of Acholi rebels the Lord's Resistance Army (LRA) and declared that it operated on the basis of a combination of guidance from the spirits and the biblical ten commandments. He filled the ranks of the LRA with abducted Acholi children, as young as eight years old. The abducted boys were forced to become soldiers and the girls turned over to LRA commanders as 'wives'. Kony punished anyone thought to be collaborating with Museveni's government forces. He condoned vicious methods that his soldiers used against their own people – like cutting off their lips, ears, and buttocks. Brutally treated, indoctrinated, living in fear, his LRA fighters were effective guerilla warriors.

The LRA was given safe haven in southern Sudan, Uganda's hostile neighbour – which was contending with its own rebellion in the south. When the LRA was not fighting the Ugandan army directly, it was assisting Sudan by engaging the Sudan government's enemy, the Sudan Peoples Liberation Army.

So the Acholi had supported Amin in his reign of terror. Museveni, who now ruled Uganda, had driven Amin from power and had also beaten down Alice Lakwena and her Acholi fighters. The Acholi had then blessed young

Joseph Kony to take on their cause. Kony and his Lord's Resistance Army now operated from bases in southern Sudan, just across the northern Ugandan border. But Kony had perpetrated so many vicious abuses against his own tribe that he had apparently lost any political support from the Acholi for his rebellion.

Meanwhile, the Acholi people had been herded from their fertile farms and rounded up into camps guarded by Museveni's government forces. The Government told the Acholi people and the international community that this was for the people's own protection from Kony. It was obvious as well that it was done to limit any collaboration with Kony and the LRA.

Acholiland was deteriorating. It had fallen into ruin: youth were unemployed, there were Ugandan army violations against innocent victims in the camps – the people were exhausted with war. Too many had lost children to Kony; too many had been looted, raped, and killed by their own son, Kony. And there was little protection from the Government forces. The Acholi were innocent people, caught in the middle.

But the war between Kony's LRA and Museveni's forces was not subsiding. Yet neither was about to achieve a military victory. And so Museveni requested President Carter to mediate an end to the war between the Ugandan government and the LRA. And from that request had emerged the Nairobi Agreement, between Uganda and Sudan.

The Nairobi Agreement committed Sudan and Uganda to cease support of rebels antagonistic to the other: they were to stop fighting proxy wars. That is, Sudan would stop supporting Joseph Kony and the Lord's Resistance Army in its guerilla war against the Government of Uganda, and Uganda would stop supporting John Garang and the Sudan People's Liberation Army in its fight against the Government of Sudan. Uganda and Sudan were also committed to return prisoners of war; to return children abducted and used as soldiers; to respect each other's sovereign territory; and when these objectives had been accomplished, to restore full diplomatic relations.

The Nairobi Agreement was also viewed at The Carter Center as a building block for peace in the region – which of course would include Sudan, proper.

So this file established in my mind what kind of challenge I was to deal with. Part of the challenge I faced, however, was the legitimacy – for lack of a better word – of the mandate President Carter had given to me. Indeed, The Carter Center was explicitly constrained in the Nairobi Agreement against interfering with the current ongoing peace process to end the war in Sudan, which I called the Sudan Peace Process. That was being managed by a Peace Secretariat located in Nairobi, Kenya, under the auspices of the Intergovernmental Authority on Development comprised of a body of states in the Horn of Africa. In fact, I had been told that President Bill Clinton had sent a letter complimenting President Carter on his achievement in having mediated the Nairobi Agreement. According to the story, however, page one of the letter was all compliments; but page two reminded President Carter to stay out of the Sudan Peace Process. And the USA remained a decisive factor in that peace process. So President Carter was asking me to get involved in something for which we had no mandate. In fact we were to stay out!

I decided not to get hung up on this. I agreed with President Carter that peace was more important than President Clinton's wishes, if the story was true.

But how would our more modest efforts on the tall order of getting Uganda and Sudan to implement the Nairobi Agreement really relate to ending the war in Sudan? How was the Nairobi Agreement a building block for peace? After all, our role was really just the role of a mediator, continuing the mediation process that Carter had used to get the Nairobi Agreement signed.

I knew that most mediators, motivated by the goal of social justice, had made a choice to place themselves as a neutral between opposing sides and contending views. They had given up their role as advocate, whether for human rights or for specific laws and services that build more equitable and just societies. And in some cases, mediation had been denigrated to a 'touchy-feely' process suitable only for 'easier' disputes. It was not seen as relevant in heavyweight conflicts. Often the more powerful party in a dispute declined invitations to seek resolution through mediation, preferring to prevail in other ways. That is, through some use of power over the other side. Even when powerful parties came to the mediation table, they often continued to dominate, playing power games at the table and away from it between mediation sessions. Facilitative mediation was not able to compensate for power asymmetries. And sometimes, countries like Sudan and Uganda would use mediation purely for political optics. They really were not serious at all about peace.

Reflecting on this, I knew I would not be practicing mediation in the conventional way. Whatever clout President Carter had, I would have to use. I would also have to draw on everything in my peacebuilding repertoire to achieve my objective.

On closer examination there were, however, some serious architectural flaws in the Nairobi Agreement. Some of these had the mark of the disquieting criticism I had heard about The Conflict Resolution Program of The Carter Center before I took the job as its Director. Some senior practitioners in the conflict resolution field had questioned why I would join The Center. They asserted that it had a reputation for 'hit and run'. Granted, they said President Carter could and would do some amazing things, especially his efforts in North Korea and Haiti. But they criticized him for a perceived tendency to hammer out a ceasefire or a peace accord, be there for the photo op, and leave. The Carter Center, they contended, had no long term commitment to peace initiatives, even when they had been forged on the moral authority, persuasive powers and technical skills of President Carter. So, when Carter was credited with mediating a humanitarian cease fire, it was devalued as having come at a time in the fighting when the warring sides needed a break to heal their wounds, fatten up, and retool for war. If a peace agreement was achieved, they criticized The Carter Center for abandoning its implementation.

The Nairobi Agreement itself was also subjected to criticism, some of which I found appropriate. Where, for example, were the LRA and the SPLA in all of this? It looked as though they had been treated as rump factions, a thorn in the side of the respective heads of state. President Bashir's removal of the LRA from Sudan would be unilateral – and so would President Museveni's stopping of support for the SPLA.

Questions arose in my mind as to why these two rebel groups were not at the negotiation table. Why, at least, had they not been brought along, showing better bedside manners than was evident? Did The Carter Center really think both would just lie down and give up; that the two heads of state, Bashir and Museveni, could just stop supporting them and render them inoperative?

I talked about these criticisms with my staff members who had been associated with mediating the Agreement. They said apparently the LRA had indeed been invited to the talks. Regrettably, the invitation had been sent only seven days prior to the definitive meeting held in Nairobi on December 8, 1999. They also remarked that while the initial request from President Museveni to President Carter was for assistance in bringing peace to Northern Uganda by mediating between the Government of Uganda and the LRA, this had necessarily brought Sudan into the picture. For Sudan harboured the LRA. To get to the LRA you must have the cooperation of Sudan. So Sudan upped the ante, requesting that President Carter intervene between Sudan and Uganda to restore their bilateral relations. The SPLA, as far as I could tell, was never factored into the Sudan-Uganda peace talks. This general line of criticism and the specific holes that I identified in the Nairobi Agreement caused me concern. As we will see, they came back to haunt our efforts, and I note this as a lesson for other peacemakers. Somehow, peace processes must be inclusive.

The answer we satisfied ourselves with at the time was that if Sudan stopped supporting the LRA, and Uganda stopped supporting the SPLA, then the destabilized region along the northern Uganda-southern Sudan border would become pacified, thus contributing to peace. More significantly, without Ugandan support, Dr. John Garang's SPLA would lose a strong moral and material ally. If President Museveni, Garang's personal friend, took a step toward peace, he could be a huge influence on Garang. Museveni could become a new statesman in the region by helping move Garang to peace talks. It was complicated. It was not perfect. And it was mine to contend with.

3

A Strategy to End War

Was I a fool on a fool's errand?

Could we really mount the type of effort required? I decided that if I was to take the order from President Carter to 'wage peace' literally, I would have to learn whatever lessons I could from those who study or wage war – Sun Tzu, Clausewitz, modern armed forces. What resources, what strategies, tactics and so forth? Who would our allies be? Who were the enemies of peace?

Our perspective and our engagement would have to go beyond the current players and current geography – that of southern Sudan and northern Uganda – the arena of conflict between Uganda and Sudan. But just how broad would our campaign to wage peace be? Who would be the key players, within Sudan, in the region, in Europe and in the USA?

How would my being 'pro' peace, and pressing actively for peace, reconcile with our role as a mediator? For 'waging peace' certainly implies using influence and drawing on a range of activities seldom associated with merely facilitative activities. Mediation is generally defined as some form of third party 'assisted' negotiation provided by a neutral actor. While we might be 'neutral' in the world of partisan politics, we certainly weren't impartial. As I had already determined in other war zones long before, I was partial to peace. And I knew my staff and interns felt the same way.

I decided to approach the assignment by enlisting the views and hopefully the support of all of the key senior personnel at The Carter

Center. I knew there was no way I and my small team could do this alone. I also knew that virtually all of the Conflict Resolution Program's resources were being poured into the job of ensuring that Uganda and Sudan honoured the commitments they had made in the Nairobi Agreement. If we were flat out on this, we'd need a lot more institutional commitment to step up our effort to tackle the war in Sudan.

While I began my internal consultations at The Carter Center, I noted that preparation for the Dayton Accord, which ended the war in former Yugoslavia in 1995, had required approximately two months of shuttle diplomacy and a ceasefire to create the space for peace talks. And the process had been marked by awkward pushes and pulls between the European Administration and the US team. The Dayton negotiations themselves had lasted some 24 days, with plenty of subplots and visits to the war zone to get defectors on board; constitutional arrangements and post-war reconstruction and peacebuilding measures were thought through ahead of time; a draft agreement was put to the parties early on; efforts were made to build relationships among the key parties; and more shuttle diplomacy was required between the warring sides. Ultimately, the primary actors, Serbia's Milosevic, Croatia's Tudjman, and Bosnia's Izetbegovic had been closeted off together, and it had been tough. I wondered if I had what I needed to get President Carter to 'do a Dayton' on Sudan.

What was the consensus view at The Carter Center? It was 'to go for it'! My staff was, however, overwhelmed at the scale and scope of the challenge as they were being asked to notch up their efforts. It took time to get them to agree to a bold initiative, to believe we could be part of the really big picture.

I pressed on and our strategic plan began to take shape. We had looked at the key political entities, both within Sudan and in the neighbouring region, including the political parties and factions, and the personalities of their leaders so that we might speculate on their motives. We needed to know what might move them to peace. We considered the main issues on the table in the Kenyan-based Sudan Peace Process: the separation of religion and state – Khartoum insisting on an Islamist state governed by Sharia law with 'opting out' provisions but the SPLM wanting a secular state; constitutional models that might accommodate the warring sides – confederation being the most recently talked about; and the role of a referendum on self-determination in the south – something Khartoum was willing to grant only after a period of rule under its central government.

22

Pivotal to our process was an assessment of the balance of power on the battlefield. Everyone judged the war as unilaterally unwinnable by either side, notwithstanding the apparent advantage Khartoum had with newly-realized oil revenues. On the other hand, 15 million dollars US was flowing into the rebel-held south in 'non-lethal' assistance, and guns were coming from somewhere. Yet total victory by either side remained unlikely. It was a grinding, protracted war. Yet, I was not convinced that Bashir and Garang had reached a 'mutually hurting stalemate'. Both seemed prepared to sacrifice more soldiers and innocent people to their cause.

We also mapped the strategic alliances of the parties: Khartoum's with the Arab world: the SPLM's with the West, including the Christian right and the Black caucus in the USA.

We noted that while all commentators judged the Sudan Peace Process to be virtually exhausted (President Carter had called it a 'sink hole'), it continued to be financially supported by a group of western countries including the UK, Norway, Italy, and Canada. The Sudan Peace Process also had at least one rival, the Joint Egyptian-Libyan Initiative. Motivated by Egyptian self-interest and Libya's desire to be a big player in the region, that peace initiative excluded the possibility of a divided Sudan. In doing so, it took a position which departed from the Declaration of Principles which was the agreed upon-basis for negotiations between Khartoum and the SPLM under the Sudan Peace Process held in Kenya. The Declaration of Principles specified that peace negotiations would be conducted on the basis of recognition of the principle of self determination, meaning that the south might choose to separate.

We knew that Bashir's Sudan was about to undergo a presidential election and Bashir had requested that Present Carter and The Carter Center monitor the election. While Bashir had the oil revenues to 'fuel' his war machine, his own position was precarious with hard-line Islamic fundamentalists snapping at his heels and mobilizing substantive opposition that gave him little room to move. It was also obvious that John Garang had not ruled over the SPLM without contest – there had been splits internally and he was drawing increasing criticism from respected southern Sudanese intellectuals living abroad. So neither of the sides in this war were monolithic, the leaders had their own battles internally; and neither leader seemed truly motivated to peace. In Garang's case, he was a de facto Head of State and enjoyed international reception and financial benefits commensurate with the position. He would hardly settle for a 'second fiddle' role in a united Sudan. If, however, he did become the leader of an independent South, he might not last long in that position.

Taking all the information that my staff and I had collected and these perspectives into account, I drafted a strategy to end the war in Sudan. It would include efforts with the United States Government, its representatives and agents in Washington and elsewhere. Rather simple, it began with the only concrete piece of the picture we had, the Sudan-Uganda Nairobi Agreement.

It was really an incremental approach, but not in a strictly linear fashion. We would have to do several things at the same time. The main effort would be to focus on successful implementation of the Nairobi Agreement and to build relationships with key actors in the Sudan war. On the basis of our credibility through implementation of the Nairobi Agreement, and good relationships, we would focus on the war in Sudan. We would know the issues, be visible but unobtrusive, trusted in the end, and poised to influence the parties and dynamics in the direction of peace. It might be two years before we ever got to the Sudan war, but we would get there. That is unless peace broke out in Sudan beforehand. And that was most unlikely.

President Carter agreed to our approach. The first move, arranged by President Carter, was to go to Washington. There we would implore Secretary of State Madeleine Albright and State Department's Assistant Secretary of State for African Affairs, Susan Rice, to take a strong, balanced policy approach to the North (Bashir) and the South (Garang). We wanted the US to press Bashir and Garang into a Washington-blessed, newly-energized multilateral peace process which we knew was the key to success.

President Carter and I left for Washington from Atlanta's Hartsfield Airport where President Carter boarded the plane before everyone else, directly from the tarmac outside. He was seated in the front row at the window, a secret service officer on the aisle. Once we were safely in the air, I was surprised to see him stand up and walk back through the crowded plane, greeting everyone as he went. His big smile was as infectious as ever. All these early morning travelers, sipping coffee, waking up, seemed really happy to shake his hand and exchange greetings. I could see how he was a political animal from the get-go, and how comfortable he was here in his home state, Georgia.

As the plane rose higher, then leveled off, we settled into our assignment. I recommended to President Carter that he press the US

Government for peace, not unlike the key role it was now playing in Korea, building on President Carter's historic initiative there. I advised him that we get our heads around oil. Rather than having oil revenues fuel Khartoum's war machine, President Carter should convene the CEOs of oil companies to get their commitment to peace. And I recommended that a multi-level intensive peace process was necessary, maybe a 'Sudan Peace Process plus President Carter', incorporating the best of the Joint Egyptian-Libyan Initiative.

He responded favorably, saying he was going to take a conciliatory approach in Washington: he would listen a lot more than he spoke. When I asked him, "what are your minimum objectives?" he replied that he wanted to achieve "maximum objectives" and he listed many, from getting the USA's policy toward Sudan turned around, sending an investigative team into Khartoum to examine alleged human rights abuses, to improving the relationship this Administration had with The Carter Center. I was impressed with his strong, clear and specific response.

At the State Department, on the opulent seventh floor, we were given a courteous reception by Secretary of State Madeline Albright and Assistant Secretary of State for African Affairs Susan Rice. Tom Pickering, the Undersecretary of State, was notably more engaging and more sympathetic to President Carter. Carter was probed for insights into Khartoum: what was Bashir's attitude, did he really want peace; what about Turabi, the Islamic leader who had so much influence in Khartoum; what kind of a peace process was required? Carter stated that peace was possible if Bashir and Garang were brought together and that the process required a concerted international effort led by the US.

But we went away with little hope that President Clinton's administration was likely to make the shift in policy that we called for. In fact, Albright's promise of follow-up contact was never realized in the months of March and April 2000, and everyone on my team suspected that President Carter was very disappointed.

Nevertheless, President Carter sent letters to Presidents Bashir and Museveni, introducing me as his representative. I was to get things moving again.

4

No Kony No Progress

Before I left on my first trip to Africa to meet President Museveni and then on to Sudan, I returned home to Canada for the weekend. My sons, Evan and Warren, were all ears, and they had good advice to offer. Evan was completing a graduate degree in post-war recovery and Warren had been working at the Institute for which I was President so he was aware of my peacebuilding efforts in the past. Warren seemed preoccupied with testing me on how we would contend with Washington's lukewarm reception. Evan encouraged me take advantage of the asset I had in President Carter. I had shared my impression that The Carter Center was not closely aligned with the US Administration in Washington. I speculated that even though a Democrat was in the White House, President Carter had only so much influence with President Clinton. Indeed, I told them that I had heard that there was strain between President Carter and President Clinton. It was a common belief at our house that politics is always a fickle business. But I strongly agreed that President Carter would be great to work with.

Ann and I talked into the night about the road ahead. I would have to immerse myself in this assignment, leaving little time for us. There would be long trips to Africa, new and potentially dangerous elements. Our hopes of exploring Atlanta and the southern USA would have to be put on hold. We had put our successful conflict resolution business in Canada in the hands of colleagues so that I could work where I might perform at the top of my game. This was my opportunity. Would Ann once again agree to support me?

"This is it," she said, "You have to give it all you have if you are going to succeed." Little did either of us know just how much I would have to give. How much it would take from both of us. But as always, Ann backed me fully when she agreed that my work was worth her support.

The night before I was to leave I had a disturbed sleep. The images of the Acholi rebel, Alice Lakwena, and her Holy Spirit Movement, and what I had learned about Joseph Kony and the Lord's Resistance Army turned over and over in my mind. The history that I had read left me believing I was about to enter a world of tribal warfare and witchcraft. How would I function deep inside Africa – next door to the Congo and Rwanda, where just six years ago the people had slaughtered each other with machetes, leaving hundreds of thousands dead?

You might think that mass communication, the internet, globalization and the impact of American pop culture would homogenize the world. But many of the changes in cultures seem very superficial and the veneer of civilization everywhere is rather thin. I had no illusions about how ruthless western countries could be and I was no stranger to rough conduct, primitive motives, strange beliefs and practices.

After all, my Grandmother Lydia – who we called 'Fat Gramma' – had been a 'white' witch. She was a white witch because she used magic powers for good ends. She was a well-known healer for a large group of people at a time when there were few professionally trained and licensed medical doctors. She had learned her healing arts in the early 1900s from her father-in-law, my great grandfather, Wilhelm Hoffman. Said to be a medical doctor, he arrived in Canada from Germany in the 1860s. One of his sons was Ben, my Grandfather, Fat Grandma's husband. She assisted old Dr. Hoffman, learning how to prepare herbal remedies from flowers and weeds and roots they collected in the countryside. When the old man died, she took on his patients. And it seems she added her own gifts of healing to what she had learned from her father-in-law. I was told that she had special psychic powers, the powers of telling the future and of discerning.

When Fat Grandma died, my Father took up where she had left off. Well into my twenties, in the 1970s, and even into the 80s, he was still seeing people from the hills who sought his advice on spiritual, psychological, and business matters. As if that was not enough of an atmosphere of magic and healing powers to be raised in, I learned one day that my Mother's mother, Ma, also had special powers. When I was about 12 years old and we were discussing Fat Grandma my Mother told me that Ma had 'the charm'.

According to this story, she could stop people bleeding! And my Mother told me that Ma had used the charm, successfully, on my Father. She insisted that Ma had saved my Father's life when he had haemorrhaged after a surgery.

So Fat Grandma was a healer – using herbal preparations and a good deal of common sense. And Ma had the charm. And my Father, I knew, had consulted people, privately, behind closed doors. Not to mention some of the dreams and visions he would recount to me. Mine was a world of mystery and magic and for a long time I really wanted to have these special powers, the power of healing. While my professional career did include some strange and gripping experiences, I never was able to enter that world the way I wished I could.

Despite this background, on the eve of leaving for Uganda, my sleep had been unsettled. What kind of a place was Uganda after all?

The next day both Ann and our boys seemed resolute. I could tell by the way they made themselves busy. I tried to keep things light and talked about what we would do when I returned with some really good stories to tell them.

I departed for London, my first step en route to Uganda. There I planned to visit representatives of Kachoke Madit (KM), former northern Ugandan Acholi. I also planned to meet with conflict resolution colleagues at two nongovernmental organizations I respected, Conciliation Resources and International Alert. I also was to meet with officials at the UK's Department for International Development.

I arrived at the small crowded KM office. There they stressed to me the importance of involving the community in any efforts to establish peace in northern Uganda. Their point was not lost on me given my experience in Mostar and the Crimea. But it was good to be reminded that Alice Lakwena had emerged from a struggle between the Acholi people and the victorious Museveni. KM argued that the condition of neglect and underdevelopment in the north, and political discord among Acholi themselves would produce another Joseph Kony if those conditions were not changed; and killing Kony would not suffice. A political solution to the LRA rebellion was needed. Kony, after all, had had the blessing of the community when he took to the bush at 18 years of age, after Alice was defeated by Museveni's army. Now the community needed healing within itself, and with Museveni.

As I listened to this historical account and took the strong point being made on the basis of it, that a political solution was required, I recalled how many times I had sat listening to people whose lives have been torn apart by violence. I recognized that people need to tell their story, and that I was embarking on a trip that would have many stories to be told. I would have to find a balance between being a good listener and convincing people of my goals and my ability to take the steps needed to be successful.

At the Department for International Development, I met with a man who devoted himself to healing, and who had the peculiar name, Dr. Dennis Pain. Dennis, an anthropologist, was a somewhat disheveled character. He shared the findings of research he had conducted in northern Uganda. He said that despite all of the trauma they had suffered, the Acholi wanted reconciliation. They would forgive Kony, his commanders, and the abducted children who were his foot soldiers. They would use traditional methods of reconciliation. The victim and the offender – people who had been abducted and those who had done the abducting – together they would drink the 'bitter juice'. This was a drink made from plant roots. Rituals would be used to restore relations.

As I listened to Dennis my thoughts wandered back to Canada to the men in Helpline. At an average age of 12, while residents in two Ontario training schools run by St Joseph's and St. John's Christian Brothers, hundreds of little boys were beaten, buggered, misused and abused. Some were confused about their own sexual identity; others were alienated from the Roman Catholic Church. Afterwards some had lost complete faith in God. Many never were able to put their lives back together. They were a hapless lot, damaged goods; and some of them who I knew committed suicide. That so many were brave enough to confront the demons that haunted them and crawl out of their personal dungeon is a testimony to the resilience of the human spirit.

Working closely with former Canadian Ambassador Douglas Roche I had designed and managed a process to assist the men, who grew in number from 142 to nearly 1400, to reach an agreement of healing and reconciliation with the Church and the Government of Ontario. As part of that agreement I recorded their stories. I found them in their homes, in prisons, in psychiatric wards – where Roger Tucker – their lawyer – had said that I would find them. They allowed me to tape record their stories. Most were prepared to have themselves identified in my report. This time they would be believed. I am going to let three of the boys – now grown men – speak for themselves:

They used me as a sexual article (shows scar left from cutting himself on bed when he tried to escape) – there was blood all over the floor the next morning, from my rectum. Brother _____ asked who did it and he told the Director. The Director cancelled my trip to the hospital and said:"Are you suggesting one of my Brothers did this to you?" The Director said to Brother _____ "This must be straightened up." I was sent to the hole in the custody of Brother _____, who hit me, hand-cuffed me to the bed and two hours later threw a bucket of cold water on me and beat me. I was beaten every day for a week. I never saw anybody touching anybody else. I thought I was the only one - when they came to get me out of my bed. The abuse started after Christmas the first year. I couldn't study; I couldn't retain anything – and I was placed out to work.

I was in the bathroom and admit that me and another student were fooling around squirting tooth paste. A Brother came from behind and punched me on the side of my head, and I hit my head on the wall. I was made to stand in front of the clock with my hands behind my back. I was very scared, crying. The Brother struck me with a closed fist on my shoulder, I fell on one knee and was punched. Later on the Brother came and took me to another Brother's where I was sexually assaulted and buggered by both Brothers. Thereafter this would occur on a regular basis two or three times a week, sometimes I was subjected to sexual assault by a single Brother, but most of the time it was with the two Brothers. At times, instruments would be inserted in my rectum.

I wonder if after all this being said if there is anyone who can really understand why I was silent for all these years. I think my reason is that I was placed in a cage or prison called fear. The fear of someone finding out all these disgusting things that happened to me. Now my fear has turned to rage and now I fear this rage held within me. I wonder will they understand all of my daily feeling of revolt, disgust and anger. Can they see this shroud of guilt and shame that envelops me and drags me down to the point of total despair? I wish someone could explain to me what I did that was so terrible and wrong to have deserved to live this life. Can it be true that I really am worthless?

The search for reconciliation and healing using mediated talks between the men and the Church and Government was unprecedented. It put aside public protest by the victims, a class action suit, ongoing denial by the Church and the Christian Brothers. It gave the men some financial compensation for pain and suffering. Some were awarded money so that their children could advance their prospects. The Church and the Government apologized. And my record of their story was written for all to see.

Of course, the agreement was not perfect. And as a non-adversarial healing and reconciliation process it has been improved upon in subsequent cases.

But it showed that alternatives to a justice system based on legal contests, on punishment and reward, are possible. It showed that impoverished and disaffected people, if respected and empowered, can act honourably on their own behalf; that a desperate past and a bleak future can be made brighter. Survivor can replace victim, as this final quote from my "Recorder's Report" shows:

> *. . . my life has changed dramatically. . . the fact that I could finally say out loud what I had experienced as a boy and suffered for all my life – to a group of people who not only believed what I said, but listened with deep compassion, acted as a tremendous release for me. From that day forward, I began to look at life from a different perspective. I had gained a greater sense of my own worth as a human being and acquired a new sense of self-confidence.*
>
> *Up until that time, in large part due to my limited education, I had worked in the restaurant business, primarily as a waiter. After the hearing, I decided to explore other avenues of employment. I finally enrolled in a university level course to obtain a certificate as a Geriatric Activity Co-Coordinator. The course was extremely difficult, really far beyond my abilities at times, and I almost quit mid-course on several occasions. I am proud to say that I passed the course and now have a university certificate entitling me to seek employment in this area. I now look to the future with hope and confidence.*

The reconciliation agreement was successful enough to attract national and international attention. Within weeks I received an invitation, from Roger again, to meet with some other victims of institutional abuse.

They were called Petabekook. They were as old as the name sounds.

They had come a long way south to meet with me; all the way from the James Bay region, near the Canadian arctic. They spoke through an interpreter.

One old man began the conversation by saying, "We are here for healing and reconciliation. We are old. It is not for us, but for our children. We were taken from our homes, our families years ago, when we were little children, when we were small. And we were punished for speaking our language. We were beaten for nothing at the school. And they took away our beliefs, our culture. And we have nothing now. We are old now."

I nodded, indicating I had understood and that I cared. Before I could speak another old man talked; then another.

All I had to do was listen. Each one spoke, including a woman who was with the group, sitting in a circle in the basement of the home of a woman who had brought them south to meet me. They all told essentially the same story of abuse, of cultural genocide.

It was a story of personal suffering, fears as a child. It was a tale of destruction of their identity; destruction of their community and culture. It was the story of abuse of power by the Sisters of Charity, an order of the Roman Catholic Church. They said the Sisters had even constructed a crude electric chair to administer shocks to some of the children.

"Thank you," I began, and thinking that I would be thought rude, but unable to hold back, I asked "can you really mean it that you want to reconcile with the church and the government after what you have just told me? After what they did to you"?

"Yes" the old man who had spoken first, replied.

It amazed me how powerful the human will to reconcile is. It seems, even across cultures, across the world, that it is easier for victims to forgive than for offenders to admit the harm they have done.

Dr. Pain insisted that the international community should put money into developing the north of Uganda. Peace was possible. Healing was needed.

His message was the same as the exiled Acholis at KM. Peace would require a political, not a military solution. Peace would have to include the community. Already the scale and scope of the challenge set out for me by President Carter was coming more clearly into focus.

Indeed, all but one of my UK colleagues in conflict resolution on first hearing it, thought it preposterous that I would undertake to end the war in Sudan. They stated even though I worked for President Carter, I didn't have the resources, that it was dangerous. Everyone else had failed, and the Sudan Peace Process was going nowhere. So why wouldn't I fail too? Hadn't I better stick to a more reasonable challenge, that of implementing the Nairobi Agreement?

At International Alert, however, an old associate, Ed Garcia, was more positive. I liked and trusted Ed, a humble former Filipino priest who was an effective mediator with lots of experience on the ground in war zones. Ed said: "If you do this, it's all or nothing."

We agreed that Bashir and Garang would not give peace a chance until each was convinced that he could not win a military victory and the pain of battle had become too much for both. Until they had reached a 'mutually hurting stalemate' the conflict in Sudan would not be 'ripe' for resolution. But I was determined to 'ripen' it; although knowing the enormity of my mission and the limiting factors made my assignment seem both real and unreal to me. It gave me pause.

Just before leaving London someone handed me a document, sealed in a large brown envelope, and I was told by the bearer of this document that it would shed light on Joseph Kony and the Lord's Resistance Army. This person told me to keep it and its source confidential. "How confidential?" I asked. "May I share it with my staff?" "No!" was the firm reply.

The document, 20 pages long, was written by someone close to the LRA, perhaps someone whose life would be at risk if their identity was known. For it was very specific in its description of Kony's military command structure and it provided relatively clinical information on some of the key, and notorious, senior commanders. In this document I learned about Otti Vincent, Kony's most senior military officer. Sam Koho, the intellectual confidante of the 'Chairman' Joseph Kony, was also described in this secret paper. The LRA, according to the document, had a vague political manifesto that blurred biblical scripture and animism. Kony's leadership was described as a search for consensus followed by personal consultation with the spirits, and then brutal edict.

What I had found in London was not a lot to go on for a mediator. Nevertheless, I had taken President Carter seriously and I was prepared to press on, against all odds. Within hours, Tom, who had joined me on this fact-finding trip, and I departed Heathrow for Uganda.

We arrived to a hot and muggy airport in Entebbe, which is miles away from Uganda's capital city, Kampala. The momentary congestion of businessmen queuing to buy visas gave the false impression that things were busier than they really were. Outside, a few cab drivers scrambled to get a fare, the inevitable placards of UN agency drivers and nongovernmental organization representatives flashed about. Arrivals searched for their names and a safe ride to their hotels, the Kampala Sheraton, the Speke, or the Grand.

Uganda lies on the Equator; its banana trees, palms and lush undergrowth springing from a rich red soil. We drove along the shore of shimmering Lake Victoria, my childhood knowledge of Stanley and Livingstone flashing through my mind. We passed some aircraft relics abandoned near the shore, several miles from the airport. Then we climbed through coastal Entebbe towards Kampala.

All along the roadside people toiled or strolled. Many rode bicycles, lugging some great load of firewood or sugar cane or water in large yellow plastic containers. Young men sat or leaned on motorbikes, perhaps they were couriers waiting for a job. I got the impression of progress, of a people who want to work, of entrepreneurial spirit. Everyone was black skinned; their clothing was mixed – from western blue jeans to colourful traditional garments. When we finally reached Kampala after threading our way through busy traffic, around round-abouts, up a hill, past a cyber cafe and a thriving business center, we were unloaded at the Sheraton. We would not be roughing it tonight. I would, however, be greeted by the photo of President Museveni, the clean shaven face of a youngish, strong-looking man. I was to discover this picture in every store and public building I would enter, and very soon would meet him in the flesh.

Everything I did in Kampala focused on my meeting with President Museveni. He had received the letter of introduction from President Carter. In a day or two I would meet him at his palace. Beforehand, however, I was grilled, educated and prepared by Dr. Ruhakana Rugunda, and members of the Ugandan delegation that had negotiated the Nairobi Agreement. Rugunda and his team were now responsible for implementing the Agreement. This was the group who had been giving their Sudanese counter-parts so much trouble in follow-up talks led by The Carter Center. I could see why, when I finally sat down with them over a fantastic Chinese meal that they hosted in a comfortable restaurant in the centre of Kampala.

Only perfunctorily courteous, they were down right interrogatory! They barraged me with questions and statements. What was my background? Was I aware of the history of the Acholi people – and more importantly, of the Khartoum government's relentless efforts to Islamize Africa? Why hadn't the Government of Sudan delivered on its commitments? Did I know about the Aboke girls, innocent students captured right out of their school by Kony years ago? Kony must release the Aboke girls! Why have Joseph Kony and the Lord's Resistance Army not been disbanded? The Nairobi Agreement was failing!

I listened for a long time. Then it was my turn to talk.

But how do you respond to this sort of thing? Of course, I was new, and in their eyes, probably naive. At least I was ignorant of Uganda and it may have been apparent I didn't know Africa. But I know people and the ways political actors behave. I know conflict and what it takes to move a violent situation toward peace. I know distrust, and propaganda, and human suffering: and I know that unless those in dispute believe that somehow you are important to them, they have no time for you.

I gave them a thumbnail sketch of my resume, emphasizing my work in prisons, with violent people and violent groups, my years in the trenches in various war-torn societies. I emphasized my professional approach.

I said, "I want to change the culture of the meetings between you and the Sudanese. I'll set it up so that we move towards real dialogue, and problem-solving. That will give you and me and the Sudanese measurable commitments."

They looked at me a little blankly. I added, "And frankly, President Museveni's hostile remarks in the media accusing Sudan of violating the Nairobi Agreement don't help. It is time for a new attitude and new behaviour. Just like you, I want results. As a neutral mediator I will hold both of you accountable."

Now their stare had turned colder. But I went on, saying "If Uganda expects Sudan to honour its commitments, Uganda will have to honour the commitments it has made. And we will need to have another meeting, soon, in Atlanta. That way President Carter can offer his assistance."

"Efforts to implement the Agreement need to be stepped up" I ended.

Ragunda paused, leaned a way back in his seat. Then he spoke slowly.

"Certainly another meeting in Atlanta is possible. Uganda wishes to comply with its commitments. But that meeting should follow a direct meeting between you and Kony. Sudan should and can make such a meeting possible. Kony should be invited to talk with the Government of Uganda. We will tell him the ways and means of coming home. Amnesty is available. He can be located somewhere safe, likely in southern Uganda." Then he added, "But these talks are not negotiations."

I replied in a matter-of-fact way that I would ask the Government of Sudan to arrange for me to meet with Kony as soon as possible. Then a meeting of the ministerial delegations to pick up the pace of implementing the Agreement would follow directly thereafter in Atlanta, at The Carter Center.

Rugunda and his colleagues seemed to accept my approach. They relaxed and got down to enjoying the excellent food, the conversation now easy. Indeed, I was pleased to listen to Rugunda, a big man with a wonderful baritone voice, regale all of us with more stories, including recounting some of his President's exploits in coming to power. And so the evening went, my hosts now fully at ease with this, Ben Hoffman, President Carter's new representative.

Later in my hotel room, I reflected on my impression of the Ugandans. They were direct, tough, wary, hospitable, and possibly paranoid about their 'northern Arab brothers'.

Before meeting President Museveni, The Carter Center's man on the ground in Uganda, Ron Gillespie, a senior consultant who knew his way around eastern Africa, arranged for me to meet with the UNICEF representative, Keith Wright. Keith is a warm and open man who wears his heart on his sleeve.

Keith told me that according to UNICEF's records, the Lord's Resistance Army had abducted some 10,000 children over the past twelve years. My mind boggled at the number. 10,000 children! Could this really be true?

As a father who cherishes my two sons, I couldn't imagine losing a child. I cringed at the pain of the parents of those 10,000. "And where are they" I asked, "What has happened to them?"

Keith said UNICEF estimated that 6,000 were still alive, several hundred had escaped over the years, and many had died in battle with Ugandan government forces and in fighting the SPLA in southern Sudan. Others had been killed by Kony and his commanders.

Then Keith paused. He had my undivided attention. He told me of how the children were abducted. The LRA would attack a village in northern Uganda at night. Everyone would be corralled at gun point. Children would be separated, and in some cases, forced to kill their parents right on the spot – as a first act of indoctrination; or be killed. This way the child would believe Kony when he said that the child could never go home, for fear of punishment. Kids – sometimes dozens of them – between 8 and 18 years would then be marched through the bush, hard, for two or three weeks back to Kony's safe haven in south Sudan. If one was caught trying to escape, he/she was killed immediately. If a child stumbled he/she was put to death on the spot by the other kids – brothers, sisters, cousins, friends from the village. A single bicycle chain would be given to the kids and each was ordered to whip the fallen child until the boy or girl was lacerated to death. There might be a ritual then of drinking the child's blood.

Sitting silent across the room and not really sure how to respond to this, I just stared at Keith. His sad eyes met mine. I could see his plea for these kids. He was asking – hoping that in my assignment with The Carter Center we would insist that the Nairobi Agreement be implemented. For the Agreement required that the Government of Sudan return the abducted children. Keith desperately wanted my help in getting the kids back home.

He reached behind him, taking a book from his bookshelf, and handed it to me. It was a compilation of drawings that had been done by kids who had escaped the LRA. I flipped through the book, noting stick figures of kids, holding rifles, some in battle; some holding rocket propelled artillery on their shoulders and firing at helicopter gunships. There was lots of red in the pictures, and gun blasts and dead kids lying in battle scenes. And the little stick figures of the kids in the drawing were of young kids, with only a few older fighters, commanders it looked like.

Keith told me the pictures, in crayon, had been drawn while the kids were in treatment centres, in Gulu, in the north. They were part of the therapy the kids went through to help them get over the trauma they had suffered, to help them put the abduction, abuse and killing behind them. Somehow the kids were to let go of being child soldiers and become just kids once again; kids who could go home and begin a new life.

That night, I spent the evening alone mentally preparing for the meeting I would one day have with Kony. Who or what was this elusive, possibly maniacal, leader of the LRA? What motivated him? What could I do to be ready?

The next day, another beautiful sunny day in Uganda, I had my meeting with Yoweri Museveni, the former guerilla fighter and current President of Uganda. While I was waiting in an anteroom, mentally rehearsing the key points I wanted to make, I was introduced to a man who apparently was responsible for the care and tending of Kony's old and frail parents. This tall, elderly man had once gone to Khartoum as an escort to Kony's parents on a planned visit with Kony. But the visit had failed, driving a further wedge between Sudan and Uganda, and between Uganda and Kony himself. The old man's presence, I assumed, was to help shed some light on Kony and the Sudanese. But as we were chatting and before I could get much information, I was summoned. I never saw him again. I followed my escorts out of the building over lush green grass and past exotic plants. There, under a great shade tree, I was received by President Museveni.

Surrounded by an entourage, Museveni was warm and welcoming. Cameras were clicking away in the background. I was seated directly across from where he sat down. I was flanked left by Ron who had joined me for this meeting, and right by senior members of the Ugandan delegation – the cabinet ministers who had briefed me two nights ago. Behind us there were rows of other officials and members of the press.

Museveni presided over our meeting with the self-assuredness that I have come to associate with the powerful. It includes an air of unshakeable confidence, a command of the environment, and an obviously personal 'presence', with its attendant charismatic qualities. Museveni was a big man, physically. He had upright posture, square shoulders, and was impeccably dressed in a dark suit. He spoke with authority, his eyes intensely focused on me, all the while sipping tea from his china teacup, chasing flies away with the wave of his white handkerchief.

I listened to Museveni's view, prompted by my questions and comments carefully inserted into his monologue. When I pressed him that his commitment in the Nairobi Agreement required him to stop supporting the SPLA, he declared he would never stop his moral support of them. He stated that Sudan could be a model country, graphically demonstrating the bridge between brown Arabic and black African cultures. Khartoum was, however, an Islamic regime intent on 'Islamizing' all of Africa. It wished to dominate the blacks in the south and he would never abandon moral support for his brothers there. As for Kony, he was an unreliable juvenile with no political agenda. Nevertheless Kony needed to be dealt with – through Uganda's Amnesty Act – and my help was welcome. I could count on him to have his delegation attend the meeting in Atlanta. Uganda fully intended to honour its commitment to President Carter.

The meeting ended – cameras flashed away again as we bid farewell.

I had heard it all before – from his senior ministers. Now I realized how deeply ingrained was Museveni's support to Garang and the SPLA. I could also feel his vitriol for Kony.

And, while Museveni had not made it a precondition for Uganda to attend a ministerial meeting in Atlanta, it was clear that I would have to meet with Kony to satisfy the Ugandans. My first visit to Khartoum would now require that I build a relationship with the Sudanese, generate enthusiasm for a renewed effort to implement the Nairobi Agreement, and ask for access to the notorious rebel leader, Joseph Kony.

Tom and I traveled from Kampala by car to Entebbe. There, from Entebbe by air eastward to Nairobi. From Nairobi, we flew north a great distance over the Sahara desert to Khartoum.

Blast furnace hot Khartoum. We were met by Doug Archard at an empty but visibly 'watched' airport. Doug was now The Carter Center's country representative after I had recruited him to my team from his post in Atlanta as our Diplomat-in-Residence. He was now our diplomatic presence working on the ground in Khartoum. He was to demonstrate our seriousness and to become informed and informative as we tried to build sound working relationships with those organs of the Sudanese government and with individuals responsible for implementing the Nairobi Agreement.

Doug had also been moving among opposition groups and human rights activists, gaining a broad perspective on the political situation in Khartoum. For, in addition to our major assignment, we had to assess whether The Carter Center should respond favorably to the request recently received by President Carter from Sudan's President Bashir for The Carter Center to monitor the upcoming presidential election. If President Carter was to agree, Khartoum would have to pass three tests that The Carter Center applies in all these cases. The election would have to be fair and free, open to the media, and all opposition groups had to agree to our role.

Doug had organized a full itinerary for Tom and me, ensuring that I got to meet as many people from different points of view as possible. Members of the international diplomatic community – our Dutch, British, and Canadian colleagues, some whose governments financed our work – received us warmly, hungry for information from Kampala, curious to learn that I might visit Kony. Over much appreciated cold beer in a country where alcohol is outlawed except for diplomatic circles, they encouraged me to press for implementation of the Nairobi Agreement. I felt we had allies; and that there was hope in our peace efforts.

However, many activists and members of the opposition in Khartoum (to the extent that they were able to mobilize and meet with me) made it clear that the upcoming Presidential election would not be free and fair. At a lavish meal held in secret in the home of a human rights activist who had been detained and tortured in the past, I was told repeatedly that the National Islamic Front, the party which governed the country, was repressive – some of those present spoke to me at their own peril. They insisted that there was not a free media in the country; the election would not be fair.

Our Sudanese government contacts responsible for implementing the Nairobi Agreement were, contrary to my expectations, most cordial, genteel, and they assured me of their cooperation. Certainly they would attend a ministerial meeting in Atlanta, providing their President approved.

And their cooperation was evident immediately. "Yes" the bright-eyed, business-like Dr.Yahia Babiker, the Deputy Director of External Security, responded "You can meet with Kony. When do you wish to go to meet him in Juba?"

Now that surprised me! I had certainly not expected to get access to Kony so easily. Juba was the Government's garrisoned city in the deep black African south of Sudan, surrounded by SPLA rebels; and Kony himself was elusive, temperamental, a mysterious figure who so few outsiders had met. I had not expected such cooperation from the Sudanese, based mainly on the picture that had been painted of them in Kampala – and the way in which they had been so negatively stereotyped in the USA.

"As soon as possible," I quickly responded to Yahia.

While that meeting with Yahia was very encouraging, Doug, Tom and I wondered how we could reconcile the likely outcome of our assessment concerning monitoring the Sudanese presidential election with our need to win over the Government of Sudan to honour its commitment to the Nairobi Agreement. For it was becoming clear to us that Khartoum would not pass The Center's tests for monitoring elections. We would have to recommend to President Carter that he decline President Bashir's request, while asking Bashir to remain engaged in our agenda.

Meanwhile, Doug took us to the Souk, the market, making his point that he learned a great deal about society, indeed about Government, by visiting a country's marketplaces. Across the Nile, in the old city of Omdurman, the marketplace was a scene of organized chaos. Donkey carts meandered this way and that through throngs of shoppers. The market concessions or vendor's booths were laid out in what for me was an unintelligible maze of tiny corridors that went on for what seemed to be miles. Stopping at various open air shops, Doug led us through an immersion course in development studies by discussing the availability and price of sugar, coffee, clothing, grains and carpets from the Middle East. At ease among the people, Doug probed merchants to tell us the origin, the method of shipment and demand for their goods. The merchants seemed happy to comply, our small assembly of white people always attracting a few curious Sudanese, and of course, scads of kids.

As we left the Souk, Doug also remarked on the safety of Khartoum – drawing our attention to the sheer absence of guns – noting that one of The Carter Center's health workers, an attractive blonde woman, had jogged each evening for three years along the Nile, never even receiving a 'cat call'.

According to Doug, Khartoum was changing, slowly. China and Malaysia were on very friendly terms, extracting oil, selling weapons and services to Sudan. European countries were beginning to warm up, too. Talisman, I was reminded, was a Canadian oil company continuing to do business in Sudan, even though it was obvious that government oil revenues went into purchasing military equipment and weapons to wage war against the southern rebels. Worse, it was alleged that Talisman knew Sudan used a scorched earth policy to drive innocent people from their homes near the oil fields. Helicopter gunships fired on unarmed civilians; then their villages were burned to the ground. But oil money was changing Khartoum's horizon; new buildings, more new cars, a new bridge over the Nile.

The demographics of Khartoum were changing also. Doug noted the colourfully dressed black southerners who were appearing in greater numbers. He pointed out the tall Dinkas and described how different tribes scarred their faces as rites of passage. While many, up to one million, lived in deplorable conditions in camps around the city, their presence in the general population suggested a government policy of simple assimilation.

In the end, I did not meet President Bashir, who apparently was diverted by official business. That may have been a nice way of saying that he had learned enough about our movements and really had no interest in meeting me at the time; or that he really was preoccupied. In any event, I was only slightly disappointed. I wasn't too excited about having to tell him to his face that I would recommend against The Carter Center monitoring his upcoming election, especially when my goal was to get to Kony. And only the Government of Sudan could make that happen.

Just before leaving Khartoum I visited the small craft shop at the back of the Khartoum Hilton. For some reason I was drawn to a disturbing, primitive mask. Leather had been tightly drawn over the wooden structure of the face. The top half, from the nostrils up, was red, the bottom black. It had blunted features – two pin holes for a nose, and the eyes were empty sockets that appeared to be burned into the face. Scorched empty holes, that neither peered out nor took you in. It was a death mask and I could not resist buying it. It was only when I returned home and the moment I hung it on the wall that I recalled a dream of weeks earlier before I had ever gone to Sudan. In that dream I had traveled into a desert landscape through a red and black tunnel, where I had found a boy of ten, myself, standing alone and naked. It had been a riveting dream, just as disturbing as the mask. The only colours in both were black and red. Obviously, this assignment was having a big impact on me personally, at a deep emotional level. Was the dream a foretelling of something? Was my unconscious mind trying to make sense of horrific things done to children, of people fleeing gunfire in a scorched earth?

Back at The Carter Center, Tom and I prepared a trip report for President Carter. In it, I recommended that President Carter decline President Bashir's invitation to monitor the upcoming presidential election in Sudan. He agreed.

At the same time my staff and interns at The Center began to make preparations for a full ministerial meeting between Uganda and Sudan. It would take place in late August. The delicate issue of obtaining US visas for the Sudanese delegation was facilitated by our diplomats-in-residence. They had contacts in the US State Department and could help cut through the red tape of an administration that considered Sudan a terrorist-harbouring nation.

Our Facilities staff, who constantly proved to be of the highest order, would have to prepare for the arrival and reception of up to thirty delegates and their entourage. They were responsible for accommodation, transportation, issues of diet, finding a meeting room and private break-out rooms, a quiet place where I might meet privately with the heads of delegation – every detail would need to be nailed down.

Our staff in the Conflict Resolution Program and the fortunate interns of that summer who would get as close as any student ever could to a real live complex mediation began work on invitations, protocol, and briefing notes. I wanted to know everything that could be known about both countries' conduct leading up to the meeting. I needed to know as much as I could about Joseph Kony and the LRA. Where had Kony come from, what was he really like? Was he a spiritualist *and* a Christian? Who and where was his family? Who were his senior officers? How dangerous was he?

Hardly settled in Atlanta, I received notice from Khartoum that Kony was prepared to meet me in ten days.

Ten days! I was both elated and sobered by the quick response from Dr. Yahia. Meeting Kony would certainly secure the ministerial meeting. Such a quick response suggested that the Government of Sudan was cooperative, maybe sincere about honouring its commitments. The Government of Uganda would have to take note, both of my ability to step up the process and of their adversary's compliance. And this would be my opportunity to build Kony and the LRA into this bilateral undertaking between two states. After all, the goal of peaceful relations between the neighbours was not all that we sought. We wanted to see a peaceful resolution to the war between Uganda and the LRA. We wanted to help see sustainable peace established in northern Uganda. And in doing this we also wanted to demonstrate our commitment to peace in Sudan. Yet there remained another party, the SPLA. Even if I had wanted to, I would never be able to forget that Sudan would be pressing Uganda for cessation of its support to the SPLA in return for terminating Sudan's support to Kony.

At the same time, I did not want The Carter Center to be any further alienated from the LRA and the SPLA by virtue of President Carter having mediated the Nairobi Agreement without their participation. For the Agreement essentially committed each neighbour to cut off support to its respective ally. Obviously those allies would not appreciate this. Yet, without the allies being brought into the equation, there could not be a lasting peace in northern Uganda nor an easily negotiated end to the civil war in Sudan.

Complex? Yes! Awkward? Yes! Doable? We had to hope so. And our hope would have to be reinforced by concrete, measurable steps taken in the right direction.

Getting Kony to enter talks with the Government of Uganda would be a huge step forward.

5

Clearing A Path For Peace
With The LRA

The record suggested there was minimal hope of success, and that my task was dangerous. With security and logistics not in my hands, and such little information to go on, there was not much I could do. That is, I had no control over the setting and conditions under which Kony and I would meet. And we had been told that Kony had just assassinated his uncle and cousin, who had come to him with a plea for peace.

I decided to ask Doug Archard to accompany me. A professional, seasoned through years of sensitive work on the front line from Vietnam to Afghanistan, he was an expert observer. And his work in Khartoum had been excellent. I wanted someone with me who would, unobtrusively, take note of as much of our surroundings and the dynamics as possible.

In our discussions to prepare for this key meeting deep in the bush in southern Sudan, we decided to take nothing with us that might put off Kony or any of his officers. No cameras, no binoculars, no maps, no electronic equipment.

I asked Doug if we should bring some gift, a token of goodwill, not unlike any meeting we might have with a dignitary, or senior official. Doug responded that he had been wondering the same, and was at a loss of what to bring.

I suggested cigars. Doug reminded me that one of the explicit prohibitions of the Lord's Resistance Army was against smoking. He also recalled the CIA debacle of a failed attempt to assassinate Castro using an explosive cigar. No, cigarettes and cigars would not do!

"What then?"

We had also heard Kony liked music. In fact, we had heard from the Sudanese intelligence officers we had met in Yahia's office in Khartoum that he liked music and movies: 'Cowboy and Indian' movies! Should we bring an audiocassette, CD, or movie? But in what format? Did Kony have a VHS in the bush? A stereo? We decided not to bother.

But we did feel a little under-prepared should this rebel, the Chairman and Commander-in-Chief of the Lord's Resistance Army receive us formally, and offer us a gift.

Our preparations at The Carter Center in Atlanta complete, including inoculations, anti-malarial prescriptions, and travel visas in hand, we embarked on the long transatlantic trip. As our plane approached Khartoum Doug remarked, "You know, when this is over we will have flown across the world, spent about 10,000 dollars, and taken six days for a two hour meeting."

"I know," I replied. "It's a lot. But it will be worth every penny if we succeed." Doug nodded agreement.

He had also booked us into the Acropole Hotel in Khartoum. No Hilton on this trip! This was a low profile mission. The Acropole is a family run hotel that is friendly, clean – and spartan. It caters mainly to low budget nongovernmental organizations and has a very intriguing group of expatriate guests. Over the next three years, I would meet a rich diversity of fellow travelers at the Acropole – a Greek Orthodox priest, Ray McGrath, the co-recipient of the Nobel Peace prize, long-haired peace workers, writers, visiting archaeologists and professional film crews. We blended in easily. But it is not the Hilton. The beds are more like cots, the mattresses thin and hard. And in July, you fight the desert heat under a modest ceiling fan.

So it was, the night before we were to fly at 6am to Juba, then travel deep into the bush to meet Kony. As I lay on my bed under the slow moving fan, I had this strange sensation that I was about to go under general anesthetic. All was calm. There were no more preparations to make. Abandoning myself to the morrow – to the future whatever it may bring. If successful I would 'wake' again on the other side.

But it was quite possible we would not succeed, and I would die, sharing a similar fate as others before me. I thought about the letter I had written to Ann, sealed and given to my secretary, Cassandra. I had instructed her to give it to Ann if I did not come home. Ann did not know what I knew about Kony and the dangerousness of this mission. She did not know about the letter. It held my last thoughts about our family. In it I told Ann that I loved her deeply. I said how impressed I was with our boys, Evan and Warren, who I was sure would do well in life if they just followed their passion.

It was dark in the early morning when we left the Acropole. With their special hospitality, George, one of the two Greek brothers who owned the hotel, had arranged for us to take lunch with us. At the airport we were met by two intelligence officers from Sudanese External Security. These men, both in their early thirties, were our hosts and guides, and were likely also tasked with keeping an eye on us. Cordial, they arranged tea for us in Khartoum's austere domestic airport. Whatever the system was, it worked. Within minutes we were sipping hot clear tea in china cups! Before we could finish, we were escorted to the small World Food Program plane awaiting us and placed in the capable hands of another young man, our friendly South African pilot. It was not yet 6am.

I had imagined the Sahara desert to be an unending colourless expanse of sand. How wrong I was! While Doug delved into one of his mammoth books which became his traveler's trademark – always some tome on any of a diverse range of topics – I stared endlessly out the airplane's tiny window from a manageable 10,000-foot perch. The mosaic of colours – reds, yellows, and copper, broken by an undulating Nile – brought back images from the highly textured movie, The English Patient, where the Sahara was a fabric of wind-swept golden dunes and shadowy rifts.

After three hours of flight, we set down in Malakal where a small cortege of UN workers exchanged greetings, loaded and unloaded supplies. We refuelled manually, two local men hand pumping the fuel from 50-gallon drums. Then we were off. Juba and Joseph Kony our next stop.

At Juba, the garrison city for the Government of Sudan deep in the south of the country, we were met on the tarmac by a military escort. Everyone was friendly, our military hosts obviously familiar with the scene and the local personnel. A Lieutenant Colonel and the local senior intelligence officer seemed unexpectedly casual and warm, yet there was still an air of business to it all. We were guided to a recent model truck and directed to the rear crew seat. The windows were heavily tinted. We could see out, but no one could see in. Four armed men jumped in the open box behind us. Three other vehicles assembled, each with four armed men, all wearing red berets, riding behind.

We were told that 'they' (the LRA) were waiting for us. We were to go directly to the camp at Nsitu. It seemed to me to be a base from where the LRA and the Government of Sudan jointly operated. It was the last outpost before the front and Sudan's enemy, the Sudan Peoples Liberation Army. Within minutes of starting off, however, we stopped at a small store. I got the strong sense of 'hurry up and wait'. Here our hosts purchased a case of Pepsi and we were offered a drink. I thought 'this is surreal' – a Pepsi break in southern Sudan – with the Sudanese Army!

When Doug opened his door to get out, two soldiers moved toward the vehicle, with stern looks that left little doubt that we were to stay inside. They left the door open a crack for fresh air, but Doug and I got the message. Obviously, two white men being escorted through a black garrisoned city were to be hidden from the public and any enemy spies.

During our unspectacular ride on a god-awful washed-out road through thick brush I began to focus myself for the meeting. We were now a long way from the elegant Norfolk Hotel in Nairobi where President Carter had mediated the Agreement between Sudan and Uganda, the Agreement I had to implement. The Agreement that required the LRA to give up abducted child soldiers. We were also a long way from Khartoum and its Arab culture. We were deep in black Africa. We passed a few military installations, some destroyed anti-aircraft guns, but as we penetrated deeper into the bush, toward the front lines – toward the LRA, and just beyond, the SPLA – the presence of war became more obvious. Tired looking soldiers returning from duty walked or rode bicycles on the dirt road; soldiers relaxed with their families near huts that could be glimpsed through openings in the bush. We were getting close. I reminded myself that my task was to be honest, to be respectful, and to win over this man, Kony; the man who was now the most notorious guerilla fighter in the world. And as for our personal safety? What could we do? The issue of physical security was in the hands of our Sudanese military escort and a function of the relationship the Government of Sudan had with Kony. Honourable intentions and authentic behaviour were all we could offer at this point. That would be our only defense.

The vehicles began a short climb and turned to a crude gateway with a guarded sentry; an LRA who waved us through. There on the perimeter, behind standing crops in an open field, I saw grass-covered huts and a woman hanging laundry to dry. Then the road wound its way through the field and a strangely empty countryside. There were a couple of checkpoints, unmanned. The road turned and we came to the camp.

As a final mental preparation, I determined to be single-minded in engaging Kony. The fate of the Nairobi Agreement and peace in northern Uganda depended on it.

A charming, beaming, handsome black man waited to greet us as we spilled out of the vehicles. Familiar greetings were exchanged between our Sudanese escort and the group assembled in a clean courtyard surrounded by impressive grass-roofed huts and larger buildings that comprised the camp. Somewhat disarmed by this unexpected cordiality, I shook hands with him, taking him for Kony.

But this man was Sam Koho, Kony's confidante. Kony waited for us inside a large thatch-roofed building. As we entered this building, I noted some 40–50 officers, mid-ranking, I thought. They were seated theatre-style on our right. Facing them, as in a bear pit, were the senior commanders – and Joseph Kony.

They all rose and we were welcomed generously. Kony shook my hand and I was invited to sit. The chairs were shaped in a small open 'U', with the opening facing the assembly. I was placed in the middle of the open U; Joseph Kony sat in the middle of a row on my left, six to eight feet away. Our hosts and Doug were seated on the right.

Quickly, the case of Pepsis was opened and offered about – a sign of goodwill from the Sudanese. As the bottles were being opened there was some 'eyeing each other up' for a few seconds. I was surprised that Kony and his senior officers were all in civilian clothing. And it was obvious that the 'peanut gallery' was taking in every aspect of this meeting. They sat motionless with all eyes on us.

Kony, taller and thinner than I had expected, was dressed in jeans and a casual shirt with a pull string that ran through the collar. His hair was short, neat and he wore dark framed glasses and carried a small book. I wondered what it might be and thought that it was the New Testament or an English Dictionary.

Sam made the introductions and recalling the secret document I had been given in London, I felt myself stiffen a bit when I was told the man beside me was Otti Vincent. Otti was Kony's most senior military officer who was reputed to be an especially vicious man and had led the assault on the Acholi village where 300 people were slaughtered. Short, sinuous, his steely eyes tried to pierce through me. Beside Otti, the others appeared benign. Two or three were quite senior; they were mature, very presentable, and far more genteel than I had expected. I tried to identify them in my mind, recalling the descriptions of the LRA senior commanders from the document. I placed the erect grey-haired man as the officer who had fled the Ugandan Air Force to join Kony. Another I took as a top military strategist.

Then Kony began, theatrically. He attacked, waving the palm-sized book – playing to his audience.

"How can we trust you if the LRA was not involved in the agreement mediated by President Carter?"

"UNICEF is abducting my children!"

"The whole world will soon see that Museveni is not the golden boy everyone thinks he is. We are not just a group of criminals living in the bush for personal gain – we are fighting for democracy in Uganda!"

"But Museveni is not interested in democracy!"

"We are not the only group against Museveni – we are connected to others – others who want real democracy!"

"Museveni rose by the gun and he must fall by the gun! Museveni doesn't understand anything other than the gun!"

He continued, "If President Carter is really interested in democracy and peace in Uganda, he should call for national reconciliation – a national conference for everyone to establish democracy."

I listened, my focus being directly on Kony. I did not argue or defend.

I waited. Although I was shocked at his remark accusing UNICEF of abducting his 'abducted' children. Sitting there, rigid, I recalled Keith Wright's story about the brutal treatment of up to 10,000 LRA-abducted children. But I could not reveal my feelings. At the same time, I was impressed that he was more articulate and engaging than I had expected, despite the theatrics, the moving about in his seat, the spearing of me with his words and gestures.

I waited – always giving him my full attention. I returned his stare, non-aggressively.

He subsided.

Immediately his commanders began, one after another. Each spoke reasonably good English, each focusing on me with intensity, their remarks direct versions of what I had just heard. Like a rehearsed script.

I listened, shifting my undivided focus from one to the next.

I waited.

The room became quiet.

I began. I spoke directly to Kony, "I would not trust me either. I would want to see action and believe what I saw. I give you my word as President

Carter's personal representative that I will do what I can. I'm here to invite you, at the request of the Government of Uganda, to enter talks with them."

Kony pressed, "If you are serious about peace and democracy in Uganda, call for a national political conference."

I asked: "What about the people in London who say they are part of the LRA, where your political manifesto is from?"

Kony laughed them off, saying he was in the bush. They were playing politics from the safety of afar.

As we spoke, I found myself relating to the man. The monster I was told to expect was not before me. I began to question the account that he was infantile, a child-like incompetent incapable of giving and keeping his word. The assumption that he had no political agenda began to collapse. The fear that I had began to dissipate. I was aware of my surroundings. I was fully present.

I made a move to engage him. I asserted that I was a mediator, that I had no commitment to either Uganda or Sudan except to see peace achieved. I therefore had to win his confidence. I needed to have a direct relationship with him. I needed to be trusted by Sudan, Uganda, and him.

I then asked our Sudanese 'hosts' to leave the room.

"This meeting is between you and me," I said. "You have to decide for yourself. I want the Sudanese officials to leave the room, now." This was an unplanned move on my part; call it a mediator's intuition. Out of the corner of my eye I could see from his curious, uncertain look that Doug was wondering what I was up to.

There was a moment's hesitation by the Sudanese, but only so. They quickly gathered their materials and promptly left the room.

Kony watched in amazement. Then he became visibly uncomfortable, unsettled. He glanced about to his commanders, seeking an explanation. Sam pulled closer to him.

I did my best to take control.

"I'm serious that to secure peace, I must have your cooperation, your trust. I need a relationship directly with you, not through the Sudanese."

He stared at me, still visibly unsettled, but being reassured by Sam Koho now closer at his side.

"I need to be clear with you," I continued. "I can act as a messenger and take your request back to President Carter; your request for a national reconciliation conference. And that will likely be the last you see of me. I'm here to invite you to talks with the Government of Uganda within the context of the Nairobi Agreement." Then I quickly added: "I'm going to step outside to give you time to consider my offer. Then I'll do as you wish."

I could hear the commotion behind me as Doug and I left the room.

Outside in the warm sunlight I found myself surrounded by LRA personnel. We were a real curiosity. A husky fighter wearing fatigues caught my attention. Perhaps in his early thirties, a very black skinned man, his hair dyed blonde and in dreadlocks, he looked like a tough Rastafarian. As I imagined the life he led, raiding and killing, I felt a presence beside me. It was Otti Vincent examining me, close up, as though I were a fascinating alien. I made some remark about the condition of the camp; indeed the buildings were spanking clean and the thatched rooftop was remarkably substantial.

"You like it?" Otti seemed to jest. But again, as in the meeting, I felt that I was under his personal surveillance. He was all business, a highly tuned fighting machine.

"Yes, it's good." I replied somewhat awkwardly, pulling back, to make my way about the courtyard – really seeking some small break after the intense session with Kony. And I saw through a window that Kony was almost supine, his head being massaged by an aide. He would need time. Sam was talking to him. I stalled outside. Minutes passed. Then, somehow, I knew it was time to go back. I invited the Sudanese, who had assured me they were comfortable with what I had done, to come inside with me.

Re-seated, I could see that order had been restored. Kony was refreshed. He began by making a gun of his forefinger, thumb, and a clenched fist; and he pointed it directly in my face. There was not a sound in the room. It was intense. I had a palpable sense of being shot in the head, the bullet entering from behind. But I kept my eyes focused on Kony, trying to show no signs of this strange sensation.

Then he looked up and said, "You are not my enemy. I don't have a fight with you." Making another gun with his other hand, he pointed them at each other. "My enemy is Museveni. I have a fight with him." Another pause, his eyes fixed on me, the two 'guns' pitted one against the other. Then, lowering his hands, he said, "we agree to talks but we need time."

The ice had broken! We turned to details. I learned that Kony wanted to prepare for the talks with the Government of Uganda by meeting with Acholi tribal elders. Not Government spies; but some fourteen to twenty elders agreed to by the LRA. They would have a conference. Here at Nsitu. Sam mentioned his elderly parents hopefully, saying he hadn't seen them since he went to the bush with Kony when he was 18, when he was about to leave for university. That must have been as many years before. My heart went out to him.

The climate in the room grew warm. We were now planning together. The Sudanese were consulted. I asked them if the elders could visit. They replied, "Yes." When I then asked the Sudanese if it could take place in the bush, they replied, "Maybe, although Juba would be better."

As the meeting was drawing to a close, I joked about needing a toilet – the Pepsi had done its work. The gallery was still intently engaged, laughing now as I made my way to an adjacent chamber where a large, clean cement latrine was to be found.

A bond was formed. I had done that which Uganda had requested. I needed to go to work on it.

As we prepared to leave and as a small gesture of friendship, I sifted through my briefcase to find one of The Carter Center's lapel pins. All eyes were on me. I stood, approaching Kony who stiffened a bit. I was about to pin it on him when he abruptly ordered 'pin it on that man'. That man was Sam Koho, who, beaming a perfect smile, allowed me to place the lapel pin on him.

We ended the meeting, shaking hands all around. They followed us to the vehicles, all of them. They gave us one of the warmest send-offs I have experienced.

When we had finished the meeting with Kony, our 'hosts' put us up for the night in a safe house in Juba. The accommodation was very modest: little water, desperate toilet facilities, a general grunge in the house that really made staying on the open-air roof-top porch especially attractive. The rough digs, however, were more than compensated for by the genuine hospitality of the two intelligence officers who had also had a long day. We feasted on grilled goat with conversation that began early in the evening and went late into the warm night. Our hosts then made us comfortable in cots covered with mosquito netting. As we all lay there under the starlit sky, still talking, they remarked how well the meeting had gone (apparently better than any recent meetings between Kony and the Sudanese – especially after Sudan had signed the Nairobi Agreement, abandoning Kony) – and they enthusiastically talked about the day when peace would be realized in Sudan. They wanted peace. The people wanted peace.

So as I drifted off to sleep I was content in knowing I had made progress with the world's most notorious guerrilla fighter. There was hope for the children and for peace in northern Uganda.

6

A Growing Sense Of Flim-Flam

We had said we were going to conduct the ministerial meeting differently. That way, I hoped to achieve the goals I had set immediately after my visit to Uganda and Sudan. Implementation of the Nairobi Agreement would require that Sudan and Uganda, hostile neighbours and wary signatories to a peace accord, develop an effective working relationship. Specific steps needed to be identified and taken within specific timelines. Bringing the LRA into the process would require unprecedented cooperation between Sudan and Uganda. Yes, this would have to be a very different mediation session if it were to be successful.

And it was. But it wasn't easy. We wanted less formality, to avoid the acrimony of past meetings, to have balanced treatment of the issues the parties had told me they wanted addressed. We wanted to change the culture of the meeting. Make it more of a problem-solving exercise than another debate veiled in diplomatic niceties and the ducking of responsibility. We did not want it to degenerate into both sides retreating to private caucus rooms or the hopeless chasing of paper as one delegation introduced some text or another, eliciting a counter-document from the other side.

To make it different, I was prepared to act more in a facilitative style, rather than assume the more traditional role of 'chair'. I wanted President Carter to open the session to give it gravity, and then to appear at key points to assist me in moving the parties along, past any impasses. We prepared the agenda items (identified during my trip to the two countries) on large flip chart paper and posted them in a clearly visible manner. We planned to start with group-generated 'ground rules', a typical starting point in conventional mediation practice. I would act in a loose-tight way; that is, remain flexible so as to encourage creativity through informality and by modelling positive behaviour. Yet, I would be prepared to be strong, even authoritative in a chair-like manner if the conduct of the parties was abusive of one another, counter-productive, or disrespectful of our efforts. I had been here before and had long ago learned to take a strong hand when I felt it was needed.

We housed the two delegations in separate hotels, took special and personalized measures to make spouses comfortable, ensured local travel arrangements and dietary issues were all in accord. We planned for the delegations to dine together at key points throughout the three-day session: first, to establish a good spirit, to build the relationship; then, to keep any positive momentum; and finally, to celebrate our success.

Furthermore, I departed from normal practice of having a lot of small working groups, so that I could be fully in charge of the process and dynamics; although we were prepared to break into small groups, with my staff having been assigned duties to assist. We also were not going to keep verbatim or detailed minutes of the meeting, something else they had chosen in the past to debate. Instead, we would keep a record of specific action items. I wanted this to move away from legalese and traditional diplomatic discourse, posturing, and division to a small but shared sense of making meaningful progress.

That was the plan. And according to good mediation practice, I met with both sides in their hotel rooms the evening before we got started. I wished to reassure them of the process, reflect to them that we would be dealing with the issues they had enumerated to me in Kampala and Khartoum; and to assert to the Ugandans that I had fulfilled their request. We were ready to move on the path of dialogue with Kony, which would lead to peace.

Immediately I met with them, my plan was at risk. A 'non paper' was produced by representatives of the Government of Sudan, a document that had been signed by four foreign ministers (Sudan, Uganda, Libya and Egypt) and was certain to be raised in the meeting. It was gingerly retrieved from a briefcase and passed to me with an air of the mysterious about it. It was entitled 'Lome Nonpaper'.

What was this non paper? It was a one-pager outlining a series of commitments and was to be the subject of a First Ministers' meeting in Kampala in September. Did it belong at our table? Not really, although it bore directly on our agenda.

I could see right away that games were being played, by both sides. Did I know about the paper, the Sudanese asked with a tone of incredulity? As though knowing meant something and not knowing meant Uganda was up to something.

"No," I replied calmly, avoiding their invitation to get agitated by its existence.

I took the paper when it was handed to me, folded it carefully, and placed in my inside coat pocket.

Minutes later, when I met with them, the Ugandans did not mention it throughout our private meeting. Only after I told them I was aware of it, and produced it, did they make some cursory remarks. Indeed, Dr. Rugunda and Minister Amama Mbabazi's body language implied that they were here in Atlanta, but barely here. They said that they had received no satisfaction from the Government of Sudan and the non paper reflected this frustration. They informed me that the First Ministers, now including Egypt and Libya, were trying to pick up the pace. I tried to appear nonplussed. I did not want these tough negotiators to think that I was in any way rattled by this tactic of venue shopping, or 'table hopping' as mediators sometimes describe it. When those in dispute aren't getting what they want from one mediator, they go shopping for another. It is a power tactic, distracting and unconstructive.

Even though I had encountered and dealt with this type of gamesmanship before in other mediations, it always comes with a soft underbelly of disappointment for me. It smacks of crass political maneuvering, a sign of the utilitarian way in which people will treat others, including those who are trying to be of assistance. For it is often the case that people, or 'parties' – as they are called in this case – will try to play mediators off against each other and will actually seek the mediator most likely to give each side what it wants. Attempts are made to manipulate mediators, by withholding information, by befriending the mediator, or by making false promises. And it is all too common to look to another process or alternative venue in the hope of getting the outcome one wishes. Indeed, that may be why Sudan had recently approached US Envoy, Harry Johnson, in the hope that another peace process would be designed to supplant the Sudan Peace Process and the Libyan Egyptian initiative. In fact, with all the peace processes competing with each other to be the definitive peace process, warring sides can just play the whole thing out, buying time, looking for advantage.

And, unfortunately, peacemakers are quite quick to compete with each other. Everyone wants to be a hero, it seems, in the world of peacemaking. Sometimes the parties don't even have to stir up competing processes; the peacemakers will come offering even when another process is ongoing.

So, what was the Lome non paper? Where had it really originated? What were the motives behind it? These things flashed through my mind but I was determined not to be thrown off track.

Of course, it was curious to me that Sudan produced the document, and Uganda acted nonchalant. It was more than curious that Egypt and Libya were now, in effect, at the table.

After my meetings and my drive home that night, I decided to stick with my plan. We had known that Egypt and Libya would be players, but I was not going to be drawn into a side-bar about which we would never be able to ascertain the whole truth. I was not, even before we got started, going to fall into the trap of the paper chase. So I resolved to start the meeting at The Carter Center just as we had intended.

I began the next day by stating that it was here at the beginning of this new phase that I wanted us to agree to a new way of doing business. This was not diplomacy as usual: it was mediation between diplomats – a more flexible, creative approach. Having 'indulged the chair', however, they now began to do what they had intended to all along. The Ugandans pressed for a review of past minutes saying they had their own document they would like to introduce. I refused (as the 'chair') to allow the Ugandan delegation to introduce any new document at this time.

I told them I would accept any document privately and I would call upon both heads of delegation to review the past minutes in private with me, during breaks or in the evening.

That put a stop to that. Immediately, the Ugandans called for a private caucus. They requested a specific amount of time. They exceeded that time, with two notices sent by me through an intern assistant. Failing to dislodge them from a room at the far end of The Carter Center, I made a personal visit and was very direct and assertive about the lack of courtesy they were showing and that I would not tolerate that from either side.

They were clearly startled at my assertiveness, and reacted by saying I had encouraged informality, and they were taking liberty with that. But they got my message, joked a bit, and promptly returned to the table.

It was a test. The process had been tested. The patience of the other side had been tested. The mediator had been tested.

We passed the test and began to work. It became clear that the two delegations would be more productive in a smaller, less formal setting. There would be less grand-standing, more focus, less formality, more opportunity to be frank and, hopefully, to be creative. I asked Dr. Susan Allen Nan, a very capable facilitator, and one of my staff members to join me and the delegations in a smaller room with a round table and a flip chart. I made a conscious choice to exclude all others – even though I knew our Carter Center interns were having the time of their lives being observers in the large-room exercise.

An agreement was reached by noon on the last day. Almost. There was one remaining contentious issue: the date by which the Government of Sudan would disarm and disband the LRA. We had an agreement that the 'path of dialogue with Kony' would be pursued, but a parallel path of 'disarm and disband' the LRA had also been insisted upon by Uganda, and agreed by Sudan.

Implementation was another matter. Now I began to see the Sudanese delegation's modus operandi. They would agree in principle to the two track process, but specificity on either would remain a mystery.

Whereas the Ugandan delegation wanted specifics and tended to negotiate from the particular to the general, the Sudanese seemed intent on generalities, the specifics of which would, apparently, simply follow. I detected and would learn for certain that these orientations, so opposed, would be a continuing source of conflict, apart from and above the substantive matters in dispute.

We broke for lunch, during which I held an intensive session with the two heads of delegation and their senior advisors. I challenged them on the practicality of disarming the LRA without force. I challenged them on the relationship of the path of dialogue to the path of disarming and disbanding the LRA. The Ugandans insisted that Sudan could disarm and disband the LRA peacefully, by administrative fiat. They said that the LRA were under the command of the Sudanese and they could not exist on Sudanese soil without their support. The Sudanese negotiators argued that it now had a strained relationship with the LRA, as a direct result of the Nairobi Agreement. Furthermore, Kony had a mind of his own and it was not possible to simply command him to surrender.

We seemed to be going nowhere. The Sudanese were pressing for time, a greater appreciation of their position, and the need for a comprehensive approach. The Ugandans were asserting that time had run out, concrete and specific actions were required now, not later.

I knew it was time to draw upon President Carter. He and I had a brief, private chat.

"It started out rough," I told him. "The Ugandans were playing games. When I confronted them things improved. But now we are stuck. I need your help."

"Tell me what you want," Carter replied, totally focused on our exchange.

In just a few minutes I laid out exactly what I needed.

"OK," he said.

Immediately after lunch President Carter entered the room where I had re-convened everyone. He called upon the Sudanese to undertake intensive activities with the LRA on the path of dialogue. A detailed plan for disarming and disbanding the LRA by other means was to be formulated. Taking my advice, he asserted that a reasonable deadline was September 15. And then he turned to address the Sudanese delegation directly.

"If Sudan agrees and fails to honour these commitments," he said, "I will be obliged to publicly condemn Sudan for not complying."

The Sudanese sat there like children who had been reprimanded. I was uncomfortable on their behalf. The Ugandans did nothing.

The Sudanese nodded their consent. But I wondered if they meant it.

These were strong words from a man whose condemnation none would wish. But it was also a firm plan. It outlined best efforts to be made on the path of dialogue, consistent with Uganda's original request to me and my successful efforts with Kony as facilitated by Sudan. It also set in motion a harder path. The path of disarming and disbanding the LRA. The dialogue was to commence forthwith; the 'D & D' plan, as it became known, was due on September 15.

It was now July 19.

We had an agreement! And now my staff and I had much more work to do at an even faster pace.

Could there have been a more exciting and challenging time? Not likely!

The Sudanese had asked for our help with the D&D Plan, emphasizing that it had to embrace peaceful means of resolving the issue of the LRA. The Ugandans were obliged to give The Carter Center the clearance to move with confidence and independence among the Acholi community so we could identify the delegation of elders who would make a first visit to

Kony and the LRA. That would meet Kony's request of me when I had met him.

I confirmed the membership of my team. Tom Crick would take on the role of Senior Political Analyst and act as my second-in-command. Doug Archard would stay in Khartoum as our Senior Country Representative there. David Lord, an old friend and colleague who was a good political analyst and knew what was involved in peacebuilding in African countries, would represent us in Uganda. Susan Allen Nam would back us up in Atlanta along with a team of student interns led by Alex Bick, an intelligent, quiet young man who had been an intern but was now a paid Research Assistant on our team. And Chris Burke was brought onto the team.

Chris, an energetic Australian, had flown from Australia to California where he had bought a motorcycle. He drove it across the USA to arrive in Atlanta in time for his orientation session as a new student intern. I remembered meeting him that first day because he looked a little saddle sore when he had walked up to me.

"Doctor Hoffman," he began with a thick Australian accent, "You don't know me and you don't know what kind of work I can do. But I want you to know that I'm not here just for an internship. I came from Australia to work for you."

"Wow, that's good to know," I had said, adding "I hear you came across the States on a bike."

"Yeah, "he grinned, "but I had no idea how far it was! It took five days and my ass is still hurting."

I liked Chris immediately. I would find out before very long just how good a man he was.

Backing us up was Craig Withers from The Center's health program, our finance and fundraising people as well as my own boss, Ambassador Gordon Streeb.

We moved quickly. Within days David Lord and Tom made their way to northern Uganda to begin the process of identifying the group of elders. Theirs would not be an easy task. So many Acholi were sincerely dedicated to peace that to be left out would hurt. Others would want to be in on the venture for nothing more than to advance their own personal political agenda. We would have to submit the list to Kony for his approval. In order to obtain passports and travel permits, the Government of Uganda would have to concur with Kony's list. And the Government of Sudan might reject someone on the list for its own reasons. Rejection of anyone would be a very delicate matter.

I left Atlanta for Khartoum and Chris Burke came with me. Our stay was to last ten days. And eight years later he is still in Africa!

Chris had given me the impression that he had street smarts and could operate in tough places. As an intern this would be his first test. He was to consult the Sudanese on the D&D Plan, keeping the path of dialogue integral to a peaceful resolution; and also liaise with the LRA on the objectives, timing, and logistics of the 'elders meeting'.

Things were going well in Uganda. Our team there was putting together a list of Acholi elders that met the test of credibility applied by key actors and our advisors in the north. From Khartoum, with Yahia's help, we established contact with two senior LRA commanders in Juba, who spoke to us on a cell phone. These LRA men on the other end of the line impressed me as intelligent and capable. We talked about the venue. It was unlikely that the meeting could be held in the bush, at Nsitu, where I had met Kony, but we all felt that something could be worked out.

Then things began to go wrong.

The list had come through and had been forwarded to Kony. He accepted it outright. But he wanted his parents to be a part of the delegation. Their names were not on the list.

Then Ugandan officials in Kampala did not want the meeting to proceed unless and until the Government of Sudan produced a D&D Plan, saying that they must see the plan first. And furthermore, they said Kony's parents were not properly part of a delegation of 'elders', which they described to me as a more 'political body'. Any attempt in the past to send his parents to meet with him had not succeeded and they would not allow Kony's parents to be a part of this delegation.

So I received a response to Uganda's position from an LRA commander at the other end of the line in Juba, who called himself 'Livingston'. He insisted that Kony's parents were Kony's 'first elders'. So how could Kony's parents not be included in a delegation of elders?

The Sudanese officials in Khartoum were looking to me, perplexed. "You see," they stated, "here we are again with our brothers from Uganda. We gave a commitment to President Carter that we would have the plan ready by September 15. There was agreement given to President Carter that you could have the elders meeting in the meantime. Now they say, 'no plan, no meeting'.

I was infuriated. Tom and David were stalled in Kampala. I was under pressure from the LRA. I was under pressure from the Ugandans. The

Sudanese knew I was under pressure and watched, with a discernible slowing down on the development of the D&D Plan.

Still holed up in Khartoum with Chris, what followed for five intense days was a mighty flurry of telephone consultations. I had confrontational telephone calls with Dr. Rugunda and his senior colleague, Minister Mbabazi. In that call I reminded them that they had made an agreement in President Carter's presence and they should not be placing conditions on the 'Path of Dialogue' by insisting that the Sudanese produce a D&D Plan *prior* to September 15. At the same time I was engaged in telephone efforts to appease the LRA, enjoining Livingston to salvage the process by removing Kony's requirement that his parents come this time. I was also making appeals to Dr. Yahia to produce a D&D Plan sooner than September 15. I asked Yahia to 'help the mediator'.

Time was passing. Pressure was building. This delay was costing thousands of dollars. I began to consider several options, one of which was to pull out. We would announce that we have suspended our efforts pending a meeting with President Carter to assess the situation.

We were at a very serious juncture. It really aggravated me that the Ugandans who had so pressed me, and Sudan, to engage Kony were now blocking the very road they had asked me to open.

I had one more frank discussion on the telephone with Mbabazi, from my hotel room in the Khartoum Hilton. It appeared that he was now taking over from Rugunda (or they were playing a 'good cop, bad cop' game with me). I reviewed in detail the sequence of events and the evidence that suggested The Carter Center was proceeding in accordance with the commitments made in Atlanta. I also made it clear that I perceived division within the Ugandan delegation, resulting in an obvious retreat from those commitments. Mbabazi is a very tough, smart and clever lawyer. After he offered a number of fairly standard, unconvincing arguments that sought to demonstrate that Uganda was not re-inventing history, but merely expecting a D&D plan prior to a green light on the visit – he mellowed somewhat. He remarked that I needed to understand Uganda's 'northern neighbour and Joseph Kony', appealing to me to be sympathetic with, and support his government's position.

I don't know if my telephone conversations from Khartoum were ever listened to by the Sudanese, or whether our email correspondence was monitored. What I do know is that the day following the confrontation with Mbabazi, I was received by a veritable delegation of senior officials assembled at Minister Ali al-Numeiri's office, the Sudanese Head of Delegation. And I was introduced to Sudan's Foreign Minster, Dr. Mustafa Ismail. The warmth and respect afforded me likely could not have been explained short of someone on their side having heard the way I had engaged their adversary.

To top it off, Numeiri handed me their D&D Plan!

I called President Carter and said I would get a copy of the plan to him, and asked him if he would phone Museveni and tell him that I was now in possession of a substantial D&D Plan. We could work out the details of the plan in New York prior to President Carter meeting with him and Bashir to finalize it on the occasion of the UN's Millennium meeting.

I then told the LRA we had stalled a bit, but that an elders meeting looked good and they should put this meeting into a larger context. I said that this meeting was hopefully the first of many to come, perhaps over a period of one to two years of talks. They should not press the point of Kony's parents attending now, but take the first step with the elders meeting based on the agreed list of participants.

The spokesman for Kony was not impressed. He assured me that the LRA was a 'mature organization' and that if there was any question of the safety of Kony's parents – or doubts of any sort regarding a successful meeting, they should be dismissed. Kony expected to meet his parents now.

Days, which seemed like weeks, dragged by. President Carter could not reach Museveni, who was traveling by plane. True or not, like it or not, a letter would have to do. So we left Khartoum. We left Kampala. We informed the LRA there were problems and that we would be back soon.

And I intended to immediately put a new plan in place. Among ourselves, we felt that if Uganda did not want Kony's parents to attend with the delegation of Acholi elders, and Uganda was indeed prepared to allow his parents to visit once satisfied that a D&D plan existed, then why not let Kony's parents go now, ahead of the elders. That way, the psychological climate for an elders meeting would be improved, the momentum of the 'path of dialogue' and a 'path of disarming and disbanding the LRA' would be maintained. Furthermore, by September 8, well ahead of schedule, Sudan's D&D plan would be finalized in New York supported by this parallel process that hopefully would enable disarmament and disbanding of the LRA by peaceful means.

Uganda agreed with us.

The Sudanese said that they would facilitate Kony meeting with his parents. The Carter Center would fund the meeting with David Lord presiding.

We pressed on but once again our efforts were thwarted!

David had, with the cooperation of senior officials in Uganda, made all the arrangements for taking Kony's parents to Khartoum from their home in Kampala. Virtually on the tarmac in Khartoum, preparing to mount the plane to Juba, he was informed by the Sudanese that Kony would only meet his parents in the bush at the camp where I had met him, in Nsitu.

When David telephoned me with these requirements I couldn't believe what I was hearing.

I felt I had no option, short of risking whatever trust I had with the Ugandans, but to inform the Ugandan Head of Delegation, Dr. Rugunda. He would have to know about this last minute development.

Rugunda refused, saying flatly, "Juba. No further!"

We scrambled. In Khartoum, David was told by Kony's parents that they were prepared to go to the bush, whatever the risks. They desperately wanted peace. They would do anything to help. The Sudanese said they would allow it, if we so deemed. Kony, however, would not move toward Juba – where he would be under full control of the Sudanese – something he had not allowed since the Nairobi Agreement had been signed.

Rugunda stood firm. He had the audacity to say, "What if Kony abducts his parents? What if they are killed? Regardless that they are willing to risk it, the Government of Uganda cannot."

I stewed in this foul set of impossibilities.

What could I do?

I could have ignored Rugunda. I could have pretended that his 'no go' message to me did not reach David in time and that they had already left for Nsitu.

But I didn't. Flooded by another wave of disappointment – frustrated – I told David that it was off.

I could hear his great disappointment in the pause at the other end of the line.

Did anyone want this to work?

When it came to achieving peace with the LRA, I thought, why had failure been pulled from the jaws of success so many times before? Was Museveni hoping to keep the LRA issue unresolved so that he could continue to support the SPLA in its war against Khartoum? Did he so dislike Kony that nothing short of a violent 'solution' would suffice? Was Kony, in the end, as unbelievable and immature as Uganda's Museveni had said? Did the Sudanese have a sweet deal with Kony, striking Juba as an obstacle, so that Sudan gave nothing to Uganda until it got more from it?

Whom could "I" trust?

I decided to pay more attention to details. To be certain that what was said was understood; to increase the level of specificity; and to be clear and strong in holding everyone, including myself, accountable.

I had always known that people or parties – whatever you call them – who negotiate with the assistance of a mediator, are likely to play dirty tricks. They are likely to inflate, distort, deny, renege, frustrate, infuriate and even hurt one another. But I had always insisted they should not abuse the mediator – or the process of mediation.

I was beginning to feel abused. I was engaged – and with engagement comes flak. All I wanted was peace. It looked like it would be achieved only if these characters were dragged kicking and screaming to it.

We set our sights on New York where the session to hammer out the details of the D&D Plan would take place. President Carter would preside over a closing meeting – planned after two full days of talks. I knew that President Carter would have to secure an explicit commitment from Uganda that the elders' meeting could proceed, unobstructed, without qualification. To galvanize the commitment, and to overcome anticipated resistance from Uganda to a meeting with Kony, President Carter would also have to obtain a security guarantee from Bashir. This would be a written guarantee that no harm would come to any Ugandan participating in the meetings with Kony chaired by The Carter Center.

Before we could take a breath our team of Tom Crick, Alex Bick and I were in New York City at the same time as the UN prepared to host heads of state from the world over. Alex had organized accommodation north of the city, in a quiet but comfortable conference center. This time, we were going to nail things down. I would be in charge. Tom and Alex would help with modification to the D&D Plan, which they had transferred to computer. We would conclude with Presidents Museveni, Bashir and Carter at a hotel quite near the UN building.

Sudan was sending its Minister of Foreign Affairs to lead its delegation, Dr. Mustafa Ismail. Minister Mbabazi and Mr. Busho Ndinyenka, Deputy Director General of External Security, would lead the Ugandan delegation.

This session would be tough. But I was happy we were getting heavyweights at the table. We were focused. We were ready.

66

Uganda came in fighting form. I had arranged time before the Sudanese delegation arrived for the Ugandans to see the plan, review it, and then query me on details. I wasn't there to 'defend' the D&D Plan, but despite its strength and the promise of peace that I had seen in it in Khartoum, it did have holes – there should and would be questions.

I was prepared to explain the annexes I had been given in Khartoum by Yahia – and I wanted to position the document in a constructive light.

Mbabazi was not going to show he was impressed or pleased – if he was. He did say, however, that I must have 'really worked on them' after the document had received his standard scrutiny.

Having situated the meeting within the United Nations' 25 mile travel limit so that the officials from pariah Sudan were legally able to attend, we awaited the Sudanese delegation.

The Sudanese were late. I worried that we were in for another round of brinkmanship. And we were.

When Ismail and Mbabazi finally squared off, we quickly moved to an interchange of obfuscation and derision. This confrontation was a far cry from the serious, focused, productive negotiation I had imagined, and which we desperately needed. I let them go on for several minutes, firing barbs at each other, saber rattling, performing for their delegations, posturing, spinning our collective wheels.

But soon I had enough. I wanted and deserved more respect. The Lome non paper, the upcoming Kampala meeting, the frustrated elder's meeting, pulling teeth in Khartoum to get a disarmament plan – it was all too much.

I stopped the meeting and requested that both Mbabazi and Ismail meet with me, now, privately, in the adjacent room.

They were surprised, maybe shocked. But they agreed, making a few jokes to break the tension I had created.

Inside our chamber I let loose. I challenged both on their sincerity. I called upon them to elevate the discussions and to bear down in good faith to produce a D&D Plan that could be ratified by their principals in a very short 36 hours.

My intensity momentarily forged an alliance in them. They dropped their masks and the theatrics. They encouraged me to be patient. They would succeed; I should be patient.

We returned to a very sober room where the others had been waiting and we got down to work. We kept at it around the clock, Tom and Alex doing yeoman's work on the text. Even as we crowded into the quiet hotel restaurant, adjacent to the UN, with the clock ticking minutes to the meeting upstairs with President Carter, they were still negotiating, dotting 'i's' and crossing 't's'. But they were stuck. We lacked agreement on the critical issue of timing. What would be done, specifically; and by what date? How would the LRA be disarmed and disbanded? Would it be through dialogue, or by other means if necessary? Sudan was prepared to say it would disarm and disband the LRA by December 31, 2000 by best efforts, but no later than March 31, 2001. The Ugandans wanted it all over by the end of November, just weeks away.

That was the problem we would take to President Carter. But before he received President Bashir and the Foreign Minister of Uganda, Mr. Eriya Kateguya (Museveni had sent his regrets) – he asked me to brief him.

President Carter, his wife Rosalynn, and their grandson Jason seemed relaxed amid the standard cortege comprised of the Center's Executive Director, Dr. John Hardman, President Carter's scheduling secretary, Mrs. Nancy Konigsmark, and the secret service officers.

Although relaxed, President Carter was focused and asked me for a frank assessment. He hadn't liked our rebuff either and intended to nail them down. I informed President Carter where we were. I told him we needed his help to formalize an agreed date; based on that we needed explicit approval from Uganda to move forward with the elders' meeting; and that a security guarantee from Bashir would be needed as well.

I returned to the restaurant and invited everyone to the meeting upstairs on the signal that President Bashir had arrived.

I introduced the agenda and I complimented both delegations – trying to put a hopeful face on our effort that had, once again, come to an impasse over the date of implementation. Then President Carter took over. He did it all. President Bashir, in traditional dress, spoke only in Arabic, refusing to look at Kateguya who was supported by Mbabazi. Carter did not elevate Kateguya and Mbabazi to 'head of state' level, but acted as an intermediary – posing questions to them, relaying answers to Bashir, searching for agreement.

And it came remarkably quickly. Bashir made some comments on the need for time to get his Ministry of Defence and bureaucracy ready for the plan. The Ugandans agreed.

Then President Carter sought explicit approval from Uganda on our proceeding with the elders' meeting, unconditionally. Mbabazi mentioned the need for security guarantees for the people involved. It appeared they were back on track. The meeting was over.

Before the dust settled from the closing of the door, President Carter wrote the text of a Security Guarantee and had us dispatch it for the signature of Bashir. That too was completed within hours.

We were all set. That was Friday, September 8, 2000. Finally we could go ahead with the elders' meeting.

On Monday September 11, Rugunda called from Kampala to inform me that there could be no elders' meeting. He said that if Kony had insisted on Nsitu, not Juba, for the meeting with his parents, how could we rely on him in the case of the elders?

He added quickly that the Kampala meeting of Foreign Ministers from Uganda, Sudan, Libya and Egypt was now confirmed. It had been delayed, but was definitely taking place in Kampala on September 27. The Carter Center was invited as observer – as was UNICEF (named in the Nairobi Agreement). After that meeting things would pick up.

I fumed!

President Carter suggested we withdraw until the parties were serious.

I was sympathetic. We were all 'fit to be tied'.

"Let's wait until after Kampala," I said to Carter. "Tom can represent us there. Then we can make our decision."

He agreed.

We imagined Kony cogitating in the bush. I began to feel that I had failed him. In doing so, I was failing the possibility of resolving the LRA 'insurrection' by peaceful dialogue. No resolution to the LRA would mean no give by Uganda on the SPLA. The Nairobi Agreement would fail. Violence would prevail again. The war in Sudan would not end. I was not succeeding in my mission.

7

A Thumb Screw For Joseph Kony

I could imagine my chief contact in the Sudanese Government, Yahia, falling off his chair. In big, bold red letters the Ugandan newspaper headline declared: LRA TO BE RELOCATED 1000 KMS FROM UGANDA BORDER.

What! Was this the outcome of the Kampala meeting of foreign ministers? Who was going to move Kony and his band? Who could believe he would go willingly? If Sudanese relations with Kony were already strained by having signed the Nairobi Agreement, just imagine what they would be like now! What about the path of dialogue with the LRA?

I had really doubted the value of the Kampala meeting, seeing it as a process of political convenience competing with our efforts to implement the Nairobi Agreement. It had been set up at the level of foreign ministers, and as such, it operated conveniently yet at a level above and beyond our peace implementation process. When issues came up in our talks that either Uganda or Sudan wished to avoid, each could conveniently refer the matter to the Kampala meeting; that is, tough issues could be deflected or deferred, which obviously frustrated our progress. And there really wasn't anything that I or President Carter could do about it. After all, we were mediators at the request and pleasure of the parties in dispute. We had no powers to bind them or to insist which matters belonged and did not belong at our table.

So now we were hit with this.

It was a turn of events that smacked of pure politicking and showed us as well the possible rifts within the Government of Sudan. For I had been convinced that Yahia's Department of External Security, the intelligence people who had fought alongside Kony and slept in the bush with him, really did want a peaceful resolution to the LRA. They wanted Kony to participate willingly in his destiny, albeit the potential demise of the LRA. The Sudanese also had shown in the first draft of the D&D Plan that they knew that peace along the southern Sudanese – northern Ugandan border was more a challenge of including the Acholi community in meaningful dialogue with Uganda's Government than any unilateral action to impose an end to the LRA. And, to be fair to a less generous sentiment, I'm sure Yahia would rather the LRA go peacefully through the hard work of The Carter Center and the Government of Uganda than by any method placing too much burden on the Sudanese government.

But this news appeared preposterous! Why would Kony agree to move 1,000 kilometres north into the desert, away from his environment – away from his chief reason for being – to wage war with Museveni? Who would pay for this? Was Kony to be permanently resettled? Was I to sell him this strange brew?

When Tom called to Atlanta from Kampala, he assured us that the foreign ministers had indeed agreed to this. The news had been 'leaked'. Libya and Egypt would weigh in. The Lome non paper which had surfaced in our July meeting in Atlanta had been the main point of departure for the Kampala talks. The Aboke girls were to be the focus of effort concerning the return to Uganda of LRA abducted children. Sister Rochelle, the brave principal of the girls' school from which the Aboke girls had been abducted by the LRA, was to travel to Tripoli. There she was going to seek assistance from Libya's Colonel Qadhafi. Egypt was to pay for tents to house the relocated LRA on land provided by Sudan. Uganda and Sudan were to place junior diplomats in each others' capital to expedite identification and repatriation of children abducted by the LRA; and Egypt and Libya would provide an observer team along the Sudan-Ugandan border, a concession to the Government of Sudan, which remained adamant that Uganda was continuing to support the SPLA in its war against Khartoum.

Tom finished his report, saying that the foreign ministers had also agreed that a technical meeting to lay plans for the relocation of the LRA and return of abducted children should be chaired by The Carter Center and take place forthwith in Khartoum. Canada, committed to the project of repatriating child soldiers, was needed to assist financially and UNICEF

72

should take the lead on identifying, processing and returning abducted children. As intelligence about the LRA, its location, number of combatants, number of women, children, sick and elderly would all need to be revealed, military cooperation between Sudan and Uganda was going to be established.

I now imagined Kony feeling the noose tighten about his neck. I worried that we would now be associated with that noose. The window for dialogue had narrowed. The geopolitics of the region were beginning to come directly into play at our table.

Indeed, we heard that Kony was not pleased with the news. He had already received the information before a team of Sudanese officials traveled to inform him and to tell him he had no alternative but to comply. He was angry that he had not been consulted; he was wary of Sudan's intentions. He nevertheless gave them some indication that he would cooperate.

In a sober discussion with Mbabazi, I informed him that President Carter had not been pleased with the developments leading up to Kampala and had actually suggested to me that we pull back. The meeting in Kampala, I conceded, although handled awkwardly, had shown there was momentum towards implementing the Nairobi Agreement – efforts to return abducted children might now improve; diplomatic cooperation was positive; and addressing Sudan's concern about Uganda's active material support of the SPLA was a balanced quid pro quo. But I insisted that a commitment to 'talking' Kony into disbanding was the ethical and pragmatic way forward. We would continue to preside over meetings to implement the Nairobi Agreement, invite Egypt and Libya to join the table, and integrate the Canadian efforts which focused on children.

When I called him, Yahia gave me the impression that he, too, found the announcement to relocate Kony incredulous. He agreed dialogue was preferred, noting that an elders' meeting could take place immediately after the LRA had been relocated en masse. They required resources to get a camp established. They would also continue to work on Kony.

So we ramped up again. This time I had the refreshing feeling that my next formal task would be to chair a meeting of technical people, not politicians. We had an agreed path and we needed to put all the pieces together in a way that ensured that the principles and larger goals driving our whole effort were preserved and achieved. I then received a discrete message that Canada was not happy with The Carter Center's role as mediator, stating that we were a nongovernmental organization, not a state actor. So they felt that Canada should lead the talks to get the abducted children back home. I was also told that Ismail, Sudan's Foreign Minister, had insisted that we stay involved; indeed, that we chair the overall process pursuant to the Nairobi Agreement.

We kept preparing; establishing an agreed agenda, confirming participation, clarifying roles and prompting specific actors to raise important technical and ethical issues in a constructive, coordinated way.

By October 3 I had a small team ready to make its way to Khartoum. There, the Canadian Ambassador responsible for Sudan wanted to meet with me to clarify roles. As Egypt was now also making noise that perhaps The Carter Center was not a legitimate mediator between two nation states I was eager to meet him. On a last minute phone call to Kachoke Madit in London I learned that they were concerned about an LRA backlash – insisting that I not abandon the fundamental idea that the Acholi community needed to be built into the talks, now more than ever. And just prior to departure, my secretarial staff informed me that the Ugandans were now going to be late for the scheduled meeting. Many hours later, these were the things on my mind as we landed in Khartoum. There would be plenty of work before we even opened the technical session to plan for the relocation of the LRA.

I awoke to more disturbing news. Dr. Rugunda had written me a letter saying that the agenda I had forwarded was broader than that agreed in Kampala. The letter stated that there were only two items to be dealt with: the return of the Aboke girls; and disarming and disbanding the LRA. My feeling of being on mediator 'easy street' with a group of technicians who like to get things done, vanished.

I was angry and, simply, disagreed. This was not the whole story. This was not the limited role that The Carter Center should play. There had been undertakings to exchange diplomats; a commitment to put an observer team along the border; the wider scope and needs of the Nairobi Agreement could not be forgotten. While I was mulling this, reviewing our strategy with Tom, I was also uncomfortably aware that my good contacts in the Sudanese delegation, Yahia and his assistant, Mohamed Hassan, were unusually quiet. Normally, upon arrival I would have been greeted by them with VIP treatment, they would have given me an up-to-the-minute report on the LRA and insights into their government's view of things. Why had they gone silent?

I met with Canadian Ambassador Shram. I raised my concerns that we avoid a situation of 'dueling mediators'. A straightforward man who was clear in stating that Canada's role was to focus on abducted children, he agreed with me.

I arranged for a joint meeting with UNICEF representatives, and the heads of delegation for Egypt and Libya, explaining to them my concern that Uganda was pressing for a very limited agenda and that Uganda's late arrival did not augur well. Was I correct in what I had understood from the Kampala meeting? Was I correct in their agreement that The Carter Center chair and they become active observers? Would they press Uganda, when its delegation arrived, to be responsive and responsible on all matters before us? They answered "Yes" to all my questions.

I phoned my boss, Gordon, to inform him that I was going to press forward and that I might have to challenge Uganda. I might have to walk away if Uganda continued to obfuscate in its excessive self-serving negotiation behaviour. Gordon stated that he supported my intuitions and informed me that I had President Carter's authority to assess the situation and pull back if necessary. I went to bed happy to have the institution behind me.

Late the next night, frustrated that Uganda had kept us all waiting, I had a very tough meeting with Uganda's head of delegation, Busho. I mean tough!

His nostrils were flared, his fiery eyes fixed on me. He leaned forward in his chair and fumed.

"You have missed the whole point of my Government's view on dialogue," he said. "You have been forcing dialogue on us when we have been saying 'No' in many, many ways. And I am insulted that you think I am not respecting the process by showing up late – we could not get a flight!"

He continued, full of steam, his face almost touching mine. "And there are only two items to talk about tomorrow – and they do not include the border observation team!"

He was really angry!

"I am sorry," I replied, "if I have seemed arrogant. Maybe I have been stupid in not hearing the real message you have been sending me on dialogue with Kony. I'll think about that."

Then I added, sincerely, "I had assumed Uganda really did want dialogue, in an appropriate way, at the right time. Rugunda sent me to engage Kony and I did what he had requested, at personal risk. And I have wondered whether Sudan is really prepared, in the end, to give Kony up. I thought a dialogue with him would entice him directly. I also fear a blood bath if talk of 'surgically removing Kony' continues and is put into play."

Then I told him I had also wondered whether we had been wrong in the way we constructed the agenda for tomorrow, inclusively and comprehensively. And then I told him soberly that I had consulted the others as a reality check. They had agreed that we had got it right. We should address everything in the meeting.

He "huffed" when I informed him about meeting with the others – Egypt and Libya, UNICEF, and Canada – in advance of his arrival. But he calmed down almost immediately, agreed to the agenda, and promised to cooperate in the meeting.

It was a difficult encounter. I think he knew I was serious about 'balance' in the construction of the agenda – both his government and the Sudanese had to have their needs addressed. I think he respected the fact that I was fighting for the process and that I was not going to be pushed around or allow the process to be pushed around. Maybe he really believed everything he had said – and having said it he too had done his job. I headed for my room as 1am approached; wanting to think tomorrow's meeting through a bit more before hitting the sack. I expect Mr. Busho's work continued into the night as well, with calls back home to Rugunda and Mbabazi, and a meeting of his delegation.

Tomorrow's meeting would be a meeting of technical experts. They had to plan precisely how to relocate the now estimated 3,000–5,000 LRA, willingly. First, to a temporary 'transit' camp, some 1,000 miles from where they lived. Then how to maintain this camp, and provide all the humanitarian supplies that would be required to feed, heal, and support this population of rebels and abducted children until they had been properly identified as to their original village in northern Uganda. Then they had to determine how they could be airlifted home. And finally they had to manage their reception at home and re-integrate them into their communities. In some cases, return them to villages they had left ten or more years before, as small children – and villages where many had returned as guerilla fighters, to terrorize their own families.

It was more than a tall order.

So I started the meeting by challenging this group of technicians. The politics were behind us, I said. Now, their task was to make a political commitment a working reality. I encouraged them to share information, their expertise and experience. Together we would design a plan that would address a very tricky problem.

And, all things considered, the meeting went well. In the morning, as committees struggled in something of an information vacuum regarding Kony and the LRA, and wondered aloud about dialogue and how safe it would be and whether Kony would go along with a mechanism for immediate repatriation of the Aboke girls, I was thinking that we would inch along at best. This would not be easy. It would not be quick. The goodwill in the room, the expressed commitments of Egypt and Libya to open their cheque books to help cover the cost of a camp for the LRA, the professional and enthusiastic contributions of UNICEF staff, the visible excitement of Sister Rochelle and Angelina, mother of one of the abducted Aboke girls and head of Concerned Parents Association, would not suffice. I thought maybe we should cut to the chase with Kony; offer him a 'retirement' package he could not refuse. Indeed, we had already thought this through somewhat, and there had been rumblings in the corridors that Libya might pay to relocate Kony and his senior commanders to a safe third country, for life.

Just then, as I was sifting through these thoughts, we had a breakthrough. Yahia declared he was willing to try, immediately, to retrieve as many Aboke girls as possible – without conditionality. That is, he would not insist that there be dialogue first and then an agreed plan on D&D; he would not insist on Uganda accepting an Egyptian-Libyan Observer Team along the border between Sudan and Uganda before he took action on the Aboke girls.

I don't know what moved him to this. Was it the physical presence of the mother of one of these girls? Was it the stalwart presence of Sister Rochelle, who had pursued the LRA into the bush for 40 kilometres to negotiate the release of all but twenty-six of her 125 female students? Was it something moving in the background now that Egypt and Libya were present?

Elated, I realized again what an emotional roller coaster this work is. I was tired, but knew it would all have been more than worth it when, not if, we succeeded. The technical team continued its work, preparing to turn political dreams into reality. My staff, Tom, Chris and Alex, did an excellent job as they had been 'volunteered' to chair individual working committees.

The meeting ended a success. I knew, however, that the action that would follow was the only real test. We had closed the meeting with Sister Rochelle asserting that Sudan could 'command' the LRA – they should be able to return all the Aboke girls now. Yahia informed the group that he would go, personally, to meet with Kony, to make best efforts. And in the background, privately, while the committees had worked, I had learned from Yahia that there were LRA commanders in Khartoum and that Yahia was prepared to allow Busho to meet them! He asked if I agreed to them meeting Busho?

I thought it might help for the following reason.

I had, prior to our meeting, proposed that Yahia, Busho and I go to meet Kony – so these proposals being set forth by Yahia were certainly very interesting. I wanted Busho to inform the LRA that once Sudan had demonstrated success (in approaching Kony about release of Aboke girls), dialogue with Uganda would quickly ensue. And that The Carter Center would mediate. So it seemed good, almost too good, to learn that Busho could meet with commanders of his arch enemy who happened to be ready and waiting right here in Khartoum. So I had my doubts.

For now I was concerned that Yahia's proposed visit to Kony was a control measure – Sudan was not giving us the full story and without witnesses or direct involvement we would never know. But had I really expected to get the full story from either side? No!

So I decided to go with the flow. That evening, after briefing a number of ambassadors at a gathering over a much-appreciated glass of wine at the Dutch Ambassador's residence, our meeting formally wound down with a very nice dinner on the Nile, provided by our Sudanese hosts. Trying not to be too obvious during the dinner festivities, I arranged an official signing of a document which detailed the actions agreed upon, and we issued a press release about the signed document. Privately, I discussed with Yahia in more detail the idea of a 'Voluntary Stand Down' package for Kony.

My work for the moment over, I slept until nine the next morning. As I showered, my phone rang. It was Yahia's assistant, Mohamed Hassan – one of the two young intelligence officers who had accompanied me to meet Kony – a man who had fought alongside the LRA in the bush and knew them well. He informed me in his dead-pan way that he had two LRA commanders in the lobby who wanted to meet me.

"When?" I asked, a little dumfounded.

"Now."

"Where?"

"Here."

"Here, in the hotel?"

"Yes, they are here with me now; in the lobby."

"I'll be down in a minute." I hung up the bathroom phone, still standing in the dripping shower.

I dressed quickly and found the two men sitting alone at a small table by the window in the Hilton's lobby. As it had become easy to identify Government of Sudan secret service types, it was easy to identify the LRA commanders. The Government intelligence men all wore inexpensive pale blue or beige safari suits, and had this look of awkward self-consciousness about them as they tried to be invisible. The LRA men were adequately but poorly dressed. They looked bush and battle ready; lean, intense. Hassan had disappeared. I introduced myself as I pulled up a chair.

Both black Africans, one man was especially handsome, tall, strong, and looked like a fighter. The other looked his part too, for he revealed that he had been Joseph Kony's personal secretary. He looked the administrative, intellectual type. They both talked in hushed tones and I was amazed how easily they accepted me, and how readily they shared information. Important information!

Both had manufactured reasons to get out from directly under Kony's control to work as LRA liaison officers stationed in Khartoum. One had feigned a stomach illness and came through Juba to Khartoum on the pretext of needing surgery. The other had made up some other excuse and had remained in Khartoum as well. Yet they were both very much in contact with the LRA, daily; but they had decided to defect. They thought it would be wonderful for all the people under Kony's iron grip if Kony would agree to relocate them 1,000 kilometres to the north, as had been announced in Kampala; but it would never happen. They said Kony was a violent, juvenile leader who had failed to meet their respective expectations. On the one hand, his assistant had hoped he would operate more politically and respond to the good strategic advice he and other senior commanders had given Kony over the years; on the other, Kony had failed to integrate the fighters whom he had brought with him from the border near Kenya to join the LRA.

They were leaving the LRA. They said the next time I heard from them, it would probably be from Nairobi. They thought the LRA might well mutate into another rebel group as Kony's band collapsed. With that in mind, in Nairobi they would assemble other LRA defectors and other Ugandans not happy with Museveni.

"Listen," I leaned forward, speaking quietly, "Will you send one last message to Kony for me?"

"Yes. No problem." the studious one replied.

"Tell him Ben Hoffman of The Carter Center wants to meet and The Carter Center still intends to mediate talks with Uganda."

"OK. Fine."

I then asked, "Do you want to meet with Busho, from Uganda?"

"No." they both answered, immediately. "It is too risky."

"Ok. Fine," I said, "can we meet again after I talk with Busho and the Ugandans?"

They said, "Yes, definitely. We are here in Khartoum. Hassan can get us."

The next day they were nowhere to be seen. Hassan and Yahia went noticeably quiet again. I met with Busho who informed me that I was to have a meeting with Kony. I began to realize Yahia and Busho had their channel of communication, without my help. This as far as I was concerned, was a positive sign.

That was October 8, 2000.

The following day I was informed that Yahia's trip to meet Kony and make best efforts to return the Aboke girls was postponed.

On the 10th all was quiet.

On the 11th Yahia told me that Hassan and General Yassin were in Nsitu, breaking the news to Kony about the Aboke girls. Yahia was to follow them to meet face to face with Kony to give him the message, "You have no alternative but to comply." Then he was to bring home the Aboke girls.

I returned to Atlanta and the days slipped by quickly as, by now, the Canadians were trying to arrange a meeting on October 30 to deal with their part of the agenda, the abducted children.

But what had happened to Kony?

By the 26th I learned from a very angry Yahia that Kony would not comply. Sudan had therefore decided to increase pressure on Kony. First, they would cut food supplies, and then take more serious measures. Yahia was of the view that there was no point now in the Canadian meeting on abductees. Rather, The Carter Center and Uganda had to get together to stabilize the environment. He had been rejected twice by Kony. Kony needed to know that the Government of Sudan was serious. Maybe some Aboke girls will come out, but he was not optimistic.

I had, in fact, already heard from David who had remained in Khartoum, that something had gone wrong with Kony. The Libyans had stayed on in

Khartoum after the Technical Meeting and it was they who had gone to meet Kony. They had returned home empty handed, frustrated.

So I believed Yahia once again, as I had many times before. I didn't know the details but there was enough veracity in it all to believe he had indeed had a problem with Kony. As we all expected, and as I had tried to convey to the various Ugandan officials since the first and only time I had met Kony, disarming him by administrative fiat was a pipe dream.

Mr. Busho, now on the other end of the phone line from Kampala to Atlanta, was sympathetic. He must have had his own sources of information about the failed attempt to get the Aboke girls. "Obviously they are having a serious problem," he offered. He agreed in principle to my suggestion that we convene a discrete meeting. That he, Yahia and I should meet quietly in Nairobi, soon, to do some creative thinking which was now required more than ever. He agreed in principle, but needed to get authority to commit to that.

Meanwhile, as had been predicted by Sudanese officials and the two LRA commanders I had met, an increasing number of escapees from the LRA who were showing up in Juba, in the south. So there was humanitarian work to do while we tried to think of how to engage Kony.

Our man in Uganda, David, contacted me in Atlanta in the middle of the night. He was upset: deeply concerned that we were providing a fig leaf to a coercive strategy against the LRA that could inflict humanitarian abuse on the LRA; drive the LRA away; and result in a military action against the LRA. Couldn't we act more independently? What about other channels to the LRA?

These were obviously good and tough questions. That was David.

My response was that we were indeed active on other channels, some of which I couldn't even disclose to him. And I was most reluctant to raise any expectations with the LRA until I had something to go with. I said that I'd been there before and got burned. Kony, I maintained, was probably in a very foul mood and would not take lightly to me engaging him in a process of talks that had no one on the other side of the conversation. No, the next time we went to Kony we would have something to take him. The Government of Sudan and the Government of Uganda would have to get behind us so we could go with something.

He closed the call saying Sudan was canceling the Canadian meeting.

I phoned Yahia immediately. It was two AM in Atlanta. I was tired, concerned and discouraged. But I was determined to follow through on this. I reiterated David's concerns. Yahia replied that his government wanted Kony to know that it was over. And I got the details of his most recent failed efforts with Kony.

They had gone as he had described. First Hassan and Yassin went to serve notice, to prepare Kony. Then the Libyans were introduced, probably following up on a commitment their Leader, Qadhafi, had given to Sister Rochelle. Kony had met privately with the Libyans, so whether money was talked about was not known. But Kony had indeed agreed to release three Aboke girls. Then he sent a message through Juba that he would release ten girls. When the delegation went to fetch them at the appointed time and place, there was no one there. No one! Kony had reneged.

But Yahia was quick to say that while they planned to pressure Kony, to make it clear that the Government of Sudan was no longer in support of him and wanted the LRA out of Sudan, he did not want bloodshed. They would cut off his food supply; they had ceased delivering ammunition since signing the Nairobi Agreement.

I was worried about this thumb screw policy. I offered immediately to go and meet Kony. I would be able to do it in two weeks. Yahia agreed to send the message to Kony – remarking, however, that it was harder to do now than before. He was telling me that there were real tensions now between Sudan and the LRA. I suggested he continue to feed the LRA until our meeting. He refused to reverse the coercive strategy.

I asked again whether in two or three weeks he would regret the strategy. He insisted not. He suggested I visit both Kampala and Khartoum before the discrete high level meeting I was trying to arrange for Nairobi. He was advising me to do the background work that would be required to make our meeting a success.

In the morning, I wondered in light of the night's talks: what to do?

As it often happens, my morning was spent on the phone in Atlanta talking to representatives from countries who gave us financial support, informing them of developments, asking for understanding and continued support. Everyone was sympathetic, and said we would get the funding they had committed so that we could keep working.

With the international community behind me, I began to prepare to meet Kony again. This time I really would have to take something or someone with me. Maybe Busho should come? Or maybe a scaled-down delegation of Acholi elders?

But back in Kampala Busho was having his own troubles. He called me to say that everyone around him (and I could imagine the hardliners) believed that the Nairobi peace process was irretrievably lost. His colleagues were angry that the Canadian meeting had been cancelled by Sudan. The cancellation had them thinking that Sudan had only wanted the diplomatic exchange all along and when it looked like they had achieved that through the Kampala meeting in September, they had dropped their other commitments.

I didn't think he really believed what he was saying. He was doing his duty this time and his own view might be different. In fact, he agreed that he and Yahia, and maybe some senior military representatives, should meet quietly. But he said that unfortunately, it would take time for him to get internal agreement for such an off-the-record meeting.

And back in Khartoum, Hassan was sending us mixed messages. The LRA weren't complying, although Kony was showing no signs of aggravation. They thought that it was likely that Kony would meet me on the fifteenth of December. He also said that there were another fifteen escapees that needed UNICEF and The Carter Center's help. On hearing this I was happy that Chris was still in Khartoum. He had proved an excellent choice and was on top of the operation to repatriate children. David had returned to Uganda, to work the southern side of the border, to be of help in Uganda's Acholiland.

Then, unhappy with the lack of progress on the commitment to exchange diplomats, as per the Kampala meeting of foreign ministers, the Government of Sudan began to play diplomatic flim flam with our efforts on behalf of LRA escapees. Sudan refused to let any Ugandan into Sudan who did not have diplomatic status. And, of course, none had diplomatic status. The process of verification of Ugandan children and returning them to their homes in northern Uganda required technical people, people who do this sort of thing. By 'upping the ante' Sudan was pressing the point that it expected to have its diplomatic representation in Kampala and when it got it, it would reciprocate. After diplomatic representation in Kampala had been confirmed, the Sudanese said they would let the appropriate people into Sudan to do their job of returning Ugandan LRA escapees back to Uganda – such an important political matter for the Ugandans.

I couldn't nail down the 'entre nous' meeting that I had been hoping for. Things were bunging up. I decided to have a three-way call between Yahia, Busho and myself. There was lots to talk about now like the exchange of information on Sudan's efforts with Kony, the method of verifying the identity and home of LRA escapees; confirming a meeting for ourselves; and a new problem of what to do with adult escapees who were not covered by UNICEF. After all, many of the abducted children were now young adults. And then there were some of the LRA's fighting force who were mercenaries and some adults who had joined voluntarily. So we had a lot to talk about, not to mention the two delicate matters: that of approaching Kony and the exchange of diplomats.

It was a very helpful call. Yahia stated that he wanted to be as transparent as possible and a mutual, indeed, multilateral process was necessary to succeed with Kony and the LRA. He repeated his story about approaching Kony and that Kony had appeared cooperative at first. He talked about the efforts of the Libyans and the failure to deliver Aboke girls. He spoke about Sudan's increasingly strained relationship with Kony and their pressure to smoke him out with a stream of escapees as the consequence. But more, Kony was now on the move. He was penetrating further south toward the Ugandan border, into no-man's land, an area beyond Sudan's control, land sometimes held by the SPLA. Yahia requested that I arrange a small meeting to determine what to do. He said that his government was committed to normalizing relations and to help bring peace to the region.

Busho did not seem at all surprised by the details of the meeting and efforts with Kony. He noted that, of course, they were disappointed about the Aboke girls, but debriefing escapees would help prepare a strategy to contain Kony. Maybe a larger delegation needed to go to meet Kony to work this out.

Even though Busho and Yahia were talking, my team and I didn't like the way things were going. Time was passing while a number of LRA escapees, at their peril, managed to find their way to Juba. (Granted, we had improved their lot, those who made it out of the camp without being killed, and those who got through the bush, under cover of night, without falling into the hands of other danger. For it had been the practice that any LRA escapees caught by Sudanese military personnel were often beaten and returned to Kony for God knows what kind of treatment. In some cases they were taken into a local home or placed in servitude to the ranking Sudanese military officer who had found them).

Now, thank goodness, we had the military cooperating in their escape. Now, these children who escaped the LRA were moved quickly and without abuse to the Sudanese military barracks in Juba. They were not interrogated at length and left without shelter for weeks inside the army compound as they had been in the past. UNICEF had insured they were treated better, on order from the Government in Khartoum. But it was still a messy, slow process. And the word coming out of the LRA camps was that Kony had really tightened security measures and was increasingly repressive. Kony had doubled the guard around his camp and he was brutal with anyone caught trying to escape.

Furthermore, the commitments made in Kampala by the Foreign Ministers of Egypt, Libya, Sudan and Uganda were not materializing. There was a growing lament about the prospects of moving the LRA to a camp within Sudan after the failed efforts to bring some Aboke girls home. No reasonable donor would open its cheque book to build a camp that would not be occupied. And I was upset about the larger political issues such as the relationship of our 'progress' or lack thereof on implementing the Nairobi Agreement and it being a building block for peace in the region. We weren't doing very well on this element of our strategy to reach our overarching goal, peace in Sudan.

Nevertheless, I had kept up my contact with the Sudan Peace Process Secretariat in Nairobi, always trying to be supportive of the moribund Ambassador Mboya, a fine man who simply was hamstrung and could not mount serious peace talks between the Government of Sudan and the Sudan People's Liberation Movement.

I was getting tired as well. We had been pushing hard since I took charge of the case in March. I had seldom been at home; virtually all of the plans and my ideas about the job I thought I had signed on for in Atlanta were unrealized. Ann had almost totally given up on Atlanta and was now spending most of her time at our summer home in Canada. We missed each other terribly. Telephone calls to her were difficult, what with the time zone changes, the cost and quality of the service, and to make it worse they were probably monitored. But I needed to press on.

After the telephone call with Yahia and Busho, it was actually quite easy to convene a First Ministers meeting on Implementation of the Nairobi Agreement. We met this time in Nairobi: neutral territory. After all, neither party was satisfied with the progress to date despite a September Kampala commitment to exchange diplomats and begin a process of normalization of relations, Sudan and Uganda's relationship was in fact further strained.

The international community too was anxious to meet. The Canadian Government had launched its Winnipeg Initiative in August in Canada and had taken some credit for the first thirteen children who escaped the LRA in September. Canada had become engaged and wished to do more. But while Canada might have thought that it had an explicit mandate to convene Sudan and Uganda pursuant to the Winnipeg Communiqué, Sudan for one was not anxious to have Canada looking over its shoulders at its efforts with abducted children. Sudan could feel the pressure already: UNICEF; Save the Children UK, active in northern Uganda; Save the Children UK, active in Sudan; the International Organization for Migration, now becoming involved in the repatriation of abductees through Khartoum to Entebbe and on to their homes in Northern Uganda: all wanted to be briefed on the situation. Indeed, they wanted to register concerns about a 'thumb screw' strategy that was sure to result in hunger and maybe illness in the LRA camps, not to mention the horror of what Kony might do if he got desperate.

So we met in Nairobi, the agenda having been fleshed out ahead, most of it during that telephone meeting between Yahia, Busho and I. And at 6:30am on November 19, before the larger group came together, I mediated a direct session between Sudan's Ismail and Uganda's Rugunda. Mustafa Ismail was 'passing through' Nairobi and would not stay for the whole meeting, but wanted to get some matters of principle resolved. Rugunda and Ismail agreed that The Carter Center would chair the overall process related to implementation of the Nairobi Agreement. I suggested Canada chair a sub-committee on Abducted Children, within the context of our efforts and reporting to our talks. They agreed. Canada's mandate was to be exactly that set forth in the Winnipeg Communiqué – an exclusive focus on abductees. On the contentious issue of exchange of diplomats they simply informed me that there was a 'dispute' (clearly there was) and that the issue was being referred to another venue, to a foreign minister's forum (the same group who had met in Kampala).

Of course, I would have loved to help them settle that pressing issue right there and then. But again, I had to live with these tactics of deflection and diversion. I was really being impeded by my own limitations as a mediator with no real clout to push these men and their governments to go where I wanted them to go.

Ismail, however, pressed to add a new item to our early morning talks. He wanted Sudanese officials to have access to refugee camps in northern Uganda that housed southern Sudanese people. These were people who had fled the civil war in southern Sudan. Ismail argued that Uganda was allowing the SPLA to recruit and train the men in the camps to return to southern Sudan to fight for the SPLA against the government's forces there. We also discussed the camp intended to house Kony and his band. I challenged the idea, saying that as a neutral and reflecting the comments I had been receiving from the international community, upon whom they would rely for funding, the idea of a camp was simply not being well received. Was it a transit camp? What kind of structures and infrastructure would be required, and for how long?

I was informed by Ismail that it would be a temporary camp.

"And by what date, exactly, will the Government of Sudan relocate the LRA to the camp?" I asked.

He said, "December 31, if possible; Kony by March 31; and all of the remaining LRA by September 30, 2001. So at that time the Nairobi Agreement will be fully implemented."

Despite my frustrations that we might have done more, my mood was elevated by these commitments. This was the big guys talking. They were putting in place a framework and a timetable. So it would be nearly a full year, I thought, before our work was done. Our private mediation session now over, I caught my breath by grabbing a coffee and sweet roll on my way to the large meeting room where some of the participants in the next session were already gathering. Now we had to get back to the immediate challenge of finding a way to engage Kony so that whatever occurred, resolution would be by peaceful means.

I came away from that large mediation session holding onto the belief that no one wanted any blood-shed. The meeting had produced a good collective strategy on how to approach the LRA. The Sudanese delegation gave everyone a fuller understanding of what they had been trying to do, and how Kony had become more difficult and evasive. The Sudanese had pressed to enlist everyone's support. The Ugandans seemed more sympathetic than they had before.

Right on the spot David had drafted a letter to Kony, signed by all present, to be forwarded forthwith by the Sudanese to him. David also drafted a press release, hoping Kony would hear it.

Privately, however, I learned the Ugandans still did not trust Sudan. They could not help but believe some deception was involved. Sudan, too, did not trust Uganda. There had been no movement on the agreed Observation Team along the Sudan-Uganda border. There was foot-dragging on exchanging diplomats.

Deutschland Radio picked up the press release and I was interviewed on Africa Report. The show would be broadcast into Africa and I hoped that Kony would hear it. In that interview my points were that dialogue is always better than a military response; that we had devised a managed approach to a complex problem which took into account the legitimate interests of the Acholi people; and that this approach was a step in normalizing relations between Sudan and Uganda.

Before too long, now back in Atlanta, I was told by Chris that the Sudanese had just sent the signed letter to Kony through the bush to the LRA. That was November 26. So we were making progress, but I reflected on likely scenarios.

If we get a no from Kony, if he refused to meet with a full delegation as we proposed, what was plan B? We didn't have a plan B. We had planned and acted and pushed and prepared for Plan A: dialogue leading to the disarming and disbanding of the LRA assuming that any political issues Kony and the LRA had would be appropriately addressed by the Government of Uganda through the talks.

So, what was plan B? I got to work, sketching out a set of options, none of which were very hopeful. These included: the 'watching brief' – continue to hold out the offer to Kony, sit tight, watch, wait and hope; 'the rifle shot' – send a small delegation (Yahia, Busho and me) to meet with Kony regardless of the obstacles; the 'notch up' – have President Carter meet with Museveni and Bashir and see what might be salvaged; the 'wind up' – call everyone together and declare implementation has stalled – as there is insufficient political will to implement the Agreement.

On December 2, I was on my way to Khartoum again. I calculated that I had slept in my bed at home in Atlanta only 13 nights in 9 months. I would meet David in Khartoum and we would go to Juba. David was a good pair of eyes, a good thinker. We were a better delegation for this assignment than involving young Chris. Like me, David was also in early middle age. Chris was young and I felt it was my responsibility to take the lead, and the risk and David concurred. We would stay at the UN Compound there to put distance between ourselves and the Government of Sudan. It would be another dangerous mission. We would send a message to Kony. I had a signed letter from President Carter, a warm, supportive letter seeking Kony's engagement. It was the rifle shot in the extreme. I no longer wanted Sudan or Uganda to be involved in this overture to Kony. This approach would be a direct appeal to Kony. David and I would also assess what was really happening on the ground. I would put my reputation on the line when I informed everyone later whether I believed that Sudan was indeed no longer supporting the LRA.

When I arrived in Khartoum, Yahia was in a bad mood. He wasn't supportive of establishing a local reception center for kids in Juba to be operated by UNICEF. He was refusing to let Ugandan technical experts into the country to explain the Ugandan Amnesty Law and how it would protect LRA returnees from prosecution and provide them with a start-up package to get their lives going once again as regular civilians.

I let Yahia vent: He said, "Why must Sudan do everything? The Observation Team is not in place. The visits to refugee camps in northern Uganda are not going ahead."

Then I asked, "What about your 'thumb screw' policy? How far are you going to take it?"

"As far as it will take us," he replied, without emotion. "We will show some relief only if that is helpful in establishing and maintaining talks."

He offered no more.

"Well," I said, "I am here and willing to do what it takes to get Kony into talks."

He fidgeted with some papers. I could see he was not keen on me going to Juba. But I pressed him. As much as I had grown to like him and as cordial as our exchanges had most often been, I was not prepared to back down.

Our meeting ended with neither of us being very happy.

David and I eventually flew down to Juba in the back of a cargo plane. It was a long, dark, uncomfortable ride. Then we stayed in the shabby UN compound just on the outskirts of Juba – although our host, Jacob, was very congenial and a great cook. As we bedded down, I felt we were far from being trusted by Kony. Drawing the flimsy bolt on my bedroom door, I thought we might be assassinated in our sleep. On the one hand the Sudanese might not want us acting so independently, getting so close to Kony and the real picture on the ground. On the other, we may have already become Kony's enemy; for I recalled his paranoia about being named a war criminal. He might think that we were there to get him.

We met with a number of local people, both civilians and military personnel, but there was no contact from Kony. So on December 8, I was back from Juba, sitting alone with my thoughts in the Khartoum Hilton. It had been one year since the Nairobi Agreement was signed. Elton John's 'Benny and the Jets' was playing, reminding me of how many miles and years I was from the great days of the 1970s when, as a young man, the same song was being played as I had worked in corrections in northern Ontario. But I realized I was still doing the same work, just now in a far off corner of the world. I was still working for justice.

In those days I had struggled with the utility of punishment as a way to deal with people who injure others, and I worked hard with others to develop treatment programs for men who abuse their wives. I believed in restorative, not retributive justice.

I had committed myself to the notion that we put people in prison as punishment, not for punishment. And I knew that there was something unsound about a justice system that focused almost exclusively on the offender. We never talked to or tried to meet the needs of victims. We thought criminals might be 'corrected' through a variety of programs: educational and vocational training, and a handful of therapeutic treatments. And we tried. But the statistics kept saying that one third stay the same, one third improve – and one third get worse. That prison doors were revolving doors with as high as 66% of the released inmates returning again to serve more time was no surprise to anyone.

Having been promoted from the rank of guard, working on the prison floor, to a senior administrator I saw all of this from a comfortable distance. But I had the sense that I was still caught up in a system that was anchored in a belief that to correct offenders, punishment was the answer. My involvement in the regime of punishment came in the form of an official document that I had to read, sign, and file away. My signature was a form of approval.

It was a punishment report.

In effect, this is how punishment worked.

When an inmate was bad you locked him up in a detention cell.

If what he did was bad enough, you strapped him. One disciplinarian I knew would demand that the inmate lower his trousers and bend forward over a table, exposing his bare buttocks. Then the disciplinarian would signal to the few guards in attendance. They would begin to shuffle their feet slowly across the floor. This made it impossible for the inmate to hear the belt as it came whipping though the air, impossible to brace for the blow.

If the inmate remained defiant you placed him in solitary confinement.

If he still wouldn't break and promise to behave, you took away his privileges – first, no magazines, then no smokes, and finally, no family visits.

If this regime failed to make him conform and behave himself, you gave him special diet. Special diet looked like soft cat food. It was a gruel that no ordinary person would eat. It was unpalatable. Yet it contained all the nutrients that government standards called for. The authorities could never be accused of not feeding inmates locked in solitary confinement.

This idea that you can get someone to act the way you want them to by taking a club to them, and then making the club larger and hitting them more and more made me shudder with revulsion. Yet I was signing these punishment forms. I was authorizing exactly that. Now Sudan was doing the same to Kony.

Three things stand out in my memory of those years working in corrections and with abusive men: how much men deny or minimize their violence; that many were able to stop being physically violent but continued to be psychologically and emotionally violent to their female partner; and how the list of men waiting for treatment never gets any shorter.

Dealing with the denial and minimization, however, has served me well. First, I had to confront my own violence, in the non-physical forms it took. I realized I could blame no one else for my behaviour. Not if it was *my* behaviour. So I had to learn new ways to express my anger and frustration. Second, I adopted a zero tolerance for violence by learning to name it, and confront it in others when it was my responsibility to do so. And thirdly, I got a clear understanding that violence is the abusive use of power. With this, I did not turn away from power, but from its abusive use.

But recalling all of this was of little compensation as I sat in the Hilton Hotel in Khartoum. I felt exhausted. And I asked myself, what really had we accomplished?

We had reached out to Kony.

But nothing! Well, not exactly. While Kony had not responded, we had done our intelligence work on the ground in Juba. We had made some key findings from which I drew some important conclusions.

I could now fully appreciate that to gain Sudan's full assistance in disarming and disbanding the LRA, Uganda must give up its support for the SPLA. That was clear to me from the remarks made by the Sudanese military and security personnel in Juba. And I understood that the more The Carter Center was effective in getting Sudan's compliance in the demise of the LRA, by putting pressure on Uganda to stop supporting the SPLA, the less likely we would be acceptable to the SPLA in any peacemaker role. This was sure to limit our ability to broker peace in Sudan.

I also began to see Kony as a vicious aberration, not capable of political negotiation, perhaps not worthy of dignifying in any way. Except for the lives of those he controlled and who suffered and died in his assault on Museveni.

I concluded that a new approach for dealing with the LRA must be articulated. It should start with me spelling out to every one of us involved with the LRA the consequences of the current 'attrition' process; that is, the current assumption that the LRA would eventually wither away through lack of support from Sudan and by abducted kids escaping from it. We needed to recognize that many innocent kids would die trying to escape and we needed to acknowledge that the Aboke girls were living under severe conditions. They would be punished or killed if there was a hint they might slip out from under Kony's control. We also had to be aware of the fact that the war-wounded, the sick and elderly in the LRA band would suffer without proper attention. And I wanted everyone to know that Kony would continue to wage war with a vengeance.

The new approach must ensure that the door is left open to Kony, with many and all channels of sending messages and opening up communication with him exploited. To take this new approach the Government of Uganda's and others' skepticism about Sudan's having cut off Kony must be addressed. This should be done by placing independent observers in Juba, if necessary, so that Sudan will get appropriate credit and support for what it had done.

We must design this approach so that efforts to assist the abductees who do try to escape from the LRA will be redoubled and put in place right at the community and village level in southern Sudan. A specific, firm time frame must be put in place to assess developments. This cannot be left to drift on its own.

I came to another conclusion. In addition to informing everyone of exactly what we had found and what I had concluded, it was obvious to me that much more was needed to get traction. I would have to go back to the drawing board, back to where I had been in March, when I had been directed by President Carter to lead The Center's efforts to end the war in Sudan.

We needed to develop a bold comprehensive strategy that would notch up this whole, harrowing effort. I would need a mandate from the institution to do more. It would include remaining vigilant with Kony; it would include shifting our resources to northern Uganda where we would try to create 'pull factors' that would entice the LRA into talks; and it would include the Acholi community. But it would also now look more intently at the war in Sudan. That war was playing hell on my process, in ways that I hadn't appreciated. And it was that war that I was explicitly directed to help end.

I badly needed the Christmas break.

But, as usual, it was short-lived. Before the ink could dry on the plan that our team put together to elevate our efforts for peace in Sudan, I received a call from Khartoum. Kony wanted to meet with me, alone.

8

Flying Blind

Kony had indeed received the letters sent through the bush by David and I. Yahia said Kony had, however, been angry that he had not been consulted on the issues discussed at our large session in Nairobi. Although, I recalled, at the meeting in November the Sudanese had insisted that Kony had been kept informed by them.

I recommended to Yahia that a smaller delegation go to meet Kony. I had in mind someone senior from the Ugandan government, a diplomat representing the international community, and myself. Yahia disagreed. We had better proceed this time exactly the way Kony wanted. I should go alone. Yahia also made a point for the record that Sudan's strategy had seemed to work. Kony was feeling the hunger pangs and wanted to talk.

I called a staff and intern meeting. What did they think? Should I go alone? What would they recommend?

They insisted that I not go alone. I should meet Kony in a neutral place, not deep in the bush where he would be in control. I should try to arrange direct contact between Kony and Museveni, excluding others who might spoil the effort. We should offer Kony a satellite phone connected only to me. That way, we would by-pass the potential manipulations of the Government of Sudan and I could build a direct relationship with Kony over time.

I decided to go, and Tom agreed to come with me.

What would we try to do? We would listen to Kony. To his laments. We would try to build trust, explain the Nairobi meetings, recent developments. We would talk about talks, about process. I would see him privately if I could, to explore whether a personal package was of interest to him. Above all, we would take our time. We would go for the duration.

But what should we tell the Ugandans, the Canadians, Egyptians and Libyans – not to mention UNICEF – all these friends of the process? How could we act discretely without appearing to be uncooperative or less transparent than a mediator needs to be?

We decided to inform the others only on the eve of our departure from Khartoum to Juba. Nothing should scuttle this extremely important meeting.

There I was back again on a long flight through Frankfurt to Khartoum. We were greeted on the tarmac by familiar faces, Hassan and junior officers who worked for Yahia. In the Hilton Hotel the staff had now come to know me and I actually felt unusually at ease. I had a sense of purpose. We were on a mission. I knew where I was. I knew what I was going to do. This could be the turning point after months of frustration and a growing sense of failure.

And our Sudanese colleagues were upbeat too. General Yassin, a silver haired man who had been a part of the Ministerial delegation to the first meeting I had mediated in Atlanta, was now the 'point'. A transition was taking place in the Sudanese management of the LRA 'file'. It was becoming a military matter. Yassin had befriended me in Atlanta, and we had exchanged brief personal stories. I had told him that my brother Alan had recently had a serious stroke. Yassin had suggested, helpfully, that a teaspoon each day of a mixture of honey and garlic would keep his blood pressure down. Now he was the man who had recently met with Kony, the man who would take me to see him.

I expected a day or two at most of preparations. What had Kony been told? What was his psychological attitude? What did he expect from the meeting?

Hassan suggested that Kony would probably ask about humanitarian assistance, phone contact and the relocation plan. In the Hilton's lobby I bumped into the Canadians who did not press me on my current assignment, but declared they supported me and did not want to be left too far behind. Then things began to go wonky – again. Our flight was postponed – the cargo plane was full and could not accommodate us. Really, we thought? What are they transporting that they do not want us to see? Then it was postponed again. And now both Hassan and his counterpart on the ground in Juba, who spoke to us by cell phone, seemed genuinely frustrated too. But were they? Was this a ploy? Were they prepping Kony in the background or was Kony not cooperating? We did not know but we did register our concern that we needed to get going, now.

Finally, and only after another 'Keystone Cops' mix-up that saw the General and me chasing around in a car on the tarmac of a military airport to find the plane on which we were scheduled (if that's not too strong a term) to leave, we boarded a cargo plane. Yes, another cargo plane. The entire great cavity of it was filled with black soldiers crammed into the tail end. These young men looked like fresh recruits taken from the black south for training in the north, obviously now being shipped back south to Juba to take their turn in fending off the SPLA. In effect, they were returning to fight their own cousins.

General Yassin sat 'up top' with the pilot, although Tom and I were given cordial treatment and the only bench that served as a seat along the side of the fuselage. It was another rough, sightless, boring flight over the Sahara and the Nile to hot tropical Juba.

There was much ado as we arrived. The local senior commander greeted us. Mohamed Hassan's local counterpart, the effusive El Fadil, scurried about looking happy to see us again. This was his beat. He was close to the LRA and we represented a humane option for dealing with them. He wanted our mission to succeed – perhaps.

He claimed that he had expected us earlier, that everything had been arranged for us to go to Nsitu again. He said that time was of the essence.

What ensued was yet again another curiosity. Instead of taking off forthwith under the escort of the Sudanese military guard, we were driven to a newly re-opened hotel – that might have been elegant one day. Here we lingered over a lovely meal as the precious afternoon hours dwindled.

"Are we going today?" I asked Yassin. "Yes," he answered. "But we are waiting for a liaison officer, a major who knows the LRA well." And the easy chatter in Arabic among the assembled officers continued.

I thought that maybe we were here to get settled in our rooms as we had been proudly shown a couple of chambers by an ancient man who had apparently returned to Juba to re-open this hotel that he had operated eons before. But no, they were only 'demonstration rooms' – we would be staying at El Fadil's safe house again – the same place I had stayed when I had first met Kony. On the last visit I had insisted that David and I stay in the UN compound. That way we could interview people in private and our discussion of the findings would be less likely to be overhead and more confidential.

Maybe my impatience was showing. Suddenly, Yassin made a move and everyone mobilized; drivers came out from behind shade trees and the red-bereted armed corps slung their AK-47s over their shoulders and loaded themselves into the open boxes of Toyota 4x4 trucks. Tom and I were shown to one of the vehicles. Then we were off.

From what I could make out, we were taking the same route as last July – heading to Nsitu. I imagined Kony, Sam Koho, Sam Livingston, and Otti Vincent. I tried to focus and to rehearse our game plan. But I had a nagging doubt – the delays in Khartoum, the late start this afternoon.

The landscape changed a bit. As we approached a rise and made a right turn I confirmed to myself that we were at the perimeter of the camp. But there was no sentry as before. Nor were there any huts with curious people peeking out as before. The crops in the field were cut to the ground. It was deathly silent. Could this be an ambush? Something was wrong.

We pulled into the great open yard of the camp Nsitu to find not a soul around. It was abandoned. No Kony. No one!

I got out of my vehicle and watched as Yassin and his military colleagues showed some signs of disbelief. But it was obvious that the LRA had not been there for weeks, or maybe longer. There was a small pile of the husks of thrashed millet in the center of the yard. The building where Kony and I had met was swept clean, as indeed was the whole yard. There wasn't even a bit of dog shit on the ground.

So, what was the point? Why were we here? To show me that the LRA had indeed moved deeper into the bush as Yahia had reported weeks ago? OK, but what about Kony? What about our meeting?

With very little to-do, as a matter of course, we loaded up and then our small motorcade of four vehicles worked its way out through what appeared to be the back end of the camp. We crawled down a grade, curved around and within minutes came to a Sudanese outpost. This was the real base at Nsitu. It was Sudan's last outpost from Juba, most likely shared with the LRA. Beyond it was 'no man's land' and the SPLA.

But here, again, there was no Kony. A senior officer reported to Yassin that the camp Major had gone to find the LRA spokesman. That Kony was sick. The LRA commanders, all of them, including Sam Koho had been there until late last night. They had been dressed in western suits and ties. They had wanted to meet me. But they had grown impatient and had gone back to Kony some miles deeper in the bush. There was a lot of talk of an action by the Ugandan army against the LRA at Mile 75 – a long way from here. Yassin offered that perhaps this had spooked Kony, and asked if the Ugandans knew that we were to meet.

I thought this was preposterous! But Yassin and everyone was making it appear to be the God-sworn truth. They all showed the right kinds of physical gestures of disappointment, confusion, even embarrassment. And the local officers were ready to fill me in on the details of the LRA entourage that had been here and had just left – and on Kony's illness too.

We sat down to tea as junior men scurried around to accommodate General Yassin and his guests. Settled in a small open-air room that served as the officers' lounge, I noticed a satellite receiver and a coloured TV. I now understood how Kony – at least while he had been supported by Sudan – could wage a guerilla war from deep in the bush and still be aware of world events including the charges being brought against Pinochet, which he had mentioned to me when we had met; and how he could enjoy 'Cowboy and Indian movies'.

From the conversation, and the casual way in which the Sudanese officers spoke about Kony and the individual members of his senior command, it was also apparent that these two military arms, that of Sudan and the LRA, had been partners with deep ties. It would not be easy to sever them, even with orders from Khartoum.

They said this was the second time Kony had been ill like this in the past year. That he was sick with yellow eyes and sore joints.

So, what do we do? Apparently the commander of this outpost had reached out to Kony four times already today. The commander had sent a liaison to the point in the bush where the LRA commanders who had been here yesterday had said they would be. But no one had shown. Now the senior officer had gone again to make contact.

Yassin asked me that if I could not meet Kony, whether a meeting with Kony's commanders would suffice? I said "certainly". And there was speculation in the air, as we sat in the officers' lounge. The officers suggested to me that some of the senior LRA officers who had been here yesterday would defect.

The afternoon's shadows were beginning to get very long. The Major had not returned. I pulled Yassin aside and put three pointed questions to him. One, what was the real genesis of the meeting – what did Kony agree to, was it imposed on him? Two, if the Ugandan army is inside Sudan engaging the LRA with or without the SPLA, The Carter Center should hold Uganda accountable under the terms of the Nairobi Agreement: what evidence could we get to confirm his allegation? Three, is Kony capable of negotiating? I said that Kony's behaviour suggests he may not be a political player and that the Government of Sudan may have to deal with him on that basis.

Yassin replied that Kony had asked for the meeting and that he had been quite enthusiastic. About the potential spoiler role of Uganda, he simply reiterated that it was possible. And he tended to agree that Kony was not a reliable interlocutor.

Long evening shadows now fell on us. And it was obvious that nothing was going to happen, so I suggested to Yassin that we head back to Juba.

The next day, as a practical measure to try to move this forward, I took Tom's suggestion that I write a letter to Kony, now, asking for engagement. I worded the letter strongly, fairly, and suggested that if he regrettably were ill that he send a liaison so that we might start talking while Kony healed. Having sent the letter we agreed to each other to stay another 24 hours.

The next day we received word from Yassin's liaison officer that Kony had requested we wait 7 days; he was sick and his commanders were spread out and unable to meet with me.

It was then that I made the following entry in my field notes: *someone should write a book about this entitled 'flying blind'*. For surely there are times in peace work, as in any other work performed on uncertain terrain, when one must just 'fly blind', without instruments, through the fog. And all you have is your intuition with no guarantees.

We agreed to give Kony seven more days. Tom and I, now guests of El Fadil, in his great house overlooking Juba and the African huts below, began to crunch endgame scenarios and to map out strategic options that would require Ugandan effort too.

A number of visitors came and went. We assumed all of them were staged by El Fadil and General Yassin, so we couldn't be certain their information was accurate or bogus.

Nevertheless, we did have a revealing meeting with two young Acholi men who had apparently just arrived in military barracks after escaping from Kony. An Acholi chief, Charlie, whom I had met privately on a previous trip, provided interpretation services, for which we paid him a small fee.

The two were handsome young men. One was 19 and the other 24. They said that they had been in the LRA for several years. They both looked well fed and fit. ("Hungry?" I thought). After we settled in a bit one became talkative, the other was very quiet, avoiding eye contact.

He said that they had just seen Kony addressing a large group before they escaped three days ago. ("Sick?" I thought). Kony had told everyone in the group not to trust me – the white slave trader.

They had been told by Kony that if they escaped they would be killed by the Sudanese military. If they got past the military, they would be seized and taken to salt mines. If they were not taken to salt mines then I would ship them far away as slaves.

If these boys were telling the truth, no wonder they were timid with me and one didn't talk at all!

But I was inclined to believe them because I trusted Charlie. I didn't think he would distort their information significantly.

Through Charlie's interpretation, we learned about the LRA camp. Conditions were very severe for the Aboke girls. They were kept in a single compound, brutalized, and warned of the consequences if they ever tried to escape. There was enough food because many of the men who weren't fighting were collecting food from the bush. Kony was building a new camp. We had heard about this camp before and that it was called, subject to interpretation, 'my last stand'. Charlie said something to the effect that Kony would go like Hitler before he surrendered.

We reassured the boys that they were safe now. They would be moved through Khartoum to rejoin their families in Uganda. There would be no recrimination against them.

The next morning as I lay in my roof-top cot I heard an unfamiliar noise coming from a long way off, out past the huts below and beyond us that marked the furthest outskirts of Juba. The noise faded momentarily and then resumed; a husky pulsating sound.

I rose from bed and went to look over the low wall around the rooftop patio. All was still in the early morning. But then I could hear it again, punctuating the calm and quiet. And it was growing louder. So I moved around, trying to locate it and as I did the sound grew steadily louder. I could now distinguish it as some kind of music, or singing. I listened, becoming more absorbed each minute as what was now a chorus rose from the edge of town and made its way toward us.

It was clear now that someone was singing and the depth of it, and the resonance was remarkable. A man's voice which penetrated the air sang a lead, followed by a chorus of men's voices that was simply spellbinding. And it was approaching.

Within minutes I saw them. Dressed in white T-shirts and blue shorts, a platoon of black men turned the corner, jogging in an orderly, easy fashion as they sang. That platoon of twenty men, now almost below me, was followed by another twenty, and then another. These were black southern Sudanese who had been recruited by the Government of Sudan to fight its war with the SPLA. Perhaps they were the soldiers who had travelled with us from Khartoum, in the back of that cargo plane. Young strong men trained in the north, returned and stationed in this garrison city to be deployed against Garang and his rebels, their tribesman.

Several looked up and noticed me on my rooftop perch. Unexpectantly gentle for soldiers, they smiled and some dared flash me a wave. I returned their waves, watched and listened in wonder as they moved down our long street, turned a corner, and faded off.

After a few days, I had a growing sense that we would not be hearing from Kony. We decided to return to Khartoum and wait out the balance of the time. I asked Tom, who did not reply, "Is the LRA an armed cult or a political movement with an army?" Although it looked like the former, my sympathy for Kony's innocent victims was growing stronger.

Meanwhile, back in Atlanta, Gordon had sent my proposal that I had developed over Christmas and which I had entitled 'Waging Peace in Sudan', to President Carter. Carter approved it, calling it a bold initiative. When I heard that, I recalled my friend Don Skilling's last words of advice to me, before he passed away from a cancer that ravaged him, to 'do something bold'. I had not known then what it was that I could or should do that would meet the spirit of Don's directive. It was a little eerie to have my proposal called 'bold' by President Carter.

After more mulling in the Khartoum Hilton, now home to me, I met with Egypt's Ambassador to Sudan, Ambassador Mohamed Assam Ibrahim, the 'loquacious', as I had come to call him. I gave him a detailed account of my efforts and my conclusions. Not missing a beat he remarked that I had done an excellent job on this 'micro' task, but that I now had to stand back. The larger political picture had to be addressed. Or, to put it another way, this micro problem I was having had to be put into a larger strategic framework. He was really saying that I could have turned cartwheels to get Kony engaged with Museveni, but it would never work. The war in Sudan was obstructing my progress. I really needed to focus all my hard work on ending the war in Sudan. Only then would I see real progress with the LRA. He was right, and I was pleased that Gordon and President Carter had supported my proposal to do just that. They had agreed to an approach, a strategy and a set of actions that would take me well beyond the role of a mediator. I didn't have a name for it then. Now I do. It is 'Peace Guerrilla'.

The few remaining days that Kony could have contacted me passed without a peep from that quarter. During that period I turned my attention to the bigger agenda. The proposal President Carter had just endorsed was focused on four elements of the civil war in Sudan: the nature of the conflict; the parties; the policy environment; and the peace process. We would have to become active on all four, trying to orchestrate the right conditions to bring about an end to the Sudanese civil war. Just to begin, we had to understand the parties better, to secure their trust in us so that we might be helpful in building trust between them. In Khartoum's case, that meant continuing to do a credible job on implementing the Nairobi Agreement and building deeper ties with those responsible for the peace process inside Sudan. Through President Carter's personal effort and the ongoing commitment of The Center to health in Sudan, we had good relations with President Bashir and his government. They would have to be protected and improved upon while not prejudicing ourselves with Dr. John Garang and the SPLA. This was going to be a delicate matter, for Garang had had some dealings with President Carter, the most successful being the humanitarian ceasefire Carter had mediated in 1996. But there had always been a hint of suspicion held by Garang toward President Carter. Rather than debate the merits of this perception, we would need to build a trusting relationship between Garang and Carter.

As regards policy, President Carter was already active with the new Bush Administration in Washington. We needed Washington to turn its attention to Sudan, to engage Khartoum and the SPLA in a balanced way that pushed for peace. The policy environment in Washington, and in other key capitals such as London and Brussels, was a long way from being properly aligned to give peace a chance.

Many felt that the Sudan Peace Process, housed in Nairobi, needed a complete overhaul and a concentration of resources to make it effective. The Joint Egyptian-Libyan Initiative, clearly self-serving, was just a convenient alternative for Bashir and Garang when they didn't like what they were getting in Nairobi. I was determined there would be a single, viable peace process. So, if we had to ruffle some feathers, or seem less diplomatic and cooperative as might be wished, that was a price we would have to pay to get a single, focused, working, credible peace process in place.

So there, in the Khartoum Hilton, with President Carter's endorsement of my proposal to step up our efforts, I began to have a series of private meetings with officials of the Government of Sudan who would have advice for ending the war. Yahia was my key ally in this, arranging the meetings, making the introductions.

The message I got was remarkably simple and clear – and this was coming from senior officials within the Government of Sudan. The war must end. Everyone had been hurt by it. The country was being held back. It is a political problem, not a religious one. Get the USA to push both Garang and Bashir to talks. Put both delegations in a hotel for three weeks and it can be done.

So that was it? The concern that perhaps peace in Sudan had to be built from the 'bottom up', rather than the 'top down'; that the elites, Bashir and Garang, could not carry the day was unfounded? The dread that Sharia versus freedom of religion was an irreversible impasse was an exaggerated obstruction? The infighting within the SPLA – the rift between the Dinka, led by Garang, and the Nuer, led by Riek Machar, was only a minor impediment? The fuming Turabi, the Islamic ideologue and charismatic leader set to undermine Bashir, was not a lethal Achilles heel?

No. I was told that there were tough challenges – apparent irreconcilables. But the USA was the key. It needed to lean on both sides and make peace 'happen'. The Sudan Peace Process didn't matter. Beefed up with American involvement, it was fine. But the peace process could be nothing like that which had ground on for these past years; what we needed now was a focused, energized, dedicated effort.

So from these conversations there appeared to be deep pockets of hope for peace in the Khartoum administration. But as the curtain closed on Juba and Khartoum, I realized I was angry at Kony and I felt distrust for almost everyone. This work, I realized, was far more than an emotional rollercoaster. That was a hackneyed phrase that simply did not capture the depth of my experience. Rather, trying to wage peace was putting me through the wringer, over and over. It was taking its toll. How was I to stay fresh, clear, wise and effective?

9

Checkmate

The darker it gets, the brighter the only light looks.

This entry in my field notes was the slogan under which we were now operating with the LRA. It may have been presumptuous to think that The Carter Center would be seen by Kony to be a light, let alone his only light in a darkening landscape. The Government of Sudan had cut Kony off. But we were hoping that our continuous efforts to demonstrate a commitment to a path of dialogue would shine through to him. As soon as I got back to Atlanta I would report that to all the stakeholders involved in implementing the Nairobi Agreement.

As the situation around Kony grew dimmer and dimmer, with lessening food supplies, more escapees, ammunition running out, limited communication and movement, I imagined he would look to us as a light. My deep concern, however, was to be sure that we did everything we could to keep the light on; and to send the message to Kony that we were true and fair.

To do this, I intended to get a satellite telephone into Kony's hands, and to release a statement to the press sending a message to Kony that we had come, we had waited, and we were still waiting to meet for talks. I also considered pressing Uganda to call upon Egypt and Libya for an observer team along Uganda's northern border, assuring Sudan that Uganda was not giving material support to Garang's SPLA. And I imagined calling upon the

Canadians to mount a monitoring team that would be placed in Juba to verify, on a day-to-day basis, that Kony was not being supported by the Sudanese Government. Then, I imagined, after 30 days of building confidence through these measures, Uganda and Sudan might exchange junior diplomats. And 60 days after that, senior diplomats would be received in each other's capital.

That is what I pictured. I even drafted the press release and thought about how we could more usefully engage President Carter in public diplomacy – in sending the messages that we as peacemakers needed to send when those messages were not forthcoming from others. But this was an imagined reality.

I had held the view that everyone has the potential to do good, under the right circumstances. My present problem was to determine who among us fell short. Was it Kony himself? The Ugandans I had worked with: Mbabazi, Rugunda? The Sudanese: Yassin, Yahia? And was it possible to separate person from position? Was it possible that we are all good people and the only problem is that we get caught up in a world of realpolitik, a world somehow on automatic pilot, responsive only to the state's corporate needs, sovereign, and responsible to no one or no thing? A world of anarchy where power is used solely to dominate and only to liberate within a very narrow self-serving view of that term?

We had already heard the talk in the corridors of the meetings I had chaired between the Ugandans and Sudanese about military action against the LRA. If Sudan was not prepared to take out Kony through a fight, then Uganda was. The talk was that, ideally, a joint military action against the LRA would suit Uganda best. We had witnessed the beginning of Sudan's 'thumb screw' policy. The thought was that Kony with no food, no medicine, and no recourse to Juba's hospital or markets would feel the pressure. He would realize he had no allies and no source of ammunition unless he stole it. He would be forced to yield.

What we had was a policy of disbanding the LRA by attrition, not dialogue, nor negotiation. Some LRA members tried to escape, as many had already. How many of those had died doing so, I did not know. Some would get sick and many had already. How many of those died in the bush, I did not know.

Dialogue, dialogue, dialogue! Surely it was the only humanly desirable and realistic way to go. Realistic because I was certain Kony would not give up without a fight, and it would be a fight to the end.

So, we would pursue peace despite the odds. We would push on with the LRA and we would notch up our efforts to bring an end to the civil war in Sudan. Maybe the Nairobi Agreement really could be a building block for peace in Sudan. If we could get Museveni to believe Sudan had stopped supporting Kony, then Museveni might stop supporting Garang. And if the USA stopped supporting Garang and began supporting peace in Sudan, then, maybe . . .

The proposal I had written over Christmas, which had been polished by Tom and Alex Little, another exceptional intern on my team, was entitled 'Waging Peace in Sudan'. It was borne of frustration, personal exhaustion with our piecemeal efforts to date, and a growing sense that President Carter would rise to a well-argued initiative. It called, however, for building relationships with Garang and the SPLA, while maintaining good relations with Khartoum, and also enhancing our credibility with the governments in London, Brussels and Oslo through vigilance on the LRA issue and on our overall efforts to implement the Nairobi Agreement. We would need broad international support in our efforts to push peace; and we would need to build momentum to break through on peace.

President Carter, however, had another plan. He wanted to hold off on my idea of calling Museveni and Bashir and invited me instead to go along with him to Washington to make a joint presentation to the State Department. We would meet with Secretary of State Colin Powell and seek a mandate to become engaged in Sudan, writ large.

I believe my proposal had stirred President Carter. Not that he wasn't committed long before I had arrived on the scene or that he lacked vision and capacity. After all, it was he who had stated nearly a full year ago that the war in Sudan could have been ended seven years ago (now eight!) if the US administration had wanted it to end. And he had tried, although we also had struck out a year ago when we met with then Secretary of State Madeline Albright. Now, Carter was more confident. He had been to the White House recently for the inauguration of President Bush. He had demonstrated bi-partisan sensibility to this new President, whose popular support was shaky. He had talked directly to President Bush about Sudan. He knew Powell personally, as Powell had previously gone with Carter to Haiti to avert US military intervention there.

So my proposal 'Waging Peace in Sudan', which he had called a bold initiative, was a stimulant. It brought a strategic direction, technical expertise, and practical steps to President Carter's well established commitment. It gave President Carter a boost to bring his passion to a head in an environment that he judged to be receptive. Bush had been responsive in the Rose Garden. Powell was familiar and judged to be a sensible moderate. We had done good work in the region. Bashir trusted Carter, and Garang could be won over. With the USA behind us, we could bring peace to Sudan.

The meeting with Powell was weeks away, scheduled for March 12, 2001. But there would be no basking in that prospect. On the contrary, Mbabazi, Uganda's tough hardliner was on the telephone and Dr. Yahia was on another line from Sudan. Mbabazi was uncharacteristically warm and asking that I be in touch with him in two weeks' time.

Yahia had more on Kony. This is what he reported. Two or three days after I had left Khartoum, Colonel Jamal, the senior officer on the ground, had met with Kony. Kony was furious. He had waited for me. I had not shown. He had heard that I had publicly announced that I was going to meet with Kony and 'bring him back'. There was a Ugandan offensive inside Sudan at mile 77 and Kony had concluded there was a conspiracy against him. He feared that I would meet with him and his commanders while he was attacked from the rear. So perhaps General Yassin, when we were at the outpost in Nsitu, was doing more than merely speculating about what may be detaining Kony. But now as then, I couldn't be sure.

Yahia said that Kony told Jamal he would have no more political contact with the Government of Sudan. No more political contact with The Carter Center. If The Carter Center wanted to talk to Kony it should be done through his representatives in Nairobi – stating "you know them".

I reacted by saying that I wanted Yahia to get a satellite phone to Kony. The phone would be fixed so that if any of the four call buttons were pressed, the phone would only connect the caller to me, no one else. It could not be used for military operations or propaganda or any other communication except to me. I also stated that I believed Sudan needed to agree to a verification team in Juba, to assure the many doubters that Kony had indeed been cut off. I told him that Canada now seemed to be behind a meeting to be convened in New York to examine our lack of progress with the LRA. A number of organizations, including World Vision, which was active with escaped LRA abductees in northern Uganda, would be there. I told him that despite my positive impressions of what Sudan had done in ending its support to Kony, others were not impressed. I stated that I had gone out on a limb, staking my reputation on the findings that I had made in Juba. Now we needed to assure the international community, especially the Ugandans, if we were to get them to stop supporting the SPLA. But I needed direct contact with Kony.

Yahia equivocated, saying that the military would have to examine my proposal about the phone. He also said that Sudan would not be happy with this New York meeting that generated more heat in regards Sudan's efforts with Kony.

I didn't even get into a conversation with him about Colonel Jamal and his meeting with Kony. And as for Kony's representatives in Nairobi, I wondered whether these were the two men I had met in the Hilton. If so, they had said they were defecting from Kony. One of them had actually contacted me a few weeks after we had met. He was indeed in Nairobi, and he wanted money to help him personally. I had refused, saying that I was not able to deal with personal matters and I never heard from him again. So I was not going to take Yahia up on this one; it was a wild goose chase I would avoid.

Instead, I recommended he have a small meeting, off the record, with Uganda. If Mbabazi agreed, we would ask the Canadians to give us a little more time, telling them that we were making progress in the background. I decided as well that David should establish a presence in northern Uganda while avoiding the contentious internal politics there.

I called Mbabazi. He was friendly again, even warm. I had caught him at home, during a dinner party with friends. An election was upon them. He was happy I was still involved, grateful for The Carter Center's and my personal efforts. But he did not share my optimism. He agreed in the end, however, that a small meeting should take place.

January turned to February. President Museveni, now campaigning for another term as president, lashed out verbally at Kony. Once again, the hope for the peace process was pounded in the crucible of political ambition. Once again, a lull in honouring commitments was justified by the needs of the political clock. Once again, Yahia was on the other end of the phone line, pressing his point that the Sudanese Government wanted an observation team along the border because Museveni was continuing to support the SPLA.

"We want Museveni to stop saying publicly that Sudan is supporting the LRA," Yahia also insisted.

Immediately afterwards I pressed for a meeting, a discrete meeting between Yahia and his Ugandan counterpart, Busho.

By mid-February Yahia confirmed that they would attend a meeting in Nairobi with the Ugandans, providing I issued a formal invitation so that the meeting was still within the auspices of the Nairobi Agreement. I understood that he wanted to work under the cover of the Agreement and The Carter Center, to avoid fragmentation of effort and to have the support of a third party. But to finesse this, I stated that we recognized that Sudan and Uganda were sovereign nations and could do whatever they deemed appropriate with regards to Kony and the LRA. My only objective was to help them find a peaceful alternative.

While we were preparing for the meeting between Yahia and Busho, Chris was on the phone from Khartoum, having just returned from Juba. He was upset. Changes were required immediately in the Sudanese military to make it safe for those trying to escape Kony. Old practices continued in some cases. That is, he had heard that certain Sudanese military officers were still beating up LRA escapees. If they weren't, their mere presence was known in the community and it inhibited those who either were planning escape or had made their way to local villages but feared going any further out of the bush. Chris said that the presence of certain notorious military officers was obstructing escape to Juba, through the Sudanese security machine, into UNICEF's hands, up to Khartoum and eventually back home to their village in northern Uganda. And there were reports on the ground that informal trade between Sudanese military officers and the LRA continued. It was not official; indeed, the orders from Bashir to stop supporting the LRA were clear. But local relationships and local practices were dying hard.

Shortly after hanging up the phone with Chris, a reliable Ugandan contact we had in the USA, someone with a direct channel to the LRA, called me. Cholera had broken out in the LRA camp. Fifty people were dead already. Obviously, we desperately needed the meeting between Busho and Yahia.

On February 27, I prepared my personal agenda for a meeting in Nairobi. I wanted a reality check on any thoughts about a military action against the LRA. Did they know the price in innocent victims that would be paid? Did they think that wiping out the LRA would end the struggle of the Acholi in northern Uganda? Would the international community not condemn such action? Why did we not get serious about alternatives? I also wanted a satellite phone delivered to Kony.

Yahia, Busho and I met in Nairobi.

Almost immediately upon giving my opening remarks Busho jumped in.

He began by stating that issues relating to the SPLA were deep-seated and complex matters that predated the LRA and the Nairobi Agreement. The SPLA had driven thousands of Sudanese people into northern Uganda as refugees, a problem Uganda could do without. He called for cooperative action, stating that the LRA was not a 'Movement' in any political sense, and that my own characterization of Kony as possibly a hostage taker only, and not a politico, was accurate.

I asked him how to move forward to which Busho offered that Sudan and Uganda had to work together – to disarm the LRA. He said trust was missing – because the Government of Sudan still supported other rebel groups antagonistic to Kampala, including the West Nile Bank Front, so something must be done to remove these bottlenecks to trust. However, Uganda was writing a draft protocol and a team could be deployed in late March to meet Sudan's request for an observation team along the Ugandan border.

I liked what Busho had said. It was direct, specific and more transparent than much of what I had heard in the past. I turned to Yahia.

Yahia asserted that the Government of Sudan was committed to implementation of the Nairobi Agreement as part of its policy to mend relations with all of its neighbours. Their way of building trust was to build confidence. He felt there had been some achievement but there remained a long way to go. He stated that all Sudan was asking regarding the SPLA was for Uganda to stop actively supporting them and pressure them to peace talks. And that peace in southern Sudan should be a great help to Uganda.

Then Yahia insisted that the Sudanese Armed Forces were not using the LRA against the SPLA. He reiterated that the Sudanese Armed Forces were not supporting the LRA. He acknowledged that the Juba-based Sudanese military, because it sees Uganda supporting the SPLA, still views Uganda as an enemy. And the enemy of your enemy is still a friend.

Yahia insisted that better messages needed to be sent; messages such as "we are working together".

Testing them I asked, "But is the political will there, in your capitals? Are we not wasting our time? Is there a way of building up the will around the politicians? Is there a role here for President Carter?"

Busho loosened up and he thanked Yahia for acknowledging Sudan's support for other rebel groups and for his offer of assistance in dealing with them. He confirmed that the Observation Team as agreed was acceptable to Uganda and that he had just put word out in the north that the Government is willing to talk to the LRA. He also said that if invited, the Government of Uganda would help in bilateral relations between Sudan and the SPLA. They would talk to Garang to encourage him to engage in peace talks.

I began to feel that we were finally making progress. We were transforming the question from blaming each other for one thing or another to recognizing that the problem – the problem of the LRA, and achieving peace – was a shared problem.

Yahia then offered to facilitate meetings between Busho and the ADF, another rebel group, if Busho wished it. But this gesture was immediately followed by a re-assertion of what his government wanted from Uganda: no military or logistical support to Garang and that the Ugandans should tell John Garang to talk to the Sudanese. He said that any initiative from Museveni to support peace in Sudan would be welcome. If Uganda showed Garang it was serious, it would be very helpful; and a discrete meeting between Garang and President Bashir convened by Museveni, even in Kampala, would be acceptable. But he said that the message from Museveni to Garang must be clear: any peace in the region is indivisible. We must adopt a 'help your neighbour' policy. Then he remarked that this meeting had been good. But it would be better if the military were here too.

Then I challenged them both by querying what, specifically, were they prepared to do to build confidence? What, practically, could be done in lieu of the publicly declared plan to relocate the LRA by March 31?

To which Busho stated that the text of the protocol for the Egyptian-Libyan Observation Team would be completed in a few days. And then it came. He added, "There will be military action against the LRA only when military targets are separated from noncombatants."

That declaration was music to my ears! There would not be the bloodshed that so many of us feared!

Seizing the opportunity, I ceremoniously called for the satellite phone which I had ready and waiting and presented it to Yahia. "Now Kony can call me directly," I said.

I think Busho was taken aback a little; at least he had an odd smile on his face. The meeting ended.

I concluded that we had made progress.

The relationship of these two men had taken a huge step forward. They had been frank and open with one another. They had begun to treat the LRA as a shared problem. The relationship of the Nairobi Agreement to other issues between the two governments had come to the surface. The relationship of the Nairobi Agreement to peace in the region had become manifest. The linkage between progress on implementing the Nairobi Agreement and progress on peace talks in Sudan had become explicit. And for me, most pressing at this moment, was the relief that the Government of Uganda was not going to force a military action against the LRA.

We also agreed to a larger meeting to be held in late March which would include the key participants who were now involved in our process: Canada, UNICEF, the Egyptians and the Libyans. We agreed to continue with these smaller meetings of the security branches of both governments but next time, senior military officers from both sides would attend.

I thought, "Now we are talking."

Shortly after that visit to Nairobi, now back in Atlanta, I received a phone call from Yahia. He was very forthcoming. He said he was going to forward a letter from his President, Bashir, to President Carter through me. He really appreciated our help and that he and Bashir sincerely wanted peace in Sudan. It had to be peace on the basis of a united Sudan, a federal system of some sort. There could be one or ten states in the southern region of the federation, but Sudan itself should remain united.

He covered a lot of territory with uncharacteristic candor. He was worried that John Garang might not be able to govern and hold together an independent south. Sharia would not be imposed on non-Muslims – there would be opting-out provisions; the think piece that had been released recently by the US-based Center for Strategic International Studies of 'one country, two systems' lacked clarity. But a positive letter was coming. Momentum for peace was building. And he added that Museveni would be welcome in a new peacemaker role.

I was elated that we were now playing an unofficial diplomatic role at a senior level. We would become a back channel for the Government of Sudan in Khartoum, the pariah, to talk to the US. The first step would be to let the US State Department see, and react to, Bashir's letter.

My elation was short-lived. Later that very same day I received a call from Busho. He had hard evidence that a weapons deal had been made between the Government of Sudan and the LRA!

We were slipping backwards!

And we continued to slip backwards for the next hectic two months. Or, perhaps I should say that we appeared to move a step ahead. And then one or two steps sideways. Then we would slip back again. This movement – or this lack of real forward momentum – was painfully apparent in more meetings and secret exchanges. There was little evidence that the noble vision and constructive steps that Busho and Yahia had hammered out with my help were turning into action. At the same time David and Chris were working hard to get closer to the community, David in northern Uganda and Chris in southern Sudan, in Juba. Their objective was to tie our efforts at the political level to practical matters concerning abducted children and community-based peace projects. But there was only so much they could do without the political leadership in each country blessing the community-based work.

Further eroding my confidence in progress, I was informed that the satellite phone had gone in to Kony only to learn later from Yahia that Kony had rejected it.

Kony had rejected the phone? Really!

Meanwhile, we had been able to share Bashir's letter with the US State Department and were able to get input from them before we responded. So some movement relating to peace in Sudan was taking place.

And on March 12, 2001, almost a year after our first trip to DC to meet with Albright, President Carter, John Hardman and I were on our way to Washington again. This time we were meeting a more friendly face – Powell. And this time our visit was following a series of focused, useful exchanges with the Administration as it grappled with the direction for policy for Sudan.

The Center for Strategic International Studies' paper had indeed stirred things up. It made a compelling argument that protracted war in Sudan was repugnant, that the US government needed to get involved, that there was a way forward through the thorny issues that seemed irresolvable. And most importantly, it came at a time when heat was being applied to the new Bush Administration to do something about Sudan's war.

What some called the 'forgotten war' was now miraculously on the radar screen in Washington. The Congressional Black Caucus was vitriolic about allegations of an ongoing slave trade in Sudan, saying that "brown Arabs were still capturing and trading black Africans as they had done for time immemorial". The Christian right in the US was adamant that Khartoum's fundamentalist Islamic regime should no longer impose its religion and

Sharia law on Christians in the south. International human rights groups were documenting a 'scorched earth' policy in the oil fields. They insisted that oil companies trading on the USA stock exchange should 'cease oil' in Sudan.

US policy towards Khartoum and the prospects of the US getting behind a genuine effort to end the war in Sudan was, thus, very complicated. Staff and policy advisors who might be pressing for peace from inside the Administration had to contend with major counterweights within the domestic USA, and within the politics of the Horn of Africa.

I had tried very hard to take The Carter Center from its narrow mandate of implementing the Nairobi Agreement to a broad and desperately-needed role as a central player in ending the civil war in Sudan. We had come a long way. Now we were going to Washington once again. This time President Carter was ready to make a pitch. This was not a courtesy call nor was it only to shape Washington's policy on Sudan. The iron, we felt, was hot – and it needed striking.

Just outside the State Department, still in our vehicle and about to step out, President Carter turned to me and asked if I had any last minute advice. I said: "This is the time, you are the man. Go for it."

And this time the meeting with the US Secretary of State was different. Decidedly different! This time Colin Powell, unlike his predecessor, was listening. So was Condoleeza Rice, unlike her namesake Susan Rice.

Powell bounded into the anteroom to greet Carter. He extended his hand and joked: "Are there any votes to count," recalling a Carter Center election monitoring mission. They laughed and we were quickly ushered inside. From the outset I could detect an air of pragmatism and openness to a course of rational action. Powell, not surprisingly, began by noting that they were just getting started at looking at US policy for Sudan. He acknowledged that the policy to date had been a disaster, and that they were under pressure from the Hill. He suggested they were talking about appointing an Envoy and that they wanted as a first step in Sudan to get the fighting stopped. He made the point of observing that he and Rice were black; and that they wanted to send a signal that Washington is concerned about and interested in Africa.

As he talked, I realized that we were way ahead of Washington. We really did have better access to Khartoum; we knew the players and the lay of the land better. And Powell was saying, "A lot of people have swung at this ball – and missed – do you have any ideas?"

Carter launched into a clear, concise and comprehensive assessment. He mentioned my role in meeting with Kony and our ability to press for success in implementing the Nairobi Agreement. Powell swiveled in his chair and took a long look at me. I added that we had kept an active engagement in Khartoum and, to explain, I mentioned the letter from Bashir.

Just as Powell returned to the idea of an Envoy, asking whether it might be better to simply increase American presence through a beefed up embassy in Khartoum, so as to re-engage with Sudan, Carter interrupted. He asked for a private meeting with only Powell and Rice in the room.

What happened behind those closed doors? I can only report what I know. What I know is that President Carter discussed the possibility of taking on the role of US Special Envoy to Sudan.

Outside, meanwhile, my counterpoint at the State Department, Charlie Snyder and I were warming up to one another. I had expected a closed-mouth bureaucrat or a boring handler. On the contrary; he was interested in what we had been doing. He expected they would go the route of an Envoy. He wanted to stay in touch and to cooperate. He had been liberated from some kind of purgatory he had suffered during the Clinton Administration and he was ready to get going.

I told him we had developed papers on the peace process. We had ideas, and we were engaged. We exchanged business cards and before we were forced into the inevitable pastime of 'small talk', the great doors swung open and our three heavyweights filled the room.

At the airport, waiting in the VIP lounge, Carter and I talked about the meeting. We agreed it had gone very well, although he was cautious, saying, "We'll see." We both recognized that this was a key moment in our efforts towards peace in Sudan. I offered that if we did not get 'traction' with Powell this time we might well end up on the margins, and Carter agreed.

Our pace, already brisk, needed to be picked up a notch or two. The number of irons we had in the fire would have to increase. We were doing our best to keep alive the path of dialogue with Kony and to hold Uganda and Sudan accountable for implementing the Nairobi Agreement without any unnecessary bloodshed. We were playing a back-channel role between the Sudan government in Khartoum and Washington. Now we were also engaged in Washington. We had a dancing partner; and a very influential one. The window of opportunity to contribute directly to ending the war in Sudan would not stay open for long. I was not about to miss this hard-won chance for peace.

On March 14 Snyder and I talked at length. He minced no words. If President Carter was to be the Envoy, the State Department would want him (and any Envoy) tied to the Department. They did not want any 'lone rangers'. We agreed to meet in Washington the following week to exchange information and to track the Envoy issue on the 'QT'.

Then I spoke with Rugunda in Kampala and Yahia in Khartoum, pressing them on their commitments to implement the Nairobi Agreement.

At The Carter Center we worked on designing a peace process for Sudan, brainstorming, and engaging our interns in the exercise. We covered the gambit of theoretical and practical issues, including who would be at the table – directly engaged in the talks; what the role of civil society in Sudan would be – and how community-based input would find its way into the formal talks; who would mediate, and how; the issues that would need to be resolved and the timing of their introduction into the talks; and the resources needed to conduct the talks.

I spoke again with Yahia and felt that I was getting 'hanky panky' on the satellite phone. Whatever he was saying was confused and confusing. Perhaps that was exactly his goal. In any event, I had little patience for it, although I half thought he had tried to get the phone to Kony.

Then David was on the telephone from Kampala. He was getting closer to the ground, to LRA agents or their go-betweens and he was worried about Uganda's sincerity. He was encountering obstacles from Ugandan officials but winning favor with traditional Acholi elders and religious leaders. The elders and religious leaders were asking him for support in repatriating kids who had escaped from the LRA and were returning home. They needed money to pay for a traditional reconciliation ceremony, so that the war spirits could be driven out. To drive out these bad spirits a goat would need to be killed, the entrails placed on the end of a spear and thrown into the bush.

I agreed to his request to fund this ceremony and our staff in Atlanta joked a bit about how we would itemize the cost of a goat in our budget. Fortunately, the accounting people worked with us so we could do this little, but important thing, to support healing and reconciliation in northern Uganda.

My staff and I completed a fully developed think piece on Sudan which we sent off to Snyder in Washington.

Then Yahia was on the phone with me. He and I were now the go-betweens on correspondence being exchanged between Khartoum and

Washington. Yahia categorically denied any collusion between Sudan and the LRA. He also reported on a number of concerns that had been raised earlier by Chris about the handling of kids who escaped the LRA. He insisted things had improved for the kids. In addition, he told me that a letter I had prepared for Kony and the satellite phone had indeed gone in to Kony through a liaison officer two days ago. They should now be in Kony's hands – so I needed to turn on my phone. (I wondered how close Sudan was to the LRA. And while I did turn on my phone, I had little expectation by now that it would ring.)

I called Uganda and spoke with Rugunda, pressing him again for a full ministerial meeting, soon. I wanted everyone to meet to keep the pressure on, and to get some more ideas on what we were now calling 'pull factors'. This was what could be done in northern Uganda to pull the LRA into talks. These 'pull factors' needed to include: better advertising of, and actual fulfillment by the Government of Uganda of provisions in the Amnesty Act; better use of traditional elders and religious leaders to conduct healing ceremonies and help re-integrate former LRA combatants – who, after all, were mostly abducted children; and the broadcast on radio of success stories of the new lives for those who had escaped the LRA or who had turned themselves in under the Amnesty Act.

But Rugunda wasn't prepared to attend a ministerial meeting just now. In fact, he growled "There are too many meetings! We need to evaluate the progress to date."

But I was in no mood for being accused of having failed to implement the Nairobi Agreement. Instead, I put the shoe on the other foot.

"Listen,' I said "This is your government's agreement. Maybe there is no political will to implement it. Maybe there is nothing more to do."

"No," he replied. "No, nothing has come as close to Kony since the efforts of Betty Bigombe (which was back in 1994). I will check about a meeting. We can talk again next week."

Later that week Tom came with me to lunch at State with Charlie Snyder. Synder said the Sudan document had been very useful, very timely. He hoped to have a policy in a week's time. So we don't re-invent the wheel he felt that it was important that we start with The Declaration of Principles, agreed by Khartoum and the SPLM in 1994. In this Declaration Khartoum had agreed to negotiate on the basis of the right to self-determination for the South.

In a telephone call I conveyed Charlie's view to Yahia. He agreed the

Declaration of Principles was the basis for negotiating. That was good, I thought, but I could hear the emphasis he had placed on the word 'basis'. This was what many of us feared. While the right to self-determination might be agreed as the basis upon which negotiation between the SPLM and the Government of Sudan could proceed, did that mean that in the negotiations to reach a peace agreement the SPLM could actually assert and then exercise that right?

I became acutely aware that the deadline of March 31 was approaching. That was the time by which Sudan was to have disarmed and disbanded the LRA. They were to be dismantled by a process of relocation facilitated by dialogue with Kony, and by whatever incentives and guarantees the international community could offer him. After March 31, it was generally recognized that Uganda could press for military action against the LRA. Earlier, we had managed to get Busho to back down from that. He had said something to the effect that Uganda would not press for military action unless the combatants and the noncombatants were separated. But we did not know if he had been able to convince his hardliners back in Kampala. Dr. Rugunda certainly had not given me any reason to believe that his government had officially come to Busho's view.

I spoke with Rugunda again. I took the initiative and laid out a number of issues and concerns. They all had to do with specific actions that were required by Uganda, Sudan, UNICEF, and The Carter Center if we were serious about resolving the issue of the LRA. I said that I would be remiss if The Carter Center, as mediator, did not note the clock: the 31st of March was approaching and I needed his view on letting it slip, or calling it, since he was in the driver's seat. Furthermore, he could suggest the type, place, and size of meeting Uganda would like to have at this time, and we would work to make it happen.

I got the impression he knew I was serious and becoming more directive in my role, for he assumed a more subdued tone and agreed to get back to me.

For the next several days I maintained the hectic pace of these past weeks, leading my team in our expanded role. I learned that Powell and Carter had spoken and Powell had reported they were still mulling.

Behind the scenes, however, in Washington and in Atlanta, the tide was shifting against Carter's appointment as US Special Envoy on Sudan. The word on the street was that Carter would be great, but this was, after all, a Republican administration; he was gifted and knew Sudan, but did he have the right relationship with Garang and the SPLA; he was a Christian, but could he reach out to, and rein in, the vitriolic Christian right; he was well liked by the Black community, but was he too generous and tolerant of those who traded in slaves?

Also in Atlanta, The Carter Center's management staff were now contemplating the consequences for the Institution if Carter became Envoy. Should he really devote everything to Sudan?

Then I received a phone call from Snyder. His mind works fast, economically, and he talks like a Gatling gun. As a former Colonel in the US Armed Forces, hardly taking a breath, he also peppers his speech with a number of cryptic phrases, insider terms that are a special kind of jargon. I was never really certain I got him altogether. But the bottom line was that President Carter was still in the running.

Still in the month of March, and still knowing that this window of opportunity to influence the big picture would not remain open long, I kept moving on different levels of activity at the same time.

I spoke with a number of officials in Brussels. Then Uganda reported back through David. They wanted a full ministerial meeting in the third week of April. They also planned to invite Generals from Egypt and Libya to Kampala so they could begin to finalize the protocol on the Observation Team, but it would still need to be approved by the Foreign Ministers after our meeting. They also wanted a Ugandan team to go to Juba to verify that the Sudanese were not supporting the LRA.

Great! David had done his job.

Things were moving as well as they could. It was perfect timing to join in on a special session being held at The Carter Center on conflicts in Africa. Dr. Steve Morrison attended our forum. He and Francis Deng, a southern Sudanese exile, were primarily responsible for the Center for International Strategic Studies' document that was getting a lot of attention around the world. I was interested in how he thought we could find our way out of the civil war in Sudan.

Morrison asserted that there was a sixty- to ninety-day window for getting a real peace effort underway. The window was open, but barely, and for a very limited time. After that Washington would yield to the strong voices on the Hill that wanted to support the SPLA and continue to demonize the Islamic government. Time was of the essence and The Carter Center should be vocal, attempting to shape the debate. The success of the Nairobi Agreement needed to be advertised and used to demonstrate that diplomacy works. The Carter Center had convening power and could bring the right people together and influence the US's policy on Sudan.

Right there, Steve and I put in motion the idea of a jointly-convened policy dialogue on Sudan. The Center for International Strategic Studies and The Carter Center would do it in Washington.

My summary of that meeting, based on input from authorities like the UN's Sir Kieran Prendergast, UK Ambassador Alan Goulty and Francis Deng, would serve as another impetus towards a credible peace process. But I'm getting ahead of myself. Back on the front lines, trying to push the Nairobi Agreement forward, I ran into more trouble with Uganda.

Rugunda was on the phone again, unhappy.

He told me that there were people in his camp who actually thought The Carter Center was being obstructive. I asked, "Who?", thinking it was probably Mbabazi, the unmovable hardliner who may well have grown tired of my efforts. But he would give no clear examples. Then he talked at length about the international community's relations with Uganda. He was looking for sympathy. There was pressure on Uganda on the issue of the LRA-abducted children. They were being pressured as to why the Aboke girls had not been released. They were also being scrutinized about their role in the Democratic Republic of Congo but there was no pressure on Sudan about the LRA.

"In fact," Rugunda bellowed over the phone, "not one child has been released freely by Kony!" He added, "And right now, as we are talking the LRA is crossing into Uganda at two points. Hundreds of fighters are coming to wreak havoc on the north! I never believed that Sudan gave up support of the LRA!"

I was not going to defend the Sudanese.

"Well," I responded "I made my observations in Juba and I've drawn my conclusions. You need to draw yours." Instead of debating him, I asserted, "The problem of the LRA needs to become a shared one – to get your kids back safely. I think we need a ministerial meeting so you can press for a verification mechanism in Juba."

He reiterated, as a concession, that he had his own internal pressures to contend with. Based on what David had told me about obstacles he was encountering with Ugandan officials I was sympathetic. Rugunda was most probably struggling with hardliners inside Uganda. He concluded by noting that his delegation was meeting soon and he would get back to me with a clear response about having a meeting.

The same day Yahia was on the line telling me Kony had returned the satellite phone. The battery was dead. What could I say!

Regardless, before I could formulate a response that would not be seen as an insult, Yahia offered that he would facilitate a meeting between Kony and me. He was not proposing that I go to meet Kony. But if I wished it, he would make it happen. "Where would it happen?" I asked. "Would it be safe?" He said he thought the security would be fine if it was held at Nsitu.

I declined and said, "Charge up the phone. Send it back. Tell Kony to pick it up and call Ben Hoffman."

When I hung up the phone I called Charlie Snyder. How would State react to a dialogue among key people on the US policy on Sudan?

He responded immediately that it would be helpful and it looked like we had more time. Afterwards, although I thought Snyder was a trooper and moving as fast as he could, I somehow felt the process in Washington had become messy.

The next day I learned that General Yassin had died in a military plane crash inside Sudan. General Yassin, the senior Sudanese military officer who had befriended me during the first mediation I had held at The Carter Center; the man who had advised me that a teaspoon of honey and garlic daily keeps blood pressure down; the man who had scrambled around his own airport trying to find the plane that would take us to Juba, to Nsitu, and presumably, to Kony. He had told me, in the bush while we waited for Kony that he had two daughters and was hoping for a son to carry the family name forward. Now he was dead without a son.

Immediately, I contacted Chris to arrange that our condolences be expressed to Yassin's wife and daughters.

The next day, Uganda was back on my radar screen. According to Rugunda, Museveni had said he was interested in talking to Bashir about implementation of "what we had agreed" – the Nairobi Agreement. Museveni is reported to have said: "I'm looking forward to talking to him."

This bit of information was shared with me to set the tone, to encourage me about the improved prospects of Uganda and Sudan actually getting serious at the presidential level about implementing the Agreement. So I took Rugunda up immediately and I proposed that Museveni and Bashir meet on the margins of a larger meeting of African heads of state, about to take place in Nairobi. Maybe I could get President Carter to facilitate the meeting. If not, what about the foreign ministers of the two countries meeting with me? Knowing Carter would be in Uganda to promote health programs, I wanted him at the very least to meet privately with Museveni. And I wanted President Carter, for the first time in ten years, to meet with Dr. John Garang.

Two days later Rugunda reluctantly agreed to the larger ministerial level meeting I had been promoting, saying it could take place in Nairobi at the end of the month. Yahia agreed, offering that at the same time Sudan's Foreign Minister might join with his counterpart from Uganda. That sounded good to me, recalling the progress Sudan's Ismail had made with Uganda's Rugunda in our early morning session last November.

Yahia also informed me that Kony did not trust Museveni and that Kony felt there was no value in meeting me.

I was a little disappointed to hear this but I had begun to shift my focus to a different level to fulfill the original assignment given me by President Carter – to help end the war in Sudan. I had become uncertain of Kony as a political actor as well as having become now more fully aware that the war in Sudan was obstructing real progress with the LRA. I also felt that Yahia was giving me only as much information as suited his needs.

Yahia did offer, however, that Sudan would welcome The Carter Center as a mediator in peace talks with the SPLA. We would be more acceptable than the American administration. On this I believed him.

I decided to hit the road. I would go to London, then Kampala, Nairobi, and Khartoum. My agenda would attend to both tracks: the Nairobi Agreement, in particular the LRA, and to the Sudan Peace Process. In London I would need to talk to British officials responsible for both Uganda and Sudan. Someone had posted a LRA Manifesto on a web site so I would also try to meet with the people who were alleged to be LRA operatives. In Kampala I would take a cold, challenging approach to Rugunda and company. I wanted to make the point that implementation of the Nairobi Agreement was their responsibility. I would go armed with a list of the commitments both Uganda and Sudan had made, and my score card of how effective they had been in honouring their commitments. And I would ask how they would judge Uganda's efforts to date? I'd ask them: couldn't more be done; couldn't Uganda shift to being a factor in favor of peace in the region, in Sudan specifically; couldn't Museveni become a peacemaker, a go-between with his friend Garang and his former adversary, Bashir?

Arriving in London, with Ann beside me on this first leg of my journey, I was determined to get the answer to a question about Kony and the LRA that had been pestering me for months. I wanted to know if there was a

123

political wing to the LRA? In other words, what did the 'M' stand for in the way Kony's rebel group was often described: LRM/A? It was supposed to mean 'Movement' but I had been hard-pressed to find a political dimension to the LRA. Kony himself had dismissed the London-based Acholi when I had asked him about them. He had said they were playing at politics while he carried the real battle with Museveni. But maybe that wasn't the case. Maybe someone outside Uganda pulled his strings. At the very least, there were questions about where he got his weapons and resources to fight an insurgency that had been going on for years. Sure, the Sudanese were a big patron of his, and the LRA stole much of what it needed when it attacked villages. But there had been suggestions that the LRA received material support beyond these two sources. And there was a woman's name that kept coming up as the author of the LRA Manifesto. I wanted to meet her.

She was not easy to meet with. I had phoned her twice from Atlanta, and it took some doing to get her to agree to see me. We met in the lobby of my London hotel where she arrived with another woman who was described as a lawyer, or law student. They were very secretive and the communication initially was not easy. But, slowly, she warmed up and told me that her family had been killed in the fighting in northern Uganda and she had to leave the country. She also said that the British authorities had taken away her passport and that she needed my assistance to have it restored and then she would go personally to meet Kony and encourage peace talks. As the chair of the Acholi Association, she would mobilize her group for a meeting dedicated to me and The Carter Center's work with the LRA. She impressed me as being a complex person.

I agreed to inquire on her behalf and to attend the meeting she was organizing.

The next evening, before Ann and I were to have a dinner meeting with Yahia, his wife and the Sudanese Ambassador to London, we went to the Acholi Association meeting place. It was set up in a tired old hotel off the beaten track in a large room upstairs. When we arrived a small number of Acholi were already assembled. And one of them had a video camera that he used to record most of the evening's proceedings.

The small group grew rather quickly to a large assembly and they packed the room with men mostly in business suits. It was clear that my female contact was a central player. It became apparent that this group was a completely different group from Kachoke Madit, the London-based Acholi group that I had been originally introduced to when I had taken my first trip on this assignment. Indeed, members of this group confided as we waited for the moment to begin the meeting that they were exiled Acholi, former members of Idi Amin's forces. They had not been able to return home to northern Uganda since their exile.

One of the men, short and well-dressed, was pointed out to me as a former colonel in Amin's army. I later learned from Ann, who had talked casually with him, that he was one of the most steely-eyed men she had ever met. She had thought to herself, "I wouldn't for the life of me want to be interrogated by this man!" She found him extremely cold with a heartless laugh, which was so unlike the other men around him. She had met many of my clients over the years, including some dangerous characters – so he had certainly made an impression.

The moment arrived, and I was formally introduced but immediately after I made a few friendly opening remarks, I came under attack. The members of this group who had been so friendly just seconds before launched an attack on The Carter Center, on President Museveni, and on the international community. I took it all in, the camera bearing down on me, and Ann sitting on the sidelines, stoically monitoring this surprising attack. Later, she told me that she was preparing to bolt!

Knowing it was not a good idea to refute anything they said, I simply restated that my goal was peace in northern Uganda, that I needed their assistance in how to bring about meaningful talks between Kony and the Government. I asked them how could they help?

Yes, they asserted, they had contacts in northern Uganda and in other countries where other members of their tribe had been exiled. They were the real thing. But they were of course constrained by their exile. Their chairwoman was credible, capable, and I should look to her for direct assistance.

Having subsided now, the group listened closely as I gave a full account of what we had done. I believe they were favourably impressed with my report. I said I would meet again, tomorrow, with the chairwoman.

Then, in the brief exchanges afterwards, as Ann and I had now clearly overstayed my time commitment and we knew Yahia and his dinner party were waiting, the 'colonel' approached me. I made a courtesy remark about the meeting and how I hoped we might make progress with the chairwoman's help. But, I noted, it was difficult to sort through who was the most helpful channel to Kony and whether there was a political arm to the LRA. He looked me in the eye and said, "Well, with an insurgency, of course you never know who you are talking to."

The colonel's remark stayed in my mind all night and throughout the next day as I sought to clarify who my female contact, the chairwoman, really was; and whether her desire to meet with Kony should and could be facilitated. Then I received a couple of calls from official sources, from two very different countries. They corroborated each other's position. No, she was not a credible player in their view and her travel restrictions would not be lifted. Most importantly to me, I was informed that she had no legitimacy with Kony.

I felt that I had come full circle. Kony had dismissed the London Acholi. Whatever the group last night thought they were and how they thought their leader could help me was not going to pan out, so I would have to tell her the disappointing news that I could not arrange her travel to see Kony.

I would also have to live with the sense of disappointment that I could not find the locus of the 'M' in LRM/A.

Ann and I separated; Ann to return to Canada and I went on to Nairobi to meet again with Kenyan Ambassador and Sudan Peace Process Envoy, Daniel Mboya, and representatives of the SPLA. Mboya had been hobbled by the lack of commitment to peace by the international community, lack of resources, and a mandate that required he operate with the consensus of the other Special Envoys from countries in the region, responsible for peace in Sudan. It was an untenable, punishing situation. I offered him sincere sympathy from a fellow mediator.

I met with the SPLA telling them again that my goal was to win their trust. I reminded them of the good intentions and service of President Carter. We would always help them in their talks with Khartoum in the ways that we could.

From Nairobi I went to Kampala where David had lined up some interesting meetings. One would be with the Paramount Chief of the Acholi. Someone else had arranged for me to meet with an informant. This informant, who I met under the cover of night in a remote bar, offered to monitor the Ugandan Armed Forces communications as well as the radio traffic of the LRA. From him I could learn whether the Ugandan army knew that Sudan was no longer supporting Kony. And who knows what we could learn from his listening in on the LRA?

Then I moved on to Khartoum to meet with Chris who was still pressing the Sudanese system (if you could call it that) responsible for the proper treatment and handling of escaped LRA abductees. He needed support in his tireless efforts on behalf of these abducted children, which included setting up a transit camp for them in Khartoum, getting them blankets and clothing, and doing some things well beyond the call of duty, such as buying soccer balls, cigarettes, and treats for the little ones. I would also need to meet representatives of the diplomatic community, including my new friend Ambassador Xavier Marchal of the EU. Marchal was keen, intense, and one of the few people who seemed to be putting real money into efforts to plan for peace in Sudan. He was also interested in the LRA, and had a constituency in Europe that was tracking the LRA issue closely.

Like all of this work, the whole thing was an emotional roller coaster. And it was a trying trip, physically. One minute you feel that there really is a chance for peace – another you feel that peace is so hard to achieve, so elusive. At one meeting your heart goes out to the person on the other side of the table. They too want peace. At another meeting you know the person you are meeting with is an enemy of peace. There is no middle-of-the-road, emotionally.

In a nutshell, after London, Kampala, Nairobi and Khartoum, I had no confidence in the whole situation. I was living in a 'no man's land'. It was a world of uncertainty filled with guerillas, obfuscation, agents, spies, operatives, misinformation, a policy vacuum, and conflicting interests.

I concluded that I may have pushed implementation of the Nairobi Agreement as far as I could. For example, there were rumors of new, active community-based peace talks with LRA commanders in northern Uganda. These rumours could just be more game-playing by any number of parties such as Kony himself, or local Ugandan political appointees, or the Ugandan army. The Carter Center was certainly not involved.

From our new informant in Kampala I had received two main pieces of information. First, he made it clear that the Ugandan armed forces did indeed know Kony was on his own. They knew the LRA had been cut off by the Government of Sudan. And while it appeared that some LRA commanders may have reached out to local government officials in northern Uganda, Kony himself had apparently changed his mind about any such local-level peace talks. Instead, he had ordered that the LRA commanders contemplating these talks pull out, and dramatically. That likely meant that they were to perpetrate some atrocity or attack a military installation.

On another front, there was a Ugandan fear that if Sudan had really stopped supporting Kony, Sudan could nevertheless reactivate the LRA in fifteen minutes.

In my discussions with colleagues in Khartoum, the Government of Sudan was described as having regressed. It was not fulfilling important commitments that it had made to various representatives of the diplomatic community. It was not sending the right signals to Washington at such a critical juncture. And the Sudan Peace Process was now clearly spoken of as a 'lame duck'.

But I believed I had made progress with the SPLA on this trip. And that was very important to our efforts. I had forged a good relationship with Dr. Justin Arop, senior advisor to Garang. We had had a frank discussion. He told me that Carter needed to be balanced in his approach. There was some feeling within the SPLA that Carter favored Khartoum. There were certain bargaining positions and preconditions for them to be involved that I needed to know. He said some of these are that The Declaration of Principles in peace talks was essential; the right to self-determination of the people in southern Sudan must be the basis upon which negotiation with the Government in Khartoum proceeded. He also said that the security situation was so complex and volatile that an international peacekeeping force would be required. He insisted that oil had to be addressed immediately – there could not be a ceasefire while Khartoum continued to exploit oil and use the money to build up its war machine. The Sudan Peace Process also needed to be strengthened to be effective and acceptable to the SPLA.

I listened, respectfully, absorbing the criticisms of President Carter. I then assured him that a meeting between President Carter and Dr. Garang would be a relationship-building meeting. It was a first step to restore a once active and mutually agreeable relationship. It was clear to everyone that the Sudan Peace Process needed to be strengthened. This I had heard consistently. Dr. Justin said that he would approach Dr. Garang about meeting with President Carter. But, he said, President Carter should not, repeat, President Carter should not push Garang towards a ceasefire.

I hoped that when the picture was so bleak on other fronts, this might be where President Carter as US Special Envoy to Sudan could really help. And my team could play a big role, too. We had done much with little; imagine if we actually received a mandate!

But back home, in Atlanta, reality hit hard again. Vice President Dick Cheney and President Carter had talked. It did not go well. I was told that in effect, Carter had been dismissed as a bleeding heart liberal.

Then former Acting Secretary of State for African Affairs, Chester

Crocker, had been approached by the White House to serve as Envoy. Crocker had declined, reportedly stating that Bashir and Garang were not serious about peace, the regional dynamics were not conducive to peace talks, and the US was not serious about peace in Sudan.

That was a strong indictment.

I felt checkmate. Could we do any more? Could we do any different?

When I had been in Khartoum just days ago, Yahia had acknowledged that we may be stalled; there would be no more progress on the Nairobi Agreement without progress inside Sudan. And President Carter would not be the envoy to advance peace in Sudan. And Crocker, whom we all thought would be an excellent envoy, had declined.

Should we throw in the towel? Had all the lights gone out?

10

All Roads Lead To Washington

Tom Crick is an eternal optimist. And President Carter is a wise man.

President Carter's wisdom manifested itself in his full endorsement of former Senator John Danforth, who ultimately accepted President Bush's appointment as US Special Envoy for Sudan. And it manifest itself when Carter made it clear to me and my staff that he was decidedly in favor of peace in Sudan, above any personal or institutional gain.

Danforth's appointment had really given me reason for pause. Deflated somewhat, I wondered what more I could do. For I wanted more for us than to be relegated to some advisory role. I had been striving to situate President Carter in a key, if not central role in ending the Sudan civil war. I had, indeed, imagined it might be an achievement that would win him the Nobel Peace Prize, something he already deserved. And those ulterior motives had become a monkey on my back. I was viewing our efforts, overall, through that narrow lens.

President Carter's positive remarks about Danforth and his willingness to keep working for peace in Sudan, without breaking stride, liberated me from that self-imposed mission. No longer obsessed with projecting Carter onto Sudan, I was free to stick to our knitting, even to contemplate an exit strategy in relation to the Nairobi Agreement. But oddly, and in an inverse way, instead of winding down, I found that Tom's optimism – he having caught fire in January when I had pressed for a bold strategy, which he then helped develop – drove me deeper into my assignment: to lead The Carter Center's efforts to end the war in Sudan.

Tom was of the opinion that we should adhere to the stratagem of his 'last man standing' theory. He had been at The Carter Center for more than eight years and had seen institutional initiatives wax and wane, only to wax again. He had seen other players from various quarters enter the fray in particular disputes, only to lose impetus, get derailed, and disappear. He knew that the staying power of state actors could be very short indeed. He felt that if we stayed at it; if we alienated no one; if we were trusted; if we were credible; if we were patient; if we were longstanding; if we were prepared: then we would be the last man standing and be able to move to the summit.

It was an *interesting* view. It was also seasoned with Tom's own wisdom. As long as we could be helpful to peace, that was what mattered most. We may not end up being visible, or given public credit. But, (and this is a real issue), funding provided, we could make a significant difference.

It really was a hopeful view. I, however, had always wanted us to play at the top of our game. I wanted us to be embraced for, and use, the assets we had, especially President Carter. And I wanted my team to be recognized and engaged on the merits of our own considerable professional competencies. I had also wanted us to know when it was time to bow out.

So now it was evident that President Carter might not 'slam dunk' a Sudan peace agreement. Or perhaps he might. Maybe he and we, my team and I, would be the last man standing.

But there were the geopolitical, structural facts with which we needed to come to terms. Our efforts to implement the Nairobi Agreement may well have been circumscribed by the lack of real progress towards peace in Sudan. Museveni would not stop supporting Garang. Sudan would never get an Egyptian-Libyan Observation Team along the northern border of Uganda. There would not be an exchange of diplomats of any rank by Uganda and Sudan. The LRA would never see peace talks with the Government of Uganda. Kony's long messy denouement was all we would witness. In fact, we would have to stand by, helpless.

As for Sudan, what had we been doing? Was it relevant, helpful? Was it anything that might approach the grand notion of 'Waging Peace'? What would it amount to in the cold light of Crocker's grim assessment and the long period of uncertainty and mixed messages which had continued to come from Washington?

To be clear, we had tried to leverage our credible effort at implementing the Nairobi Agreement into a role in Sudan. We had been working on four elements of the civil war in Sudan: the conflict itself, the parties, the policy environment, and the peace process. I believed that this was still a sound approach. I felt we were down, but we were not out.

Who knows, we might end up being the last man standing. But now, we would have to settle for pushing as far as we could to help end the war in Sudan. We had to push the Sudan peace rock like Sisyphus, who was condemned to pushing a huge rock up the hill only to have it roll back down, over and over again – forever. Hopefully, we would also overcome those obstacles that stood in the way of a peaceful resolution to the war in northern Uganda. In that regard, I clung to a stubborn notion that Kony, given the right environment, could and would respond to the opportunity for legitimate talks with Museveni.

May 2001, therefore, looked busy. There would be the Sudan policy dialogue co-hosted with the Wilson Center in Washington. The Carter-Museveni meeting in Kampala was scheduled. I would mediate a full Ministerial meeting in Nairobi to keep the international community in the loop, and I would mediate a meeting that was shaping up between the Foreign Ministers of Sudan and Uganda. We also would have the meeting between President Carter and Garang. To top it off, we would hold another 'off the record' meeting of the security branches of Uganda and Sudan.

As it turned out, we learned that Colonel Qadhafi was about to launch his own peace initiative between Museveni and Bashir. Having air-lifted forty cars into Entebbe airport, Qadhafi entered Kampala with a huge entourage and a self-supplied motorcade. He then presided over an historic meeting between Bashir and Museveni. But more importantly, he obtained a commitment (allegedly for a price paid to Uganda) to the exchange of diplomats between the two countries. He had nailed down what was to be the icing on the cake of a successfully implemented Nairobi Agreement! That which, I had been told again and again by the Ugandans, was only to be secured once Sudan delivered on the LRA.

My staff and I all shook our heads. Yet we all believed this was indeed a good development. We figured that Qadhafi had capitalized in his own way with Museveni on Sudan's having cut off Kony. Qadhafi might also have felt the burn of his earlier efforts with Kony in his failure to free the Aboke girls as had been privately requested of him by brave Sister Rochelle. As Yahia had reported at that time, the Libyans had come home empty-handed. Qadhafi therefore had something to prove. I also reflected on the persuasiveness of power, and the power of money.

Without question, however, this development was an infusion of new and good energy. And we capitalized on it.

First on the list was to have President Carter and President Museveni meet. They met in Kampala and had a constructive exchange. Then I arranged for Libya's ambassador to Sudan to meet President Carter so that we could thank Qadhafi for his effort. Shortly thereafter it was confirmed that Sudan's Foreign Minister, Ismail, was coming to Nairobi to meet Uganda's Rugunda and would participate in an early morning mediation with me, before the larger Ministerial meeting was to begin. And Dr. Justin, Garang's man, assured me that Garang would indeed meet with President Carter, providing Garang was in Nairobi on the appointed day and not on the front lines.

We were making progress. Push, push, push.

To top it off, when we arrived in Nairobi from Kampala for our series of meetings, the headlines on the front page of the State-run Ugandan newspaper, in huge print, read: SUDAN STOPS KONY SUPPORT.

I must say that David, Chris and I took real pleasure in reading this! I had gone out on a limb nearly five months ago, declaring the same. I had been informed weeks earlier by our Ugandan informant that the Ugandan army knew this to be true (and of course, so did the key Ugandan political actors who I had recently faced in Kampala and who had denied this). Indeed, they had been accusing me of no progress and just days before would not give an inch on my assertion that Sudan had cut off Kony. So now, more than ever, we wanted Uganda to begin to give some concessions of its own.

But we knew that even without Sudanese support to the LRA the war in northern Uganda was still a fundamental problem and we could not let down on that front. Innocent people continued to be victimized, kids continued to be abducted, the north remained lost. There was work for us to do. Furthermore, Museveni had agreed way back in September in Kampala, prior to Qadhafi's involvement, to exchange diplomats. But nothing came from that commitment and we were not sure that the recent commitment that Museveni had given to Qadhafi would be honoured. We would therefore have to nail this down. Who would be exchanged, when, and how?

President Carter had to settle for a telephone conversation with Garang, rather than a face-to-face meeting. Even this brief episode, however, was not without its drama.

I had visited the SPLA as part of our strategy to build relations so that we might be helpful down the road. The SPLA's perception, however, was that President Carter favoured Bashir. They had also insisted that if and when President Carter met with Garang, Carter was explicitly not to raise the issue of ceasefire. In fact, about this time, Garang and the SPLA had begun to use the phrase: 'cease oil, before cease fire.' That is, the SPLA was not prepared to uphold or agree to a ceasefire while the Government of Sudan continued to exploit oil, realize revenues, and strengthen its war machine. In fact, it went deeper than that. The SPLA was not interested in a ceasefire until it achieved an acceptable measure of progress on political issues with the Government of Sudan.

So 'ceasefire' talk was anathema. And the last big thing President Carter had done in Sudan, in 1996, was to mediate a six-month humanitarian ceasefire between the SPLA and the Government of Sudan. We were told that this time the SPLA did not want to consider it.

My team and I were on alert to this. I had briefed President Carter on these two key matters. I was frank, stating that there was a question in the SPLA's mind about his perceived impartiality and that he should build a relationship here, slowly. Moreover, he was not, repeat, not to press for a ceasefire at this time.

As the meeting approached we moved from 'alert' status to 'tenterhooks.' We all knew that President Carter is his own man, and would do what he wanted when he wanted to. I also saw him as a thoroughbred racehorse – and one that was champing at the bit. This horse was built for speed and for success. He wanted out of the stable and would have little patience for our efforts to simply get him to the gate. And the fact was that we were yet a long way from the gate. I was trying now to just get him fully registered and in the race.

Would he blow it? Would he bolt and cut to the chase? Would he press Garang for a ceasefire? Could he stay cool and build a relationship?

As the hours closed in on the meeting, we were informed by the SPLA that Garang would not be able to make it. He was 'out of town'. He was prepared, however, to talk on the phone. Of course, Tom, Alex Little and I wondered if this was really the case. Nevertheless we set up the phone call in a secure room in Nairobi's Serena Hotel. The SPLA's official spokesperson, Dr. Samson Kwaje, was present as we made last minute preparations to get a dedicated line so that this opportunity was not lost.

The call went ahead swimmingly. President Carter made a few friendly remarks, recalling earlier visits and good relations. He then noted that Garang seemed to be having new military success. And he kept the call altogether exactly as we had hoped. He engaged and welcomed and encouraged Garang to keep their good relationship. Not a word about ceasefire. The call ended. We tried not to make any visible sighs of relief while President Carter was swept out of the room to be interviewed on health issues by the Kenyan media.

Kwaje and I made eye contact, congratulating ourselves.

Then, as a complete surprise, Kwaje suggested that perhaps President Carter could assist in arranging ceasefires in a number of areas, for humanitarian reasons.

What!

I couldn't really believe my ears, and I was thankful President Carter was out of the room.

What kind of ceasefires, we asked? Where?

Kwaje offered that there were two or three communities where, for health reasons, it would be helpful to have a ceasefire agreed to by Khartoum. This would allow health workers, including our own health program staff working on the Guinea Worm Disease, to get in and provide health services to villages that couldn't be reached because of the war.

While this proposal had a certain amount of appeal, giving Carter an explicit role at the request of the SPLA, I had my doubts. Maybe these were areas that the SPLA simply wanted to stabilize from a military perspective? Maybe the excuse of humanitarian ceasefire would cover for a more strategic advantage?

Just as I was formulating a response, President Carter burst into the room. He was stirred up. He loves this kind of action. He queried me, "What are you talking about?"

I explained Kwaje's offer but tried to signal my caution to him in front of our SPLA colleague. It didn't work. Carter took the bit and wanted to get back on the phone to Garang immediately.

Uh, oh, I thought, here we go.

Thankfully, we could not reconnect immediately and Tom and Alex were tasked with putting a call through to Garang ASAP. I had to withdraw as I was scheduled to fly out of Nairobi that evening. But before I left, Tom and I mulled this over and hoped this next call would not undo what it had taken months to achieve. As Tom pointed out, it had been the SPLA who put ceasefire on the table, not us, and not Carter. So when the call did take place that evening, and Carter introduced ceasefire, it had come from the SPLA itself. But when Carter notched up the SPLA request to consider establishing ceasefires in a few specific areas to a 'comprehensive ceasefire' Tom was afraid he may have lost it. For President Carter asked Garang, why not a comprehensive ceasefire? To which Garang flatly refused but agreed that Carter's staff and Garang's staff could look at a map and see where limited ceasefires might be established for humanitarian reasons.

The call ended and Tom relayed the conversation and the outcome of it to me.

We hoped that there had been no damage done. We would remind the SPLA, just in case, that it was they who had raised the issue, not us. We had done our job. We had focused on restoring Carter and Garang's relationship. We had kept ceasefire off the table. President Carter himself had done the same until they had asked for his help.

And so it goes when you are trying to manage a thoroughbred racehorse bent on peace.

I was determined to ride the wave of good fortune and the positive results we had going for us. It had taken about five months to get all these meetings lined up and behind us. I reminded myself that time, and timing, were key factors that could not be ignored; but I also sensed that we had to become the pacesetter. The Carter Center would have to fill the leadership vacuum that was so obvious, and for which there were a number of contenders, including Qadhafi, Egypt, and the moribund Sudan Peace Process.

We would need to have President Carter use his influence with the Christian religious right in the USA; and it was time to canvass the key actors in the international community.

So President Carter called Reverend Franklin Graham, the founder of Samaritan's Purse, a humanitarian agency active in and very sympathetic to the SPLA rebels in the south of Sudan. Franklin is world-renowned Reverend Billy Graham's son. Both had close relationships with and influence on George W. Bush. Both had huge constituencies. Both were independently wealthy. Both knew and influenced like-minded members of congress. We knew that they could be directly helpful in moving the Christian right off the hard-ball agenda it had against the Islamists in Khartoum, so that peace could have a chance.

While President Carter prepared the way with Graham, I headed out to London, Brussels, Berlin, and Oslo. These cities were the centers of influence; indeed, they were the main support of the Sudan Peace Process. Initially called 'friends' of the Process, they had become a 'Partners Forum'. Their governments kept the Sudan Peace Secretariat in Nairobi alive, but barely. They each had their own history with Sudan and reasons for involvement there including, for some, an interest in oil. For that matter, Canada was also included among the partners, and I would also go to Ottawa to gauge its views on peace in Sudan.

The trip to Europe was grueling. Alex Little showed no mercy, sending me first to London on the painful overnight red eye, then the same day, after my London meetings, over to Brussels and on to Berlin for a short sleep. The next afternoon, after meetings with German officials and with Gerhard Bauum, the UN Envoy on Human Rights in Sudan, I proceeded on to Oslo through Stockholm for another short sleep before meeting with Ambassador Hans Freydenlund, Norway's Special Advisor on Sudan. Freydenlund was a solid supporter of our work with the LRA and the Nairobi Agreement.

By the time I got back to Atlanta and summarized my findings, I was scheduled to fly to North Carolina to meet with Franklin Graham. But in the meantime I was in contact with the Sudanese ambassador in Washington, Ambassador Khidir Ahmed, who called to ask for Carter's help with Graham and the Washington set that was pressing hard for the passage of the Sudan Peace Act. This was legislation that was not friendly to his Government in Khartoum. Ambassador Ahmed wanted Carter to inform Washington of Sudan's good behaviour and discourage the passing of the Act.

So I was fatigued, with a lot on my plate, but the trip to Europe had buoyed my hopes – although it had confirmed the disappointing fact that the whole world seemed unable to do anything without the USA. They said that all roads lead to Washington.

All of the technical experts, the foreign relations and peace policy advisors, and the peace advocates I had met with on that whirlwind tour were in accord, that the Nairobi-based Sudan Peace Process was the vehicle through which peace talks should take place. The Declaration of Principles, with its recognition of the right for self-determination, and the legitimate role of regional actors, were embedded in the Process. But the USA must lead. It was the key. Nothing would happen without the US leading, from behind. The consensus was that it should not presume to be the mediator of talks between Khartoum and the SPLA. Its weight was essential though,

138

to lean on both sides; to weigh in on Khartoum and to hold it accountable; to offer carrots and have sticks that were real; to influence Garang and make him aware that the status quo was not going to carry forward in perpetuity; and to hold Egypt and Libya in check, so that talks were not spoiled from that quarter.

And as for US's Special Envoy, Senator Jack Danforth, the consensus was that he should not merely be a fact finder, but he should stimulate peace and revitalize the Sudan Peace Process.

They felt the role of The Carter Center was to keep pushing for a single, viable peace process. And that The Carter Center should take on the dirty issue of oil, over which so much blood had and was being spilled. Everyone agreed that this was a war about power and not just religious belief and cultural differences.

Back in Atlanta, I summarized these findings and sent them to everyone I had interviewed, with a copy to Danforth's team.

If the US State Department was peace-shy in any way, and in reality it did have many domestic obstacles to peace in Sudan, this would be ammunition that should help.

The relevant actors in the West were all behind peace, behind a revitalized Sudan Peace Process, and waiting for the US Government to move.

I hadn't really recovered from the long, rushed trip to Europe before I had to get back on a plane and head to North Carolina.

Deep in the woods there I met with Franklin Graham at the headquarters of his Christian charity, Samaritan's Purse.

Upon arrival he greeted me warmly and was visibly pleased that I had brought along a young Christian intern whose parents had been missionaries in Africa. Dressed like a contemporary high tech professional, Graham was wearing blue jeans, a sport shirt and a ball cap. After a brief description of his facility, which was a large compound with storage sheds and an airplane hangar large enough to repair their cargo planes on-site, he offered us a light lunch in the staff cafeteria. We hurried our meal and were quickly taken to his opulent offices where I noticed rifles and a grizzly bear he had shot in Alaska mounted on the wall, and on a side table a photo of him in prayer with President George W. Bush. As I sank into the plush leather couch, getting serious now, his first question of me was, "What is your religious belief?".

Now my Mother had raised me in the Pentecostal Church. She was a born-again Christian. And my Father was what I would call a Christian mystic. In Mom's view of the world there were only two possibilities: either 'a' or 'not a'. Both 'a' and 'not a' cannot exist at the same time and in Mom's view, people had to choose one or the other. Mom believed that the Holy Bible was literally the Word of God, that Jesus was Lord and Savior and that anyone who did not accept Jesus Christ as Savior would rot in Hell. Dad had turned away from Christian fundamentalism to embrace Eastern Mysticism. He believed that both 'a' and 'not a' could exist at the same time. So I went to church on Sunday with my Mother, but when I was alone with Dad he taught me yoga, rhythmic breathing, and spoke at length of the 'sound of the universe'.

Feeling tested, I answered Reverend Graham rather abruptly. I said that both my parents were dead but my father had been a mystic and my mother had been a born-again Christian. I said that I would be described by him as a backslider. I thought that I might as well be as direct as he was. And I wanted him to know my Christian credentials, which he should be able to identify as fundamentalist.

The interview with him was very tough. This was a man who saw Sudan in very simple, black and white (or should I say, 'brown' and 'black') terms. We had scheduled a one-hour meeting. Two and a half hours after we began, having had a tour de force unlike most of the meetings I have had in my long career, we ended only when his secretary opened the door and reminded him of his other obligations. We discovered in that meeting that his view of the government in the north of Sudan and the people in the south was clearly stereotyped: the north was oppressive brown Arab Islamists and the south was victimized back African Christians. He took a hard line against Khartoum and Sudan's President Bashir, offering that Bashir should be taken to the Hague, as a war criminal. His demeanor was tough, the issues cast in terms that allowed him to stake out and assert an assumed moral high ground.

Of course I listened as sympathetically as I could. But I quickly found that he was not responsive to a rational argument. Rather, I found myself digging into my past experiences that I could share with him by way of an object lesson, to make my point, to challenge and rebut him. It was a strange metaphorical way of communication. I told him my view of punishment and retribution: how I had found that taking a bigger and bigger stick to an offender was not as effective in the long run as engaging him and building a relationship. A good relationship was the bond that

140

reduced the offender's alienation and encouraged identification with others. That elicited the behaviour from offenders which I had hoped for. I said that the people in the south of Sudan could be helped by engaging the north, by getting both sides to participate in a viable peace process, in which reasonable accountabilities should apply.

Finally, and to my surprise he said that he would give peace a chance.

Once we were in the car the intern who had been thrilled to attend the meeting with me, was flabbergasted. The man we had just met, with whom I had debated and enjoined to bring his influence to bear for peace, had been one of his heroes. He had now seen, first hand, the reasoning of a powerful, self-assured fundamentalist Christian. It took a few miles drive through the Blue Mountains of North Carolina for both of our blood pressures to come down.

But this was needed. We needed Graham. Graham might get to Bush. Bush ran Washington. All roads lead to Washington. Somewhere on the other side of the world, in Sudan, we might see peace yet.

11
9/11

When my colleague, Chuck Costello, who directed the Democracy Program at The Carter Center burst into the room, he stated, "The world will never be the same."

Of course, others were as quick to state this as we watched the second plane explode into the World Trade Center towers and the simultaneous attack on the Pentagon. But Chuck was right in more ways than we would know that fateful day.

And the implications for all of us exceed by a great measure those that my team and I worked through for Sudan. We thought instantly that Sudan, already on the US's list of terrorist countries, was now going to come squarely into the cross hairs of an angry and retaliatory United States of America.

We knew that the US had unofficially just given Sudan a clean bill of health on terrorism. In fact, we had been hoping that President Bush and Secretary Powell, now satisfied that Sudan did not harbour terrorists, would be stronger in their resolve to push for peace in Sudan, despite continuing opposition from tough-minded members of the Black caucus and the Christian right.

But perhaps, now pre-occupied with Osama bin Laden, Washington would simply lose interest in Sudan as it took on this assault from an unprecedented threat.

We still had our job to do. We still had our mission. We wanted Danforth to remain seized of his assignment. We wanted to keep pushing for peace.

So we kept on. We stayed with our strategy to establish a credible peace process. We redoubled our efforts. Tom worked closely with Danforth's advisor, Ambassador Robert Oakley, keeping tabs on Washington's approach and keeping President Carter and The Center in the game in Washington. Chris pressed on in northern Uganda, supporting the development of community-based peace forums, and serving as unofficial 'glue' in what was often a host of very uncoordinated nongovernmental efforts to do peacebuilding in northern Uganda. He also worked hard to establish our credibility as an organization that cared about the connection between high-level talks and grassroots reality; the connection between policy and real people.

Doug and I took to the road again. This time we visited Cairo and Tripoli where we pressed for a single peace process, exploring ways that the Joint Egypt-Libyan Initiative might be integrated with a revitalized, US-supported Sudan Peace Process. We also went into southern Sudan, deep into rebel-held territory. We wanted to learn how connected John Garang and the elites of the SPLA were to the grassroots. Did the people think a united Sudan was possible; was the Sudan Peace Process in Kenya viable, indeed, did the people even know what it was; what was their perception of the US; and how could The Carter Center help?

But here in southern Sudan we encountered a new world. It impressed us as a separate reality distinguished by nineteen years of fighting and a culture so unlike northern Sudan that one was hard pressed to think the two could ever be truly united. We had the privilege of getting deep into communities accessible only by light aircraft, devastated by, and yet habituated to war. We met key members of the SPLA, some women but mostly men who had fought as soldiers and then became officials in the political wing of the rebel movement. Now they occupied quasi-political posts, or acted in a humanitarian capacity, controlling the flow and delivery of relief to the war-torn south.

One of them gave us a tough reception. Leaning on his ceremonial walking stick, at ease in the world he controlled, he came quickly to the point. President Carter was not trusted in these parts. He said Carter had failed to speak out against the bombing of civilians in the south, some years ago, on an occasion that they thought he should have. Doug and I reacted non-defensively, remarking how we had been working to re-establish President Carter's formerly good relationship with Garang. We stated that we wanted to listen and to learn. How could we correct that injury?

As we moved about in this community and at every turn in the road, we were met with needs. These people had nothing. They were cut off from markets, so they were no longer able to be productive; they needed peace. They told us that they had lived as neglected, underdeveloped people during the British control of Sudan; and that they had not fared any better under the rule of their Arab oppressors. They said they were fighting a war of independence. They wanted a peace that no longer kept them second-class citizens in an Islamic state. They felt that they had been forgotten. They said that if the US after 9/11 was worried about Islam and Al Qaeda, why would it not be concerned about those who were already living under an Islamic regime? They pleaded with us for the US and the rest of the outside world to take their plight seriously.

Then they told us how we could help. Their list included: schools and teacher training; assistance with developing the judiciary and establishing rule of law; financing small businesses and establishing access to markets; building systems of governance; and creating opportunities for youth. I now had a grounded view of their drive for self-determination and I had strong doubts about whether the north and the south could ever really coexist in a workable, equitable, united Sudan. But I had long since learned to keep my personal opinions to myself.

Nevertheless, in Mundri, near Lui, where Franklin Graham's well-equipped and well-run hospital lies near a bombed-out bridge, I was deeply moved and made a promise. Our local contacts had arranged for a village meeting. Some sixty or more people sat for hours waiting for us as we had been delayed getting back from the visit to Graham's Samaritan's Purse Hospital. They had waited for hours in the heat, and they were not young people. But once we arrived, they spoke at length through an interpreter about their past, their dismal present, and their prayers for peace. Some had been educated years ago to a grade eight level, and they had been teachers and leaders in the community. Now, aged, they were the last of those who were literate, most of the young people had been killed in war or were off fighting in the war. These old people said that when they died there would be no more of the educated class in the whole society. As Doug and I listened an ancient woman rose and with assistance made her way to the front. She looked us directly in the eye, and said that there had been some other people there not too long ago, asking about peace. Now that we Americans had come, asking what we might do, she stated that we should not return to the village again unless we were able to take the message of peace out and make it happen.

I promised her that if there was no peace in two years, I personally would not return. I also promised that we would work hard during that time to help bring about peace.

With those promises made, Doug and I made our way back to Nairobi, en route to Libya and Cairo.

In Libya, we were hosted by a small senior delegation who had booked us into a comfortable, Soviet-style hotel. It was very spartan, cement grey, and virtually empty except for a small group of visiting archaeologists. The hotel had no telephones in the rooms and offered a modest buffet, the menu of which had all the boring predictability of institutional food. Happily, in complete contrast, our hosts took us to dinner at an excellent seafood restaurant on the waterfront, after which we were given a tour of Tripoli. I was impressed with the city's huge modern expressways and housing tenements and suburban homes that looked very comfortable. A TV satellite dish was mounted on each home!

After Doug and I settled in, we prepared to meet Foreign Minister Treki, who I had met in passing in Ismail's office in Khartoum months before. At that time Treki had suggested that The Carter Center and Libya team up, but I had asserted that I was worried about too many cooks in the kitchen and that I was more interested in a single viable peace process. I expected a similar line from Treki this time.

And so it was. Recovering from a mild illness, he met us in his rambling home, where the courtyard seemed to lead on one side to the family dwelling, and on the other, to more formal or functional rooms. We met in a living room off what seemed to be the kitchen. There we were warmly greeted by Treki and introduced to his son, a man in his late teens or early twenties who looked quite intrigued by these Americans in his home. After some small talk, Treki asserted that Libya and Egypt were indeed going to go ahead with a peace summit in January, and that The Carter Center would be invited. I re-asserted our line that a single viable process was required and that it would be hard to imagine the SPLA entering into any talks that departed from the Declaration of Principles, which it cherished. (And having just come from southern Sudan, I now knew that the people all wanted this principle of self-determination acknowledged; indeed I knew that many would choose independence from Sudan immediately if they could.)

Understandably, Libya and Egypt were opposed to self-determination; they could not countenance an independent south. Treki made it clear to me that he had been that transparent with Garang, who had just visited Tripoli. Treki said he feared any arrangement that would endorse the breaking up of Sudan, as the Declaration of Principles allowed. He maintained that separation in Sudan could easily usher in a whole series of fragmentation of African countries. (He notably did not mention Egypt's coveted Nile River water.)

I asked Treki what Garang had thought about his offer to hold peace talks based on the principle that the south could not separate. He brushed off any resistance Garang may have expressed and affirmed that Garang had said he was indeed interested, ideally, in a united Sudan. Treki insisted that Garang was prepared to have Egypt and Libya mediate. But I left Tripoli doubting that Treki would get Bashir and Garang to the table in January.

When Doug and I traveled on to Cairo, it appeared from our discussions that Treki's Egyptian brothers, partners in the Joint Egyptian-Libyan Initiative, were not even aware of Treki's plans for a January summit. At least these Egyptian officials played it down and, throughout our interview, were more inclined to receive than to give information. I nevertheless gave a brief summary of the findings I had made on my European tour and the developments in Washington. We pressed for a single, viable process and asked the Egyptians to think of ways that their interests could be guaranteed in a revitalized Sudan Peace Process.

Notwithstanding that I was able to visit the pyramids and linger in a perfume shop while buying various essences for Ann – flowers along the Nile pressed to make scented oils with exotic names, Nefertiti and Cleopatra – I felt unsatisfied with the Egyptian visit. It did show, however, how fragmented the 'joint' Egyptian-Libyan Initiative was. For unless the Egyptians wanted me to be confused, they and their Libyan brothers certainly did not seem to be on the same page.

In the meantime the Danforth initiative was beginning to move. His advisors, it seemed, were telling him to take advantage of 9/11. What better climate would there be to press Sudan? After all, it remained on the US's list of terrorist nations and with the strong retaliatory mood in Washington, now directed at the Taliban in Afghanistan, it wasn't a great leap of the imagination that Sudan could come under the US knife as well. So, Danforth was in an excellent position to establish a number of 'tests' to determine if the Government of Sudan and the SPLA really were interested in peace. That most of the tests bore down more heavily on Khartoum than on the SPLA was not a real issue for the US; after all, Khartoum was the seat of the government of Sudan and the Government of Sudan should do most of the heavy lifting.

Not surprisingly, too, all those countries and nongovernmental actors who had really wanted the US to become engaged in peace efforts in Sudan were now worried that it might become too engaged. They feared that the US would take over and that they would all be shoved to the margins. This was not good, they noted, because it removed partners who knew the conflict and had long-term commitments to Sudan and the neighbouring region. It also suggested that a heavy-handed US 'Daytonesque' outcome-oriented peace process might be imposed on the parties. Based on hard lessons from the former Yugoslavia, marked by serious struggles to implement the peace agreement there, they feared such a process would reduce real ownership of the 'peace' in Sudan and that it would unravel as soon as the US lost interest.

Nevertheless, Danforth was ramping up. Oakley had said to me that Danforth would be neither mere fact finder nor fully peacemaker, but something in between. Oakley had remarked how many other pieces of paper (peace agreements) had been developed and had gone nowhere in the past. This time, they would require tests. Furthermore, he said the US would lead from behind and not necessarily be the mediator. I took some satisfaction in this, recalling that I had delivered just such a message to Synder and Oakley after my round of consultations in Europe. The Americans had been listening.

Now in Atlanta, as the fall of 2001 changed to winter in North America, I sketched out a plan for peacebuilding and peace support activities that would take us into Sudan, both north and south. The plan would also have us prepare delegations from the Government of Sudan and the SPLA for peace talks, if and when a process came together. President Carter had also met privately with Danforth and talked about our assistance with the highly contentious issue of religion and state. Danforth hoped that President Carter could be of particular assistance with that thorny obstacle to peace: how could the Government of Sudan's insistence on Sudan being an Islamic state governed by Sharia law be reconciled with the SPLA's insistence of separating religion and state?

And we also remained vigilant in our efforts to bring about a peaceful resolution to the LRA.

By now we were holding quiet meetings of the military and security arms of Uganda and Sudan in Nairobi. In actuality, my role as mediator of these meetings had almost become that of a facilitator. It was lighter lifting for me and my team as the two security arms of these former enemies began to work together, building on some of Yahia and Busho's accomplishments months earlier. But more so, 9/11 was again having its effect.

With US pressure being placed on Sudan through Danforth, Sudan was becoming more compliant on the issue of the LRA and on Sudan's relationship with Uganda. In fact, as Sudan felt the US pressure, its military seemed more prepared in our secret meetings to tolerate, if not accommodate, Uganda's pressure for a military action against Kony. When that type of discussion began to dominate the meetings, with only token efforts being made now about talks with Kony, I withdrew our immediate services. I suggested they should meet elsewhere. They could resume meeting with The Carter Center's assistance if and only when they were not going to talk about a military option, whether it was to be undertaken by Sudan alone, by Uganda alone, or – as the Ugandans were hoping – jointly.

Our hope for peace with the LRA was fading. Our relevance in the context of the Nairobi Agreement was declining. Uganda and Sudan had increased their level of diplomatic cooperation. Any LRA escapees who still managed to find their way to Juba in south Sudan were now routinely processed, thanks in large part to Chris, David and UNICEF. More and more were able to safely find their way home to northern Uganda. Uganda's Amnesty Act and its provision for a small package of assistance to those who gave themselves up was working after a fashion. Centres operating in northern Uganda, in Gulu, run by World Vision and other nongovernmental organizations were providing treatment for war trauma to the kids; and job training when they were ready and able to take it.

And the word was out that in January, 2002, Museveni would make an historic visit to Khartoum on the occasion of the annual East African Intergovernmental Authority on Development Summit meetings. Museveni and Bashir were scheduled to have private bilateral talks. This was big news, for Museveni had not visited Khartoum in twelve years. Many people in the international diplomatic community gave us credit for this, remarking that without our efforts to implement the Nairobi Agreement these two former enemies would never be meeting, certainly not in Khartoum. But it was a bittersweet accomplishment for us.

Danforth's team was now in high gear. I clearly witnessed the tempo change and saw how representatives of different governments were galvanizing around the Americans. But, I thought, isn't this what we all had said was required? Like a mantra, I had heard over and over again that peace in Sudan was impossible without the Americans. President Carter and I had worked hard to bring them in. Now they had arrived. And just as Bob Oakley had said to me months before, Danforth would proceed by setting tests for the two parties. Danforth's tests, remarkable for their incisiveness, included a full six-month ceasefire in the Nuba Mountains, a remote area laid waste by war for the past nineteen years; a prohibition against the bombing of any civilian targets, worthy in its own right but also responsive to the domestic USA Christian right's allegations that the Government of Sudan targeted civilians in the oil fields; a prohibition against, and a US eminent persons' investigation into abductions (read, 'slave-trading' by the Sudanese), a measure responsive to the US Black caucus; and finally, a requirement that humanitarian relief not be restricted in any manner by either side.

There was much ado about Danforth's tests, and while there were some cheap shots from the diplomatic sidelines, and some griping by Sudanese Government officials about the imbalance of the tests, it was obvious that the US was becoming seriously, yet cautiously, engaged. One day, we knew, the US would take over the dormant Sudan Peace Process. Egypt's fears about water and its general reluctance to support a change in the status quo would have to be overcome. The US could do this. Getting Bashir and Garang to the table for serious talks could be arranged by the US.

Yet, those of us who make our professions in peacemaking were aware that the Americans alone could not do it all, even if they wanted to. And I don't think they did. This was a hugely complex challenge which would require multiple levels of activity with multiple actors. All of us knew that a piece of paper with an agreement written on it was only just the beginning. Getting the agreement would be a challenge and implementing it would be an enormous undertaking.

So, we and others who were now less involved on the main stage did not retreat from our commitment to peace in Sudan. We took on tasks that would support peace. We made investments that would help make any peace agreement sustainable. In our case, we were still concerned with the relationship between the parties, between the official delegations from Khartoum and from the south, who would one day negotiate peace. We were also concerned about key obstacles to peace, including the nature of the peace process itself.

At a very practical level, Norwegian Ambassador Freydenlund pressed me to provide negotiation skills training to the two delegations, the Sudanese and the SPLA. And he strongly urged me to keep up our effort on the Nairobi Agreement, that it was a building block for peace, as President Carter had envisaged it more than two years earlier. Freydenlund also thought that The Carter Center might help on the contentious issue of wealth sharing; and that would necessarily demand that we get engaged on the issue of oil.

So we began to work on these things as well as finding our health program staff taking an active role in the Nuba Mountains, their path having been cleared by Danforth.

But we would not be at the head of state summit scheduled for Khartoum in January 2002, and we had little direct connection with Danforth's team as the New Year approached.

Then, on the eve of the summit, I received a curious call.

It was Busho, from Uganda. He informed me that his President and President Bashir would meet during the Summit and that there were only two items on the agenda. One was the LRA; the other was the civil war in Sudan. It would help if I could bring his Ugandan team of technical experts together with Yahia's Sudanese team before the Presidents met. It might make the meeting between them more productive. Would I come, now, to Khartoum?

I must say I was extremely cautious, despite my warm personal feeling towards Busho, based on his track record. I had already distanced us from Busho and Yahia's meetings with their military teams when I believed they had shifted from 'how to talk to Kony' to 'how to fight Kony'. While we had kept Chris on the ground in northern Uganda to keep alive the hope of talks with Kony, bolstered now by a new member of my team, Jeff Mapendere, an experienced freedom fighter and soldier from Zimbabwe, we were not going to be a party to killing. Wasn't this just a trap to give the appearance, in Khartoum, during a well attended and closely watched summit, that The Carter Center blessed a military action against the LRA?

Or, perhaps, just maybe, it was Busho's signal to me that he did not endorse a military option and hoped against hope that we could influence the upcoming talks between Bashir and Museveni in that direction. I called Yahia.

It did not sound good. Always gracious, he welcomed me to come to Khartoum, noting how busy it would be and that I may have to wait around for some time before we could meet. If that wouldn't offend me, then, yes, come. But he also said that his government had made a decision: the situation with Kony was stalemated. They had made a renewed commitment that the LRA must go. They were willing to develop a bilateral approach with the Ugandans and, while a military action wasn't what they wanted, it may be the end result.

Tom and I left for Khartoum immediately. We would run the risk of seeming to have been associated with a decision to take military action against Kony because we were adamant it should not happen. We went to try and reverse the tide. Maybe Busho was with us, maybe Yahia too. But they were servants of the State and of their Presidents. We wanted to help them avert a presidential agreement to remove the LRA by military means.

For us to be able to achieve this we would have to be sure that the technical teams from the two countries preferred a non-military solution. Then we would have to mobilize the assembled international community to deter Museveni, who we expected would be pressing for military action. We would have to bolster Bashir, who we expected would much rather not get tangled up in a messy fight against Kony, a former ally who posed no real threat to him. And we would have to change the impetus, arguing that the 'path of dialogue' with Kony had never been given a chance. We felt that it could work, especially if it had presidential weight behind it. That is if both Bashir and Museveni said, aloud, we want peace talks with the LRA and directed it to happen.

When I met with Yahia, I could tell instantly that it was all over. In fact, he was so resolute that I sensed that his President had already made the decision. Indeed, after I pleaded with him on behalf of the innocent victims of the LRA – for virtually all had been abducted against their will including the elderly, the women and the children – he turned the tables on me. He said that if I felt that way, it was my responsibility to convince the Ugandans.

That night, I confess, I cried for the first time in years. I could foresee the coming blood bath. I saw women and children and young men dying by the thousands. Shot dead, hacked up, and dying alone in the bush. And I felt the pain of their loved ones.

The next morning I felt depressed after having summarized what we were up against, so I suggested to Tom that we should leave. I said that it would be better to leave now and not be seen in any way to bless the inevitable.

Tom, on the contrary, was more impassioned than I had ever seen him.

He insisted that we must stay to fight this one and mobilize the international community. He listed possible contacts who were here at this meeting and might help, saying "The Norwegians are here and they are our friends and would want peace; we might be able to meet with the Americans and see if they could help; Xavier Marchal, the EU's representative is here, surely he will help; and Ambassador Mohammed Sahnoun who had served as the UN Secretary General, Kofi Annan's Special Representative is here and our friend, maybe he will help."

I was moved by Tom's determination to fight this thing. It is something about Tom that I will always remember and respect. Typically he was analytical and reserved and was slow to act. I saw now what the man was made off.

I agreed. We needed to start immediately and not quit until we had done every thing we could.

The Khartoum Hilton was a swirl with Summit comings and goings. Delegations from all the countries in the region had arrived, high officials were deposited from expensive chauffeur-driven cars, their entourages including secret service men, fashionably dressed wives, and in some cases, their children in tow. Representatives of the international diplomatic community and businessmen who had an interest in Sudan and east Africa were there, as well. I also noted a small number of reporters and camera crews.

We encamped there, in the Hiltons' foyer, operating in the midst of the Summit. For three days we worked, meeting people, lobbying, explaining that, given the right opportunity, Kony would talk. We met with Sudanese military officials and found some sympathy. Certain ministers in the Ugandan delegation surprised us in their willingness, indeed, in their plea to us that we find a peaceful route. Someone from the Ugandan delegation claimed he had been brought along for the express purpose of going with us to meet Kony and secure talks. We worked that angle. The Norwegians suggested they had a channel to Kony and they would help. Sahnoun said he was meeting with the presidents privately and would state our case to them.

The hours rushed past us. The appointed time came. Bashir and Museveni were to meet. We stood by. They met. And there was a great silence. Great silences like that tell me the decision has gone the other way. And it had. And it got worse.

12

Operation Iron Fist

It was sold to the people of northern Uganda as a rescue mission. The Ugandan army would now enter southern Sudan and rescue the abducted children from Kony. Sudan would cooperate. The armed forces of its former enemy would be permitted to operate on its sovereign soil and the Sudanese would give the Ugandan army logistical support.

This outcome, itself, was truly remarkable. Some members of the diplomatic community insisted to me that it was a strong indicator of our success implementing the Nairobi Agreement. Our success would have an impact on the dynamics of the Sudan civil war; indeed, it augured well for peace talks. After all, Museveni and Bashir were warming up to one another. Museveni would likely be more persuasive with Garang in return for this favor from Bashir.

We thought it remarkable for other reasons. It was remarkable, or actually terribly sad, that the Acholi people in northern Uganda were so desperate for peace that they would believe this story of a rescue mission. For one thing, virtually every abducted child that could carry a weapon in the LRA would be armed. There were no unarmed, 'abducted children'. For another thing, we were certain that Kony would fight to the bitter end. That meant that every child to be rescued would be armed and under orders to fight. The rescue mission would become a slaughter.

It was also remarkable how powerful the influence of the United States of America was. For it was my assessment that 9/11 was having its impact

155

here as well, on this marginal issue in Sudan, as well as on matters more central to Sudan, as initiated by Danforth. Sudan, it seemed, could not shake off the stigma of a terrorist nation. The US was going to press this point as far as it could, ostensibly for good purposes. After all, they stated, didn't we all want peace in Sudan? Didn't we all agree the Islamic government in Khartoum was an aberrant regime? Didn't we all agree that only real and sustained pressure was the way to motivate such regimes to change? Wasn't a strategy of holding the stick firmly above Khartoum's head with the promise of carrots at the end of proper compliance the most effective strategy in this case?

As January 2002 turned to February and March, it was apparent that this was indeed the attitude and orientation of the US toward Khartoum. Most of my colleagues and contacts were inclined to agree with it. Certainly there were doubters, and some worthy doubts. These included concerns about the extent to which Khartoum could be leaned on without a backlash, the most probable being a re-emergence of true Islamic fundamentalism in Khartoum. That would make it very hard, to impossible, for Bashir to cooperate. Those with a longer view wondered about the ability of the US to remain focused on Sudan. They questioned if this house of sticks would fall apart as soon as the US lost interest. Others worried that any peace agreement between Khartoum and the SPLA would be fragile at best if it really was the product of unreasonably one-sided pressure on Khartoum. I wondered how could one get to an agreement if Khartoum never received a carrot but only and always faced the stick?

Naturally, we were upset about the precise impact of this larger dynamic upon our stubbornly held hopes and tireless efforts for peace talks between Kony and Museveni. Sudan was yielding to Uganda because it was under pressure from the US, not simply because it wished to be a good neighbour. We were also beginning to see the window close on our own efforts to end the war in Sudan. But what could we do that would help?

I thought hard about this. The prospects of drawing on President Carter for direct involvement as a peacemaker were quickly diminishing. By now the US was joining up with the UK and Norway, emerging as a 'troika' that would ultimately orchestrate the Sudan peace effort. They were keeping the Sudan Peace Process in the forefront, now. They asked President Moi of Kenya to appoint the head of his armed forces, General Lazaro Sumbeiywo, as the Special Envoy and mediator for the peace talks. My old friend, Ambassador Daniel Mboya, had been retired. There was plenty of motion in the background as other countries and nongovernmental actors positioned themselves to take some piece of the action.

We wanted to be of assistance, but at a level that was commensurate with our institutional strengths, and comparative advantage. To be most effective that would have to include President Carter.

So we took advantage of a trip to Khartoum that President Carter had planned for some months. He was to attend a high-level conference on health, which would dwell upon The Carter Center's efforts on eradicating the Guinea Worm Disease. So, with Carter in the region, we went back to our planning documents and decided it made sense to take the Norwegian ambassador's advice to offer training in negotiation to both the Government of Sudan and to the SPLA. We would exploit that to combine with our own goals of building up the relationship between Garang and President Carter.

Not only were Garang's associates expressing antipathy to President Carter but when Doug and I had been in southern Sudan the people we met there expressed antipathy towards President Carter as well. We needed to mend this fence. In fairness to President Carter, we needed to give him the opportunity to make it clear to Garang and the SPLA that he was indeed as supportive of their aspiration to peace as he was of Khartoum's. He really did not favor one over the other. What had happened, I think, is that the US administration under Clinton had been clearly biased towards the SPLA, and President Carter was vocally against such bias. His stand was interpreted by the SPLA as being a bias against the people of the south. This was not the case. It was his preference for even-handed treatment of all the people in Sudan and his hope that the US would take a balanced policy of peace, not war. His statement though had distanced Carter from the Clinton Administration. Being distanced from the Administration, I suppose, could be seen as being distanced from the Administration's friend. In this case, that would be Garang and the SPLA.

Regardless, I saw it as imperative that we address the perception. We wanted to position Carter to be of assistance to both Bashir and Garang when it was needed. I knew that once President Carter met with representatives of the SPLA, and then Garang himself, the truth would emerge.

We also thought that Norway's Ambassador Freydenlund had struck a key note in advising me to offer negotiation training. It was a simple thing, but as is sometimes the case, we fail by overlooking the simple things. So we offered our services to both Khartoum and the SPLA, to provide them with training in negotiation and preparations for peace talks. We also invited the Government of Sudan, the SPLM, and the Government of Uganda to participate in an unprecedented week-long workshop on conflict resolution and peacebuilding.

Our idea was that these needed skills would make for better peace talks, when they took place. But more immediately, the simple, non-threatening opportunity to have training in negotiation, conflict resolution, and peacebuilding would give all three of these key players a chance to explore sensitive subjects well before they got into the real, and politically charged, peace talks. And finally, spending a week with each group would give us and them a chance to get to know one another, to build the kind of constructive relationship we had always intended. And of course, if we could arrange for President Carter to meet the leadership of the SPLA during our session with them, this would help on the most important matter of trust in President Carter.

We were lucky, really. President Carter's schedule is so fully booked that it usually takes months of lead notice simply to get a few hours of his time. The fact that he was going to be in Khartoum, not long after the Summit, during the early days of Danforth's 'tests', and at a time that we needed new energy in our campaign to end the war, was perfect.

I made a case to President Carter that regardless of how pressed he was for time, he really must visit the south of Sudan. I was quite frank about the perceptions of him that we had encountered. I knew he deserved to know, would want to know, and would most probably respond constructively. And he did. Even though his visit to Khartoum would be the first of several intensive days on a HIV/AIDS trip through Africa with a delegation from the Gates Foundation, he was prepared to go with me into southern Sudan, to the SPLA capital city, Rumbek. He and I would take a small plane from Khartoum to meet Garang or whoever was assembled for the training event that we planned to hold there in Rumbek. From Rumbek President Carter could proceed to rejoin the others waiting in Nairobi. But more, after I completed the training in Rumbek, I'd go to Nairobi to have a meeting with the Sudan Peace Process's new mediator, General Sumbeiywo, in advance of a meeting between Carter and Sumbeiywo to be held on Carter's return from the South African leg of his journey. It was a full program. And it worked perfectly.

When President Carter arrived in Khartoum for the health conference, the issue of peace dominated from the outset. He was greeted by Dr. Ghazi al din, President Bashir's Senior Advisor on Peace. And the media scrum at the airport was virtually all about the prospects of peace in Sudan. Indeed, as we were to learn the next day, Khartoum needed Carter's help. Reports that the Government of Sudan's air force had recently bombed civilians in the south were threatening to topple Khartoum's performance on one of Danforth's tests. So early in the process, this was not helpful to anyone – except perhaps the SPLA who would gain sympathy. Ghazi needed Carter to communicate with Washington, to put things back on track as Khartoum wished to comply with the US demands and eventually move forward with peace talks.

Even though President Carter's agenda in Khartoum was jam packed he was ready on the appointed day to go to Rumbek. We squeezed into the tiny King Aircraft as dawn was breaking. President and Mrs. Carter were accompanied by a personal physician, their scheduling secretary, John Hardman, and three Secret Security officers. Alex and I rounded out the passenger list. Already deep in the south, in Rumbek, Doug would receive us, accompanied by yet another Secret Service officer who had gone ahead to prepare the way.

The flight was rather uneventful, with quiet chatter as Mrs. Carter read and President Carter played with his laptop computer, locating Rumbek on a map of southern Sudan for all to see. We also had a brief, telling conversation. He wanted to know how the training session for the Sudanese delegation had gone in Khartoum these past days, what I was planning for Rumbek, and how we were going to move forward with Sumbeiywo.

I explained how the training which I had given in Khartoum and would repeat in Rumbek was designed so that the first two days focused on the theory of negotiation and learning practical skills, and the next days invited the participants to talk about their views of peace. I said that the last day was focused on mediation: what kind of mediation was most effective; what did mediation require of them; and finally, what should a peace process look like?

I informed him that we had also already done another type of training session, held on neutral ground, in Nairobi. It had been unique in that it had been attended by representatives of the Government of Sudan, members of Garang's SPLA, and some key people from Uganda. I explained that it was during the joint peacebuilding training session held in Nairobi that I had received a call from Sumbeiywo, asking for our assistance. I told

President Carter that what really mattered today in Rumbek was to establish ourselves with the SPLA. I asked him if he knew that the SPLA was going to kill a bull upon our arrival and ask him and Mrs. Carter to jump the bull for a ceremony in his honour? He said he was ready to jump the bull.

What was most telling for me, however, was his response to my general plans for more work in Sudan. I wanted to deepen our programming efforts, as a result of the discussions during that joint workshop on peacebuilding which we had given in Nairobi. I was of the opinion that in addition to, or more accurately, in order to give credibility to our efforts at the higher level of diplomacy, we needed to be more active on the ground. As far back as my work in the Crimea and Mostar I had believed that peace talks need to be informed by the community and peace agreements need to be implemented through long and hard work that 'wires' the agreement to reality on the ground.

President Carter was not sympathetic. Not that he overtly objected to this strategy. He simply wasn't sure it was where our strengths, our efforts, and our resources were most advantaged. He said that he would think about it and that he and John "would decide after their trip was over."

Ouch! Apart from the hit to my ego, and the sense that he had not really appreciated what we had done to get this far and how valid my views were in getting us further, I was aware of something more important. It has something to do with the old adage: 'Be careful of what you ask for, you might get it'. For just as I had led our charge to get the US involved in Sudan, and I had developed reservations about the way in which the US was proceeding, I was having a similar feeling about The Carter Center. I had tried to get President Carter into a key role and I had always pressed the institution to be supportive. Now both were becoming engaged. Both the man, Jimmy Carter, and the institution itself were more alive to my efforts. I was asking both to help, calling upon The Carter Center to raise nearly two million dollars a year in funding to do what I proposed in Sudan. As The Center confronted my request to help raise the money to do the job right, it was moving from intelligent, but relatively benign support, to engagement and it would want to share being in charge. The dynamic of my peace work was changing; the game was becoming the kind of game in which Carter could personally participate. He was taking charge. I felt the initiative slip from me at that moment. I had wanted my cake and to eat it too. Carter's remark reminded me that I was one player on one of the smaller teams in an international league with rules that are set largely on the basis of power and self interest. Indeed, to be fair, President Carter smiled a wry smile, saying to me that I had been trying to take over the whole peace process. Not that he minded, but he wasn't sure it was doable. What would our financial supporters, Norway and the UK, and others, think?

We landed in Rumbek to the beating of drums, colourful dancing, shouts and cheers as a tightly tethered bull pressed to the ground under the weight of four men had its neck slit. As the blood ran out on the tarmac, President and Mrs. Carter, assisted by the Deputy Commander of the SPLA, Salva Kiir, leapt the dying animal. Then we assembled for a ceremonial kick-off to the session. President Carter appeared keen, giving a touching speech, encouraging democracy and introducing me as an expert on negotiation.

We worked our way through that hot week, overcoming their scepticism about the usefulness of our instruction to the practical realities of negotiations with Khartoum. We learned and developed trust with these determined, friendly people who had been fighting a war of independence for nearly nineteen years. This good relationship that was growing between us was galvanized one afternoon. I was lecturing to the assembled group which included Salva Kiir and many of the SPLA commanders. Suddenly, we heard a burst of gunfire. Everyone reacted immediately, standing up and going to the open windows that looked out to a few small buildings across the way and the open fields beyond. Then there was more gunfire. We poured onto the low veranda and could see dust rising off to the left, in the direction of the town centre. There was obviously some kind of scuffle happening. And then the sound of gunshots resumed, the exchange of fire more rapid, and louder.

Instantly all of us ran for our vehicles and Alex and I quickly drove off toward the UN compound at the other end of town. Within minutes we were there, safe, while now, nearby in the town centre the gunshots continued, but sporadically. Then a silence fell over the town and we learned later that some of the body guards of the commanders attending our training session had gotten into a fight. These men, loyal to commanders of different ethnic groups, had been drinking. A fight broke out, gunfire followed.

This had taken place in the mid-afternoon so I sent out word that we would cancel the rest of the day's session and resume in the morning. We did, and all went well. In fact, that week of training in negotiation was so successful that we were hosted to a wonderful dinner on the last night under the starlit sky. The menu was traditional food and the conversation turned to next steps. I was assured of their friendship; we were trusted. Garang would be encouraged by Kiir to meet with President Carter on Garang's next trip to the USA. They wanted us to press the new mediator, Sumbeiywo, to move quickly to concrete negotiations, with a document to be put before the parties to get things going.

We left Rumbek for Nairobi. The next day, at 7am I met with Sumbeiywo to prepare him for our 8am meeting with President Carter. I encouraged him to be frank, to be comfortable, to ask for assistance with resources and to disclose the challenges he had encountered thus far. When Carter arrived he was revved up on his return from the South African leg of his trip with the Gates Foundation. There he had met Walter Kansteiner, Powell's man for Africa and the 'point' on Sudan.

At the meeting Sumbeiywo explained to President Carter that he continued to be responsible for Kenya's armed forces while taking on this new role of mediator of the Sudan Peace Process. Indeed, he needed the armed forces, as he had insufficient funds to run his mediation efforts and was taking administrative support from the army. Money was needed to kick start his team, and to pay for expert advice as he proceeded. But more importantly, having shared this with me earlier, he took President Carter into his confidence regarding his first effort to elicit explicit commitments from the SPLA and the Government of Sudan to participate in serious, focused talks. He referred to a document he had drafted and the resistance he had met to it. He also was refreshingly direct in reporting to President Carter that Garang had dismissed Sumbeiywo's proposal that The Carter Center convene and conduct a series of workshops on the topics of wealth-sharing, power-sharing, and state and religion. Garang had said there was an issue of trust. Carter took this on the chin, without chagrin. And I was able, in good faith, to explain that we had known about this reluctance but that I was certain now that the relationship with Garang was changing course, especially after the successful week we had just had in the bush in Garang's homeland.

I reinforced the need for a document, explaining that just last week Kiir had pressed me to get a document in circulation. Sumbeiywo's transparency and my reference to Kiir's request was more than enough to prompt a lesson from President Carter on mediation techniques. I recall the intensity and clarity with which President Carter walked Sumbeiywo through the concept of the 'single negotiated text' procedure. He gave a step-by-step description of how to draft and use a text that would become the agreement of the parties. Sumbeiywo was a sponge, taking in every nuanced bit of the lesson from a master.

This push from Khartoum to Rumbek to Nairobi was clearly a success. We had done a lot in a series of relatively simple, yet deliberately taken steps. We were building momentum for peace. We were in the game and usefully so.

Meanwhile, relentlessly, Operation Iron Fist in Uganda was moving into full swing.

The 'rescue mission' had, of course, not succeeded. In fact, Kony had lashed out as we had predicted. He attacked Sudanese bases, killing former allies and driving villagers from their homes in southern Sudan. The US agreed to Museveni's request to designate the LRA a terrorist group, elevating its notoriety and legitimating closer collaboration between Washington and Museveni in the hunt for Kony. We were informed that the US was now providing satellite intelligence on the movements and location of the LRA. Museveni was mobilizing up to 10,000 troops to find and destroy the LRA fighters, whose numbers were estimated to be between 1,500 to 2,500. Ten Ugandan soldiers for one LRA fighter!

Horror stories were coming from the bush. The LRA were reported to have attacked a funeral procession in southern Sudan, forcing the mourners to cook and eat the corpse. Refugees were spilling from southern Sudan into northern Uganda. Kony was mounting a counter-attack in a response to Operation Iron Fist. LRA fighters had penetrated behind the lines of the Ugandan army, coming close to Kitgum and Gulu, the government garrison town. Villagers were fleeing their homes for safety. A humanitarian crisis was taking shape.

Yet no one in the international community, it seemed, was concerned any longer about peace talks with Joseph Kony. Maybe the international diplomatic community in Kampala had simply become resigned to the inevitable. Our German colleague and sponsor, Ambassador Claus Holdenbaum, remained our only official exception. He continued to worry about Museveni's challenges on so many fronts, from difficulties in the Congo to political rivalry at home. Holdenbaum thought peace talks with the LRA remained a humane and politically advantageous route for Museveni.

However, the Government of Sudan was still under extreme scrutiny by hostile US domestic interest groups. It was still in the early stages of having to demonstrate compliance with Danforth's tests and was now facing the added pressures of taking peace talks seriously under Sumbeiywo's lead who was backed by the US, UK, and Norway. Giving an increasingly freer hand to Museveni's war against the LRA, even on its sovereign territory, was a matter of administrative necessity for the Sudanese. Sudan's compliance was determined in the crucible of realpolitik. Operation Iron Fist continued for the next twelve months when it had been originally presented as a rescue mission that would take no more than a few weeks.

Was our work done? Was this not proof positive that, with the assistance of The Carter Center, Sudan and Uganda had successfully implemented the Nairobi Agreement that had been mediated by President Carter?

Certainly, bi-lateral relations between Sudan and Uganda had been restored, and then some. Clearly, we were making progress on our original larger goal, peace in Sudan. Furthermore, our funding had dried up, except for the Germans. Wasn't that a clear message from our sponsors that our work was indeed done? Was it our concern, let alone responsibility, that northern Uganda was being put through a bloody, protracted war? Wasn't this just one more cruel but inevitable manifestation of politics, not as usual, but as enhanced by 9/11? To repeat, wasn't our work done?

My team and I did not think so.

13
Endgame

Is there ever, really, an endgame?

I had thought from the outset that characterizing the Nairobi Agreement as a 'building block' for peace in Sudan was far too mechanistic – too Newtonian. Reality seemed much more convoluted and unpredictable. Peace needed to be 'woven' rather than 'built'. And that was long before 9/11 and a world increasingly, and dangerously, impregnated with American angst and American hubris, American omnipotence. But terms such as 'building peace' reflect the way we deconstruct reality in our aspiration to control events.

By now, however, I realized that neither President Carter nor the best efforts of a small and dedicated world-class peace team could control events. So it seemed pretentious to think and talk about the 'endgame' of peace efforts in Sudan.

Nevertheless, Chris had pressed me one time, arguing that it seemed to him more that we were 'making up' what we were doing as we went along rather than having any command of the process. I recall how angry this had made me. No, I had insisted, we were adhering to the science of conflict resolution. A body of theory informed our efforts. We were operating on principles that had been distilled from practice, reflection, research and theory. It may seem to him, so close to the ground, that we were making this up as we went along, but we were not. We were strategic in our approach. We were flexible, of course, but we certainly weren't without discipline and merely reactive.

To prove my point, I had shown him an outline I had sketched the first day I had stayed in the Khartoum Hilton. It clearly showed that we would push through stages to completion with 'the endgame'.

I had thought the endgame would see President Carter and our team deeply involved in the mediation efforts which were now in the hands of General Sumbeiywo. I was also aware that we would have to exit Uganda at some time, either having successfully won Museveni and Kony over to real peace talks, or having challenged both but having failed to bring them to the table.

My plan, however, had not foreseen 9/11. I had not envisaged how strong forces which were external to our four factors would be. I had worked on four key elements: the conflict, the parties, the policy environment and the peace process. These remained important, but we were clearly now swamped by the policy environment as it was being determined in the aftermath of 9/11. Simple Newtonian endgame scenarios that had served to guide me were now clearly being tossed aside by circumstances unpredictable and unprecedented; and yet to be fully realized. Chris may have been right, but not for reasons within my control or within our dexterity.

After all, we had overcome the initial obstacle of the US having cut Sudan off and from taking an even more hard-line view of Sudan as a terrorist nation after 9/11. If the US had done that, the hope of peace in Sudan would have been dead in the water. We had also taken advantage of the scrutiny Sudan attracted after 9/11; we tried to push for peace talks when the US was paying attention. In fact, we sensed the apprehension towards Americans in the Horn of Africa and tried to exploit that to an advantage. We pushed for the US to lead from behind and we put our eggs in the Sudan Peace Process basket. We supported and tried to shape, and give resources to, a single viable peace process. I had envisaged peace talks as the endgame; and they were materializing.

But Operation Iron Fist undermined any sense of achievement I could garner from nearly two and one-half years of non-stop work. A military 'solution' to the LRA 'problem' was a sad, albeit virtually predictable development.

Chris, who now had been working between Kampala and northern Uganda for nearly two years, had taken over from David (who I had asked to leave after his life had been threatened), felt the same way. In fact, I had begun to worry that Chris was 'going native', so deeply into the weeds had he gone on our behalf. He had spent hours with the people, listening, learning, informing, and being informed about the entire situation. He had continued to help escaped LRA abductees who made their way back to the north, for he now knew the situation from Juba to Khartoum to Kampala to Gulu.

Chris had convinced me to engage Louis, a former Ugandan military intelligence officer, as our 'community liaison officer'. I went to Uganda and one of my tasks was to meet and confirm Louis in his new job. I was picked up in Kampala by Chris who drove us directly north towards Gulu. I had arrived late so before too long evening was upon us and as it happens on the Equator, darkness came almost instantly. About two hours out of Kampala, Chris slowed at an intersection and came to a full stop beside a grungy old building that looked like it was a bar, a restaurant and a grocery store all in one. A small crowd immediately surrounded our vehicle, curious onlookers in a landscape that had very little diversions. Chris jumped out of the truck and disappeared into the crowd and the black night. Returning just as quickly, through my side view mirror I could see he had a couple of live chickens bound together, up-side-down, and he threw them into the open rear compartment.

"What are the chickens for?" I asked him in some amazement.

"You'll see," he said, grinning at me as he shifted into low gear and took off like a bullet.

In Gulu he didn't waste any time, saying we could check in to our hotel after he dropped the chickens off. So we wound our way down a narrow, dark alley through a collection of poor houses. We stopped and once again Chris scrambled out of the truck, grabbing the chickens with a farmer's efficiency, and then he ducked inside a doorway.

Two hours later, after we had registered and settled in at the hotel, we were now back at the same place. It was Louis' home.

Louis, a friendly looking man in his late thirties warmly greeted us to his humble abode. The doorway opened onto a small poorly-lit room with a low ceiling. This living room had one dilapidated couch that I was invited to sit upon and where I remained for the evening. Then his wife, a very young woman – perhaps just 20 – entered sheepishly from what I took to be the adjoining kitchen. She was very shy and kept her head down as he introduced her to me. Her name was Daisy and she quickly excused herself to finish preparing the meal.

Chris, Louis and I tried to make small talk but Louis seemed determined to talk about the LRA and Museveni. He gave me the impression that he was very intelligent, informed and seasoned by the war.

He said, "I want to do this work for The Carter Center because I am so tired of the war. I love my country but I want the war to end."

Curiously the last remark reminded me of something similar another informer had told me once when I asked him why he was willing to help us.

I told Louis that I was pleased with Chris' work and that I valued Chris' judgement. I said I believed Chris was making progress with the LRA but that we needed to get Kony and Museveni to talk to one another.

Just then, Daisy returned with a large platter with two golden brown fried chickens upon it. I was invited to take my serving first and they treated me with that respect throughout the evening. The scrawny chickens turned out to be very tough, although tasty. I ate my fill and could hardly manage the special desert Daisy brought out.

Louis explained that the honeycomb we were having for desert was from wild bees. He said that it was very difficult to get, very delicious, and being served in my honour. As I took the overly large chunk of honey comb from Daisy I thought to myself that it must also have been very expensive. So I ate all that I could but I really was unable to finish it. I had been a beekeeper myself one time and I liked honey. But this was extremely rich, the dark honey squeezing out of the natural comb as I chewed down on it.

Soon afterwards I formally welcomed Louis to our team and, thanking Daisy, we excused ourselves.

Of course we knew well that he might double cross us but we had to work with what we had. He helped Chris and Jeff to make contacts with LRA go-betweens and field commanders. They all helped community-based peacebuilding organizations get established. They covered the waterfront, and Chris soon became the most reliable, impartial source of information on the LRA and Operation Iron Fist in the international community in Uganda. He was in demand for his insights.

But the situation looked bleak. Thousands of Ugandan soldiers were pouring into northern Uganda. The LRA was counter-attacking. The local community was undergoing increasing trauma. There were abductions, rapes, killings. Villages were being burned to the ground. The local religious leaders, elected members of parliament, government officials – all were in varying states of stress. Some were embarking on peace efforts, reaching out to the LRA. Some were rallying around Operation Iron Fist. Some were tending to the injured and fearful community.

I decided to visit northern Uganda and assess, one last time, whether there was anything we could do. Or should we simply pull out? We had been trying to conduct a series of workshops with the community-based nongovernmental people working for peace in the north of Uganda. We had no intentions of replicating or competing with their efforts. But we were trying to do a little where and when we could. I thought it would help if we brought along an independent consultant to assess what, if anything, we might try to do under the circumstances.

We would seek the views of Sylvia McMechan, adding to Chris' insights and Jeff's views based on his experience as a former freedom fighter and member of the Zambian armed forces. Sylvia was a conflict resolution practitioner who had been a professor at Royal Roads University and she had valuable experience with Canadian aboriginal people. She also did not know Uganda or The Carter Center. Any naivety she had would be an advantage. I also knew her to be objective in these matters.

Chris, Sylvia and I met in Kampala and embarked on a wonderful, informative, and dangerous trip through the north. We started by holding a conflict analysis workshop in Gulu facilitated by Sylvia, and attended by some thirty participants from all over the north; Acholi people working on peace and conflict resolution. The message I took from that day was that 'band-aid treatment' was useless. The Government had to be pressed into peace talks.

Having received security clearance from the Ugandan army, as the roads were being attacked by the LRA, we made plans for a trip that would take us from Gulu Town north toward Sudan to Kitgum, then southeast to Pader, and further south to Lira and then back to Kampala. Before leaving, I called Ann and informed her that we would be out of contact for a day or two but that if she had not heard from me after four days, to alert The Carter Center. I can only imagine the stress she felt upon hearing that.

The three of us and our liaison, Louis, visited an internally-displaced person's camp where his parents resided. We witnessed the desolate conditions, our hearts going out to these Acholi people driven from their farms and villages by the war. These were the people caught in the middle. These were the victims of a civil war, one day preyed upon by the LRA and pressured by the Ugandan army the next. Their camp housed 20,000 people in huts crammed so tightly that only a footpath separated them, hut upon hut upon hut; and the camp received a water supply sufficient for only half of the population.

The camp literally abutted Louis's family farm. So it was that his elderly parents were able to go to their farm during the day, like many other Acholi did, and then return to the camp at night to sleep. We found them at home, on a few arable acres of land that rose slightly above the camp. The driveway to their homestead wound its way through several mango trees, the fruit ripe and hanging in the hundreds.

Our visit was brief, but very telling. His old father and mother were so pleased to see Louis, and they took our presence in stride. Very quickly, Sylvia and his mother wondered off to the hut that housed the kitchen, where Sylvia was given a good look at a traditional hearth, various cooking implements, and a review of the spices that were grown locally and used in meal preparation. Meanwhile, after a dozen kids climbed the mango trees to throw down more fresh mangoes than I could eat, Louis, Chris and I followed Louis's father. He took us to a hut in a clearing, not far from the mango trees and the kitchen hut. Then he quietly left us. We gazed about, looking far over the land past the camp and over fertile fields. It was lovely, pristine and peaceful. But when I turned back to survey Louis's home more closely I noticed three mounds in front of the hut. We walked towards them. They were simple graves where Louis told us his brothers were buried. I ask him how they had died. Looking down at the graves, almost under his breath, he answered, "In the war".

His father, such a humble man, returned and Louis and he wandered off to have a private chat. Speaking quietly in their absence, Chris told me that the brothers had died from AIDS, and that many young men had died that way. Saying 'in the war' was a common way to say that someone had died from AIDS, and did not necessarily mean they had died in battle.

Before long, we re-grouped and got ready to leave. I was given a large bag of mangoes to take with me, as they noticed how much I had appreciated eating as many as I possibly could when we had arrived. As we drove away Louis explained that his father was a tailor. But his sewing machine had been stolen years before and carted off by the rebels. Later, when I offered to buy his father a new sewing machine, Louis discouraged it, saying that his father was now too old to sew, his vision was too poor.

Further north we visited a refugee camp that housed Acholi and Dinka tribe-members who had fled from southern Sudan, either escaping the war between Sudan and the SPLA, fleeing Kony, or escaping the war between Kony and Museveni, now being fought in Sudan. At the entrance to the camp a few women were selling ground nuts and we bought a little from each of them.

We visited community leaders whom Chris knew; people who, despite their grief and suffering, or because of it, worked for peace through dialogue.

Just outside Kitgum, Chris took us to meet one of the most remarkable women I have ever met. Aunt Irene.

Chris had been talking about Aunt Irene for days now, building to this rare visit. He had said only that she had an orphanage of sorts that she ran on the outskirts of Kitgum, in the midst of LRA rebels.

We pulled off the main road to Kitgum and made our way toward an odd-looking, sprawling cement block building. The dusty grounds, relieved by a few leafy shade trees, were quiet. There was no sign of the life I had expected, of orphaned kids running about, screaming and playing as kids do. But Chris knew his way around here, and slowly drove past the main, elongated cement building and turned at the end to a quick stop. Right there, sitting in a dilapidated chair and cradling a young child in her arms, was Aunt Irene. Standing beside her was a teenage girl, a striking image in her own right. Aunt Irene, a white woman, stood and smiled a warm welcome. I noticed her teeth were decayed with some missing. And as we shook hands I could see that she was an older woman, in her late sixties, with years of stress on her face. The young, very black girl beside her, Irene's assistant was truly remarkable. Barefooted, she was decked out in a flowing pink gown, the likes of which young women from the southern US wear to a debutant ball; a coming-out dress. I had to take a double look although I tried not to show my amazement. But there she was, as innocent as can be, unselfconsciously adorned in this grand flowing gown, barefoot and all. As she took the child from Aunt Irene I thought the dress must have come in some shipment from the US, clothes donated to Africa by the members of a church. Wouldn't they be struck by this image; to see where one of their daughter's dresses had ended up!

As we settled down to a relaxed conversation I could of course not resist asking Aunt Irene how she had arrived in Kitgum.

"I went to the bus station in Kampala," she said "and I said to them 'take me to the end of the line'."

She was from Australia, she explained. She had been a schoolteacher and she was a grandmother. And she said that for years she had been sponsoring kids in developing countries through an international organization. One day, she said, it occurred to her that her own children and her grandchildren were well and did not really need her as much as kids in countries like Uganda did. So, she told me, she convinced the small congregation in her church in Australia to support her.

I looked about and now realized that we were sitting just beyond a caravan, a camper trailer she must had secured somewhere else and brought here to be her home. But in the most remarkable way, it was now embedded in a building. She had started there and quite literally built on to it so that it was encapsulated by concrete bocks.

She must have noticed my disbelief. "Do you want a tour?" she asked.

"Definitely," I replied, standing. "That would be great."

And so I walked alongside her as she told me about her activities and showed me the building, still (and perhaps always) under construction.

"Over there," she pointed to a shed-like smaller building on the horizon "is where our trades shop is. Older boys and men are learning to fix bicycles there and do some craft work. And in here," she said as we entered the larger block building, "I am going to have a meeting room and a place for visitors to stay."

She explained that while she relied almost totally on her small church for funding, some American groups had visited and many had said that if she could build accommodation, she would likely attract volunteers who would stay longer and help out. So that was what she was doing.

As we walked through the empty building she pointed out how she and the men who were doing the masonry work had designed the sleeping rooms. We entered one, a small chamber, and she pointed to the wall adjoining the next room. The wall went up only so far, and there was a gap at the ceiling, between this room and the next. And it was like that between each room in the long run of some eight to ten guest rooms.

"I left the gap at the ceiling," she said, "in case the rebels come. This way, the guest might have a chance of getting away."

Outside, I asked her where the children were, and she explained that hers was a day program. 1,500 kids came each day at noon for a meal.

I couldn't believe the number, and asked her if I had heard her correctly.

"Yes," she said in a matter-of-fact way. "It started with a lot less. But then as the war got worse, it grew. And now we feed 1,500 a day. And I am starting an AIDS hospice. And we are going to get a radio station going too."

She said that she was registered with the Ugandan government only as a day care centre, and so she would just run the hospice in a low-key way. She said the radio station would never broadcast anything political; she would stay out of politics. But, she explained, the local community could use a radio station – for weather reports and music.

I asked her, "On top of all that you are doing, can you really also manage a hospice?"

"It is not that difficult," she replied. "It is not that hard to sit and hold the hand of someone who is dying."

I left Aunt Irene believing that I had met a real saint. Her dedication and sacrifice put mine into perspective in a humbling way.

Further on our journey we met young people who had escaped the LRA. Young girls impregnated while with the LRA, now mothers, trying to rebuild their lives. We met young boys, returned fighters, who were trying to find a future with so little to go on, with a past too horrible to remember; but in some cases, because it had provided a role, a place, a way of life, it was too powerful to forget.

But the war, this ramped-up, American-blessed phase of it, was only just beginning.

What, if anything, should we do?

What could we do? We had little to no support from the international community. While the UK and Norway were weighing in with the US on peace in Sudan, through Sumbeiywo in Kenya, they were not interested here. I believed that mere conflict resolution workshops and any community-based efforts that we might undertake in the north were worse than palliative. The World Bank might be thinking about 'post-conflict peacebuilding', anticipating an end to the LRA, but in my opinion it was too early. The people had told us they needed more. They needed to influence peace talks with their needs being added to the mix. More importantly, we had been told almost to the person that a military victory against Kony would not bring a lasting peace. A political solution was needed.

Sylvia recommended that we stick with our strengths. That there must be something we could do that built on the success we had had in implementing the Nairobi Agreement, maybe something at the official diplomatic level. Chris pressed me to get President Carter involved in an effort to influence Museveni or Washington. Chris was convinced the LRA wanted talks, or they would soon. I had Kony in the back of my mind. He had agreed to talks two summers ago. I knew this because I had asked him.

In these matters, things take time. Professor William Zartman had coined the phrase, 'ripe for resolution'. He argued that in many disputes a hurting stalemate may be needed. Both sides must reach an impasse, but more so, they must feel sufficient levels of pain to be motivated to peace talks. The dispute has to be 'ripe' for 'resolution'

Were we there?

No.

Could you 'ripen' a situation that wasn't yet ripe for resolution? Theoretically, yes. And yes, because we had ripened it in Sudan.

Could we ripen it here in northern Uganda? Maybe, but not very likely. The Carter Center did not have any leverage that would move the USA, Museveni or Kony. As we ended our trip and headed home I was left wondering what if anything we could do?

With the security situation getting worse in the north, I told Chris to withdraw to Kampala, far south and removed from the violence. But he was idling away. His informal probing of the international community verified things were exactly as we thought. With the exception of a couple of sympathetic political officers in one or two embassies, Operation Iron First was a given. We would find no support to bring influence upon Museveni. In fact, my old friend, Mbabazi, now Minister of Defence, was making routine visits to Khartoum and the Government of Sudan was, whether reluctantly or not, extending its authorization to Uganda to find and fight Kony in Sudan.

More time passed. And as it did, we managed to host Garang to a visit at The Carter Center. He not only had a cordial and productive private dinner meeting with President Carter and our team but was also given a public forum to present his views to a standing-room-only crowd.

Later, at a senior meeting at The Carter Center, President Carter asked me to write the draft Sudan peace agreement. Now this was something I had not envisaged! I had thought that maybe one day, way down the road; but now? Before talks had begun? I hesitated, worried about the timing and the handling of such a sensitive document.

This, however, was vintage Carter. He was going to kick-start this peace process. He had always been of the mind that an elite-centered peace process was needed. In this case get Bashir and Garang in a room, with adequate US backing and international support, and an agreement could be achieved. I had begun to believe he was right about that. Despite my agreement with the assertion made by peace scholars about the need for community-based bottom-up peace processes, inclusiveness, and ripeness to ensure the sustainability of a peace accord, I was inclined to agree that with the right amount of effort and methods to bolster and sustain it, an elite-centered process could be effective. After all, Yahia had said as much, so had Kiir, Garang's second-in-command.

So Carter's request was not out of the question. Instead, I questioned his timing. My experience, which I had shared with Sumbeiywo just as Carter had shared his view, was that the mediator's 'single negotiated text' should be introduced about 60 per cent of the way into the negotiations. Both sides should have ample time to get preliminary views on the table, to explore each other's positions and interests, and begin to look to the mediator for assistance. The 'single negotiated text' should remain in the mediator's hands so he/she can manage it and amend the many critical drafts it will undergo. Then a well-drafted text that reflected, literally, language and views and options already asserted by the parties, embellished by insights and options put forward by the mediator, would most likely be accepted by all parties as the final agreement.

But Carter wanted me to write a draft peace agreement now!

We could do it, although I had real reservations about doing it now, before the talks had really begun. President Carter could see I was resisting. I didn't want to disagree with him on such a fundamental technical judgement call in front of my colleagues, his employees.

So I asked him, "Do you really want to get into this now, here?"

"Sure, why not?" he had responded, smiling at me.

The room went silent as I explained my reservations and as I was doing so it occurred to me that he had promised this document to Walter Kansteiner! He must have told Kansteiner, the Africa lead from the US State Department, Powell's man, that he would write up a draft peace agreement to get things going. In fact, that was probably why he had returned so energized from his tour of countries in the south of Africa to Nairobi. Whether or not Kansteiner had really wanted the document, Carter was going to do it. He was charged up in having a piece of the peace action. And of course, that was why he had taken great pains with Sumbeiywo, giving him a lesson on writing single text peace agreements.

As these thoughts flashed through my mind with Carter's penetrating gaze upon me, I nevertheless continued, trying to make my point on technical merit. And I could feel some tension developing between us. He persisted, acknowledging my concerns and saying we would talk about the details of how and when to give it to Sumbeiywo and Kansteiner after I had written it. He obviously wanted the document, but he had also heard me. I acknowledged right there that he was the boss, saying that I appreciated he had heard my concerns and that I appreciated his willingness to consult on how and when we introduced it. I said I would write it.

As to the technical task of writing a draft peace agreement, although I felt challenged, I knew we could do it. I prepared to take the lead on it, set the direction and tone of it.

I flew home to Canada and I walked around for two days, on that weekend, thinking about the draft peace agreement that I was now responsible for writing. I had written a number of agreements over my years as a mediator. One had been the very comprehensive document outlining the terms and details of the healing and reconciliation agreement in The Helpline case. I had also crafted agreements that dealt with complex land use and public policy disputes. At least a dozen times in the past I had used the 'single negotiated text' procedure. But I had not written a peace agreement intended to capture all of the elements that would secure a lasting peace in a war-torn country.

Two days later I had a draft outline, with most of the preamble well developed and nearly all of the eventual sections anticipated. I returned to The Carter Center and I assigned sections to my staff according to my assessment of their strengths. As I gave my assignments to my team members, setting timelines I insisted that I retain control of the drafting. Everyone delved into his respective task and at the end of a week we had a good draft. But we had policy questions galore. Questions such as: were we going to stick with a united Sudan as the overall goal, with adequate and legitimate means by which the south could realize its aspirations; would there be an interim period before a referendum on self determination; should we specify what the referendum would ask, and of whom; would Garang contemplate being the Vice President of a united Sudan; what would happen to internally displaced people; would there be a ceasefire and when; what about oil revenues and wealth sharing; and who would monitor and who would guarantee the commitments made?

We produced a final draft document that I asked to be annotated for President Carter's review. I met with him and he said that he liked it. He asked me if I agreed with him to send it to Kansteiner.

"What about Sumbeiywo?" I asked.

He said that it could be released simultaneously. So I sent Tom to Washington to walk Kansteiner and his staff through it and I went to Kenya. And we all agreed that no one need ever know that we had drafted this document.

Tom reported that the Washington team was attentive, agreed with some of it, and had other views on other parts. That seemed reasonable.

When I presented the draft agreement to Sumbeiywo he was shocked. He was genuinely surprised and grateful that we had worked with such focus and such speed. He was keen to read it and talk about how to introduce it to Garang and Bashir.

Other than this telling now, for years I never mentioned to anyone that we had done that. It was almost six months later, however, that someone approached me and said they thought that the agreement that was circulating from the Sudan peace talks looked a lot like the draft my team and I had written. Are there any secrets!

As it turned out, however, my meeting with Sumbeiywo was indeed on the eve of historic talks between the Government of Sudan and the Sudan People's Liberation Movement.

They began on July 18, 2002 in Machakos, Kenya. We were not there. Rather, on July 21, in Atlanta, I was one of several speakers addressing one of The Carter Center's regular audiences, a group of supporters called the Ambassador's Circle.

I stood up and noted that while we were not at the talks, and not mediating, that on July 18 the first ever serious talks that have the promise of peace in Sudan had begun in Kenya. They were being mediated by General Lazaro Sumbeiywo with the active support of three key international actors, the US, the UK, and Norway. And while there may never be any public recognition of the role The Carter Center had played over the past ten years, and especially the past two and one half years, they (members of the audience) could be assured that we had helped make peace a possibility. We had started with a flawed, indeed, moribund peace process in Kenya and helped give it credibility and focus. We built and maintained relationships between the warring sides. We overcame a hostile policy environment in Washington. And we had been vigilant in tracking and understanding the complexity of the conflict so that the elements of the parties, the process and the policy environment were in as good an alignment as we could influence them to be. A forgotten war of nineteen years with two million dead and four million displaced now might end, in part, through our efforts to 'wage peace'.

14

The Work Of Sisyphus

Late in July and early August, 2002, we received written notes from the LRA stating that they wished peace talks. One, from Vincent Otti, identified as Brigadier Vincent Otti (a copy of which I now keep posted on the bulletin board in my home office) is a letter addressed to religious leaders, traditional leaders and all other leaders. In it he refers to a total of ninety-nine women, girls and boys being returned to the community by the LRA so that they may start a new life. The letter requests from the leaders to: "Please receive them well to show solidarity that you are really interested in peace. However should we hear that they have been harassed or mistreated in any way then that will show that you the religious leaders, the traditional leaders and other representatives of Acholi are not serious about the peace that you have been talking about in Gulu, Kampala, and other parts of the world."

This letter itemized the number and condition of the ninety-nine returnees. For example, some were listed as 'pregnant', others as 'infant'. And the letter ends "We are ready to receive anyone who is interested in meeting us in regard to peace."

Therefore the evidence was mounting that ours and other efforts to reach out to the LRA were having an impact. Some more skeptical people said that they saw the release of these LRA abductees as an indication that Operation Iron Fist was having a deleterious impact on the LRA. The LRA, they asserted, were hurting and trying to shed dead weight. These skeptics thought that being hunted by the Ugandan army with the support of US surveillance, the LRA needed now, more than ever, to be mobile and fleet of foot. The pregnant women and infants were just unneeded baggage.

Chris, who had now returned north and once again had penetrated deep into the community in Gulu, had recruited contacts in the camps for internally displaced people. They said that their information was that Kony wanted peace talks. Although these contacts clearly walked a fine line between the government and the LRA and their information may have been false, I was inclined to believe this.

To test whether the LRA was serious about peace, I orchestrated a number of moves with Chris and Jeff's help. Louis first made contact with two men who were identified as LRA couriers, and they were quietly introduced to Chris. Then, through them, a message asking for a meeting was sent to senior LRA Commanders. The two couriers took separate routes, in case one or the other was killed by government troops or by LRA warriors suspicious of us. After painstaking secret arrangements handled again by Chris and Jeff a meeting took place in the bush. And then, to test whether these alleged LRA commanders really were who they said they were (and they were also the ones who had said they wanted peace talks) we pushed further. I prepared an information package for Joseph Kony and I prepared it in a way that if the Government learned about it, it would not impair our perceived impartiality. It was a description of how peace talks should proceed: the steps; timeframe; and the role of a mediator. Although we knew it might take weeks for the package to get to Kony and weeks for us to hear a response, we waited, expectantly.

In October, still waiting for a response from Kony, I flew with Chris to meet President Museveni in Gulu. We wanted to inform him that we were in contact with the LRA. The flight to the north was arranged in a hurry with the assistance of the Government's head of external security. He was a man who I had never felt comfortable with but he was also an opportunist who had political ambitions and he could move on things if he sensed there was a pay-off for him. So he had manoeuvred with Museveni's staff to get us an appointment immediately in Gulu.

The plane we rented had a single prop, not a recommended craft to take, but the only one available for hire. As we flew at a low altitude through a clear blue sky I could see the Nile flowing below. Unlike the way the Nile snakes slowly through Sudan, the water was rushing here, white foam spraying up. The vitality of Uganda always energized me. But later, as we descended, approaching the small runway, I could see two military gunships sitting like iron dragonflies on the tarmac below us. They were being loaded for another attack on the LRA. And in the distance, as we banked for the landing, I could see clouds of smoke on the horizon, just beyond Gulu. I wondered whose hut was being burned, what horrors were going on in a battle zone so close to the town. I wondered who, really, wins a war like this one; and what child might be dying now.

We landed, and waited in the courtyard of a make-shift military base on the outskirts of Gulu, where Museveni was now encamped. A woman in the compound offered us fried chicken and a drink as we sweltered in the hot sun. Then I got the signal: Museveni would see us. In full military uniform, Museveni had taken charge of Operation Iron Fist. He looked more at home in a military uniform and here in a war zone than I recalled him at his palace in the centre of Kampala. He recognized me, and welcomed Chris and I to sit in a row of chairs that had been assembled in front of a crude desk where he sat. The President at war.

I told him that if he wanted to test whether Kony was serious and was capable of talks, we could assist because we had made inroads to the LRA senior command. I believed talks were possible. At the very least, I urged, Kony should be tested as to whether he really was capable of talks. If given a real chance, and he failed, then Museveni would surely have the sympathy and support he needed to continue his military action against the LRA. I described my approach as a 'rifle shot', with our focus only on Kony. We could help him if he would give us time to get to Kony and let only one process proceed with both leaders in direct contact. He accepted our offer.

And thereafter ensued another series of secret moves with LRA contacts, and high level meetings with Museveni's senior officials, all directed at the goal of holding peace talks with the LRA. Somehow, however, something always spoiled our efforts. I received desperate calls by cell phone to my home in the middle of the night from LRA fighters. They were under attack and there was the sound of battle in the background. In those brief calls they pleaded with me to get The Carter Center to lead talks. But nothing solid materialized.

Then, just after Christmas 2002, Kony phoned in to an open air radio talk show on Gulu FM. His remarks about Museveni, and about peace talks in particular, while not strictly in conformity with the package I had sent him months before, accorded enough to suggest he had received our material – and that he wanted meaningful talks. He mentioned The Carter

Center and the foiled plans for an elders' meeting and emphasized that he doubted Museveni's sincerity for talks.

Of course, Chris, Jeff and I all hoped this would be a breakthrough. But no.

The hope of talks were spoiled by signals from the Government that it did not take seriously our contacts with the LRA. On more than one occasion the Government launched its own peace initiative, confounding the community and interfering with our progress. People who pressed for peace were attacked and some were killed, always under dubious circumstances cloaked in a veil of misinformation. No one could tell exactly who had done the killing. And now Chris and Jeff were beginning to come under pressure. It came to a violent head. On a crowded road in Gulu, a crazed motorcyclist charged down the road forcing people to dive into the roadside ditches, so Jeff and Chris did the same. But then, looking up, they could see the motorcyclist coming right back, his engine revving. Before Jeff could get out of the way for a second time, he was struck and he was thrown several feet as the bike careened. Everyone was in shock. Jeff lay on the road, a huge slice out of his calf, his leg badly broken. His injury was so serious that within hours he was airlifted to South Africa for emergency surgery. The motorcyclist was arrested and when asked to produce identification, provided a card from the Ugandan intelligence agency.

Now both David Lord and Jeff had paid personally for peace. And despite an increasingly bloody war whose pace was accelerated by Operation Iron Fist, which extended from dry season to wet, and back again, we came no closer to real talks than we had been nearly a year before, in July, 2002. I realized that we were now struggling unsuccessfully for peace three full years after Kony had told me personally that he would talk to Museveni.

I was 99 per cent certain that Operation Iron First would grind on. And I knew Kony would retaliate with ferocity. There was no 'hurting stalemate' in sight. This grueling war was not 'ripe for resolution'. Indeed, I concluded that Museveni was committed only to achieving a military victory. I believed that it was now time to pull out. I was convinced that by staying engaged, without success or even small steps that suggested peace talks were possible, we were becoming a part of the circus of war, a potential foil to whomever our presence suited their ends. We had to leave the country – the responsible thing to do, as difficult as it was. We had failed. Why stay around to witness and in any way aid and abet the horror!

But Chris pressed me to not abandon our peace efforts, and the people. So in June, 2003, I made a final visit to Uganda to test, one last time, whether there was any hope of peace talks – of any sort, involving anyone.

It didn't take more than a half day of meetings with representatives from the international diplomatic community, with government officials, and with Chris to conclude it was all over. And it pained me to meet with a traditional Acholi elder that evening and to tell him we were pulling out as he pleaded with me to stay. He had just come from a UN office where he had asked the local UN representative to send peacekeepers into the north.

Of course, I knew his plea would not be heard. The deck was stacked against peace in northern Uganda. The US was backing Museveni. The war in Sudan was still a big factor. But I did not tell him. Instead, I suggested he mobilize efforts to bring the war in the north into the homes, minds and hearts of the people right here, in Kampala. I said that the people of Uganda must want peace; they must press their government to enter talks. For the war in the north, not 400 miles away, despite newspaper coverage, was somehow beyond the pale of consciousness in the country's capital. How could the UN take it seriously if the international diplomatic community didn't, if the US was lined up behind Museveni, and if the people themselves did not care?

Sudan, to the credit of everyone who had pushed for peace there, and after false starts and setbacks, had come to the brink of peace. It took a lot longer than the 'three weeks' I had been told would be needed. But it was done!

General Sumbeiywo and his team, with backing from the US, UK, Norway, and Italy too, had pressed on and in the spring of 2004 an historic agreement was signed by the Government of Sudan and the SPLA.

All of us who had been relegated to the margins, yet were watching the whole thing from afar, celebrated this victory for peace. I sent congratulatory notes to the people I knew, and who had been involved in the talks. The world took note. The US prepared to host Dr. John Garang and President al Bashir to a signing ceremony in Washington over which President Bush would preside. It would be a signal to the world that even though the US was now perpetrating war in Iraq, and had alienated many Arab countries, it had done a good thing in Sudan; that it was capable of promoting, mediating, and supporting peace in that troubled, indeed, increasingly delicate region of the world.

Then a new war came on everyone's radar screen. This time it was in Darfur, in western Sudan.

Festering for years, and replicating so many of the features of the war that had been waged for some 20 years between Khartoum and the SPLA, Darfur had turned into a humanitarian crisis. Upwards of 200,000 people had died as African villagers were being driven from their homes by militias in the employ of Khartoum. It all sounded too familiar!

As the crisis in Darfur continues to worsen the Government of Sudan in Khartoum is losing the high ground that it had achieved with the international community by forging peace with the SPLM; and that peace is precarious.

How easy it is to see that those who work for peace do the work of Sisyphus. We push the peace stone up the mountain of human suffering, so often to find that it rolls back down. But when, for a moment, we push that stone to the mountain's peak, and it stays there, perhaps teetering, we celebrate that which is in the heart of good people everywhere. We see ourselves in others, and our fears are replaced with a capacity for great civility and tolerance.

Our fingers are still crossed for Sudan.

15

Transformation

There is a joke among former employees that, 'Yes, indeed, there is life after The Carter Center'. But it is a hard act to follow. You play at the top of your game there and you can have an impact far beyond that of so many other people in the peacebuilding field. But there comes a time to leave and it wasn't long after the signing of the Sudan Comprehensive Peace Agreement that I knew my time had arrived.

I left with mixed feelings. Not about whether I should move on, professionally, but about what I had or had not accomplished in those intensive three and a half years. I was angry at President Museveni. It was my firm view that he wanted to hunt down and kill Kony, and it did not matter how many innocent children were mutilated and killed along the way. I felt terrible. I felt I had failed in northern Uganda. I could not let go, and for months afterwards kept checking the internet daily and with Chris who was no longer active but living in Kampala, keeping abreast of every move. Indeed, Chris too must have stayed engaged because one day he called to say that Louis had died of AIDS. He had gone the way of his brothers. We agreed to try to help his widow, Daisy, as a personal gesture. But my time had passed and I was out of the game.

I had retreated to join Ann at our home in the Canadian hills, deep in the woods on a lake. I had begun to hand-carve bowls from wooden burls found on the hardwood trees in the forests surrounding us. The weeks passed uneventfully. I was enjoying the fact that for all intents and purposes

I was finally unemployed. I had no commitments. And I wanted none. No more calls in the middle of the night from rebels in the bush. No more urgent trips to conduct a mediation session half way around the world. No more staff to direct. No more people to impress. Instead, I kept a low profile and worked on my carving, finding great pleasure in working with wood.

Then the call came.

It was like the popular TV show 'Murder She Wrote'. Nine people were invited by a wealthy older gentleman to collect at an inn on the US Atlantic coast. No one knew who else was invited. Instructions for us were in brown envelopes at the inn's front desk. Our assignment, which had been given to us when we were invited, was to answer this question: 'Can mass violence be reduced?'

In the hours alone at the inn the night before the meeting I thought about the theories on the causes of war and the many opinions about how to stop wars and to build peace. Bottom-up; top-down; middle-out. That is, take a lot of time and construct peace from the grassroots up; or get the leaders together and hammer out a peace agreement at the top, hoping it will trickle down; or find people in a society at war who are in the middle, connected to the grassroots but also influential with the leaders – and help them sow and nourish the seeds of peace.

My opinion was that different cases call for different approaches and really tough cases like Sudan require a balance of all three approaches at the same time. But I'm inclined to look for the leaders; the war lords and the peace lords. The war lords are the ones prepared to use power abusively. And I look for would-be peace lords in peace loving countries, like the US and the UK, those from middle powers like Norway and Canada – who are needed to stop the violence and to help transform the way power is used by the war lords. I think more can be achieved faster if leaders are brought on board. Expediency is critical in eliminating the violence and the pain that people perpetrate on others.

In reality, I had found that war lords and peace lords, as political animals, share many similarities. The task of getting peace lords to take up peace and war lords to give up violence is a central challenge. Both are self-interested. Both often have a narrow short-term focus. They are committed to what has worked for them in the past. They love power and don't like to share it. They are moved by cold calculations of what will be best for them and their constituency. Thus, there would have been no US-led peace effort in Sudan unless someone could persuade President George W. Bush to act like a peace lord. That is why we worked to get the crucial meeting with Reverend Franklin Graham, who could persuade Bush to act in the interest of peace.

I had come to this conclusion about violence and power and leaders in a cold sweat in Mostar, years before. I realized then that violence, not conflict, is the enemy of peace. The term 'violent conflict' is an unhelpful conflation for those really seized with the challenge of ending violence and nurturing peace. Why treat 'violent' as an adjective when it is the removal of violence itself that should be our focus, when we work for peace? Why say 'post-conflict peacebuilding' when we know it is really post-violence peacebuilding – as though conflict is now over with the signing of a peace agreement?

Some have said that this is really a semantic issue and that I am misguided in my diagnostic obsession with 'Violence'. They questioned me saying that conflict can be expressed non-violently and what is it that I see as being wrong with the goal of 'conflict transformation'?

But my point is that I have come to believe that conflict is really a *symptom* of violence. In trying to resolve conflict in war zones, I found over the years that I was confronting violence itself. I was becoming so clearly aware of the impact that violent people had on others as well as coming to appreciate the real implications of the term 'structural violence'. This occurred to me when I began to look at the root causes of 'violent conflict'. In addition to the nasty deeds of violent people I discovered that structural violence was a profound factor in the emergence of most 'violent conflict'. Indeed, conflict emerges as a symptom of the underlying violence. Those who suffer this underlying, persistent, structural violence find themselves in conflict with the source of the violence. They experience conflict (tension, disharmony, incompatible interests) with the oppressor or with oppressive structures. Failing to resolve the symptomatic conflict through peaceful means, and suffering continued violation, it is not surprising that some groups turn to violence in an attempt to rise out of their violent circumstances.

So, clearly, violence can beget violence. If we are to build peace, my working assumption is that we should focus on its enemy: violence. That means that I now focus on the actual actors and factors that are in themselves a form of violence, or are likely to violate someone. Of course there is conflict in these cases. And on the positive side there are actors and factors that are peaceful or auger well for peace. But I no longer worry as much about the conflict (the symptom) and I pay less attention to trying to 'transform' the 'conflict'. It is something deeper that requires transformation.

Now, when I look at violence closely, whether it is open hostility or structural, I realize I am confronting the way in which power is being used. For my purposes, power is the ability to affect outcomes. Power is intentional. The product of power is not merely a 'change' that occurs by chance. Embedded within this definition of power are the actor's values. The values the actor holds give license to the actor to use power abusively or foster him to use it non-abusively, constructively and collaboratively.

My efforts at violence prevention (and building peace) are therefore aimed at the goal of transforming the way power is being used or expressed, by individuals and/or systems. The transformation of power from abusive to liberating forms is deeply challenging. Underlying it, however, is the deepest of all challenges, dealing with values. I assume that those who use power abusively must hold a set of values that 'enables' or 'permits' them to use power to violate. Systems that are oppressive likewise are sustained by an implicit set of values condoning oppression. Preventing violence and building peace must inevitably turn to the issue of values.

This set of beliefs had left me feeling alone. I felt like a renegade, a traitor to my friends and colleagues in the field of conflict resolution and peacebuilding. I was not talking about semantics. I was talking about hating violence as the stubborn enemy of peace. And after Sudan and my dealings with Joseph Kony my language was changing. Targeting, eliminating, and neutralizing became the words of choice. I had little time or patience for dialogue processes that seem to go nowhere, or building empathy, or for nonviolent resistance. I had concluded that I would not lie down in front of the tanks if they were moving in to capture my town, to rape Ann, kill our sons. I would get a gun and resist them with force. Likewise in my peacebuilding work I would use whatever legal means available to neutralize any war lord who refused peace talks and kept killing with impunity.

Most peace workers, however, I have found, make a good number of false assumptions when they are dealing with war lords and peace lords. They assume that what is of importance to them should be important to war lords and peace lords. They assume that their values and their positions on issues should be shared by war lords and peace lords. And they assume that when their issues are or become important to war lords and peace lords they will remain important. They make the mistake that access to leaders implies influence over them. That their information will change leaders' behaviour because they are rational and surely what they are being told will be persuasive. Not so.

In a nutshell, that comprised the answer I formulated for the meeting of nine held at the home of Milt and Helen Lauenstein, down the road from the inn on Cape Ann, in December, 2003.

The group Milt pulled together changed a bit over the first few meetings and in the end we answered his question in the affirmative. We said war can be prevented.

Milt wanted evidence and was prepared to put his money where his mouth was.

"Show me," he challenged. "Show me that prevention works."

So after The Carter Center that is what I am doing now. Dr. Michael Lund, a colleague, put together the initial approach we would take to prevention, based on his research into best practices. The goal was to pick a country likely to become openly violent if left on its current course. We wanted to get in early, long before the predicted outburst of violence and diagnose the problem with local leaders and other actors such as the UN agencies active in the country. We intended to work behind the scenes as a catalyst, stimulating preventive action; and stay involved until the causes of violence are removed and sustainable peace is predicted.

It sounds clear and straightforward enough. It isn't.

Thank goodness we picked a small country. One that most of us thought would be less complicated than others on our list that are predicted to explode, or collapse into anarchy.

We picked Guinea-Bissau, a small country of about 1.5 million people situated on the western-most tip of Africa. This was a country that none of our working group had heard of, let alone knew anything about. To the north is The Gambia and Senegal, and to the south is Guinea-Conakry. Guinea-Bissau is largely an agricultural society, and its coastal waters are rich in fish stocks. Since fighting a long war of independence from Portugal in 1974, the last war of independence in Africa, Guinea-Bissau has suffered recurrent military coups, some bloodless, and some bloody. This has kept the country in a state of chronic instability, thwarting its development. When we identified Guinea-Bissau as a candidate for violence prevention it was still staggering from the destruction of its economy that had been caused by a short, violent rebellion in 1998–99. It is the sixth poorest country in the world.

So I'm back in Africa again. This time, with Milt's money, I'm working pretty much on my own. I have a small hand-picked team but we are operating on a shoe string. We don't have the trappings of The Carter Center. I did not automatically have the access to political elites – presidents, ambassadors, top UN personnel – that President Carter was able to give me. And this time my job is to prevent a war, unlike my assignment at The Carter Center where I was explicitly tasked with ending one.

I knew that to be effective I had to take a 'whole of problem' approach, which I had wanted to do in Sudan but in the end I had not received Carter's support. In Guinea-Bissau I resolved that we would have to target our actions to remove or neutralize the actors and the factors likely to create violence; those that stand in the way of peace. That would not be so bad if you were able to get a clear sense of who the good guys are and who the bad guys are. And if the situation was relatively stable; maybe desperate, but relatively stable. But it is has been anything but stable in Guinea-Bissau.

Just as we were about to leave on our first trip to the country the head of the armed forces was assassinated. I thought to myself, well so much for getting in early!

Nevertheless, I led my team of five into the country under a 'yellow alert' from contacts we had in the US Embassy in Dakar, Senegal, the major country in the region. We were told to proceed with caution. So we went, a political scientist, a security expert, a woman with expertise in development, a logistics man, and me. Through the one solid contact we had on the ground, an American aid worker, we were introduced to a local woman, Macaria Barai, who has become the 'go-to' person for us. Within a day of our arrival she had arranged for us to meet all of the people that we would need to give us a true impression of Guinea-Bissau, and its suitability for the type of violence prevention activities we had planned. We met government people, the few key foreign aid workers, a handful of business people still active in the country, local peace activists, and a couple of academics. Four days into our mission in the country, however, I ordered that we pull out early, for our own safety.

An informant from the army had asked if he could meet me, alone. Dressed in civilian clothes, in hushed tones he had told me that there would be a coup within days. He urged me to immediately alert the international community to how serious the inter-ethnic rivalry would become. He said the Balanta, the 'warrior' tribe, comprised 95 per cent of the army – they had all the guns. He informed me that they wanted control over the politicians. Assassinated General Seabra had been a professional soldier, and because he was not playing along with the politicians, he had been killed. My informant, visibly shaken, predicted a bloodbath if things did not go the way the Balanta wished.

It was an extreme view, perhaps. But how were we to know it wasn't accurate? Especially when other people began to make the same noises. A coup d'état was a real possibility. And it could be bloody. So we retreated to Dakar on a heavily packed airplane. Others obviously thought the same as us. There were some pretty high-placed people on board and not an empty seat.

A few days passed and I realized we should return to the US and wait for the dust to settle. We believed we already had enough information to make a decision about whether we had anything to offer Guinea-Bissau. Two months later, although unstable, without any further violence occurring in the country, we decided to return to Guinea-Bissau. Our clear aim was to show that political violence can be prevented. Three and a half years now, with fourteen visits behind me, it has been a roller coaster ride from the get-go.

There have been triggers for violence at every turn in the road. These are actors and factors that if not neutralized, have the potential to 'trigger' violence. In my view, they are more often than not a form of violence themselves: people who have or will act violently to achieve their objectives; or structural conditions that are a form of violence, similar to what I had found in the Crimea.

The first trigger in this country that had to be neutralized was the presidential election, which was scheduled for the spring of 2005, just a few short months after General Seabra had been murdered. One of the candidates in the election was Kumba Yala, a former president of Guinea-Bissau who had been removed from office by a bloodless coup d'état. He was bound by a legal charter that he had signed to stay out of politics for some time. Certainly by signing this charter he was to keep out of the presidential race. He claimed, however, that he had signed the charter with a gun to his head, that he was the rightful president of Guinea-Bissau, and that he did not have to honour the charter.

Another candidate in the election, former president 'Nino' Vierria, literally dropped into the country out of the sky. Forced into exile after being defeated in the rebellion in 1999, Nino returned in a helicopter. Without official approval to enter the country he landed to a large group of supporters assembled in the local football field and announced his intention to run for president.

Now Kumba Yala and Nino were in the race.

It was obvious that we had both loaded and loose cannons on our hands. Violence could have easily erupted right there and then; especially if the Armed Forces, still simmering from the recent assassination, decided to get into the mix. And the country was now in the hands of General Tagme Wai, a war of independence hero who was a member of the Balanta Tribe. No one knew where Tagme stood.

What could be done to prevent violence?

The answer was easy enough to say. Make sure the presidential candidates acted responsibly. Keep the armed forces out of politics. Do whatever we could to ensure a fair and free election. But with limited resources and no access to the ruling President or the Prime Minister, I acted on my intuition and the assessment I had made on our first visit.

On that visit, although we had been in the country only a few days, I was struck by a powerful sense of déjà vu. The difference was that I was in an African country, not one in Latin America. But the similarities were striking. It had only been a year or so before, when at The Carter Center I had been called in to assess conditions after the failed coup d'état in Venezuela. I had met with President Chavez at his palace late one evening just after he had been released from custody. Charismatic, although visibly shaken, he chain-smoked throughout the meeting, even dropping his cigarette one time as he fumbled nervously with it. But he was very hospitable as I am sure that he had fond feelings toward President Carter, who had sent me and a colleague to meet him. We were friends at a time when he must surely have wondered who, if anyone, he could trust.

What I noticed during our work in Venezuela, however, was that a handful of families ran the country. It was a good old fashioned oligarchy that Chavez was trying to turn on its head. Even the labour party seemed to be in the hands of a few well-heeled leaders. Labour certainly didn't have the 'blue-collar' feel that I had expected.

And Venezuela had reminded me of Ecuador, where I had gone just a couple of years before that; another coup. This time the President was driven out and we were working with the Vice President. In both cases the need for national reconciliation was the buzz-word. My job was to determine how to make that happen.

So, the dynamics in Guinea-Bissau were similar to what I had found in

Venezuela and in Ecuador. That is, a few families, the elite, run the country with the majority of people left outside the palace gates, outside the circle of power. The majority barely subsisted but the few rich lived at the pinnacle of wealth. The rich, that is, who were currently in power. Guinea-Bissau looked like another small country run by a few families who drove Mercedes, sent their children to university abroad, and lived lavish lifestyles while the general population barely survived.

It was like a Shakespearean play. The curtain is down. The audience – mostly peasants – have no idea what is going on behind the curtain. Then the curtain rises. Caesar has been killed. The people gasp, but have little information or insight into who killed Caesar. And they know they can do nothing about it in any case. They wait, working their fields, or fishing, just subsisting. Some things take place on stage, visibly, for the peasants to see. Then the curtain falls again. And the people are left to wonder what might follow. Who will be killed next? How will it change their miserable lives, if at all?

On our initial trip, just after General Seabra had been assassinated, and having been told to be ready for 'act two', I concluded that we would have to get to those in power, and soon. We would have to get behind the curtain. We would have to work with the few elite actors who rose and fell from power in an endless struggle that might this time be bloodless, the next, bloody. If we didn't get the elite to change the way they used power abusively, and at the same time empower the people, I maintained we would waste a lot of Milt's money and our time.

Given this scenario, I was surprised to hear a news story that General Tagme Wai, the new head of the armed forces, was talking about the need for reconciliation in Guinea-Bissau. That was not a term I had expected to hear in a country whose political culture was violent, marked by a pattern of attack and revenge. He was talking about the need to get the various tribes within the armed forces working together and to get factions within the dominant Balanta tribe to agree to stay out of politics; to stick to soldiering, united under his command.

That was the first real sign we had that there might be a conciliatory mood in the military, at least at the senior command. Furthermore, to my mind he was touching a theme that applied to the whole country. The need for national reconciliation. And I decided that we would have to build on it, fast. So I met with General Tagme as soon as I could. I wanted to reinforce his commitment to reconciliation and his commitment to stay out of politics. I wanted to support his professional military conduct. I wanted to be his ally because I believed he held Guinea-Bissau's future in his hands. If he could unite the armed forces by overcoming inter-tribal rivalry; if he could keep the military out of politics; and if he could stabilize the country enough that it could go down the path of healing and reconciliation, then we were on the right road to preventing mass violence.

I met him at his headquarters not far from the centre of the city. I could see that he was a physically strong man, in his mid-sixties. He wore his uniform proudly, his shoulders square and his head held high. He was reputed to be illiterate, although as I had entered his office he had made the appearance of reading a document lying in front of him on his desk. As we shook hands I noticed he had a disfigured left eye, I thought perhaps a war wound. It is off-putting at first but as you come to know him, as I have, he just comes over as the 'real McCoy'. There is no nonsense with Tagme and he wastes no words. Everyone around him is deferential, almost subservient.

We had the first of many good meetings. I believe that my background as an officer in the prison system in Canada years before, and all the work I had done in war zones and with security and intelligence people in Uganda and Sudan, served me well. We communicated instantly, even though it was through an interpreter. I told him how much I admired and respected the stand he was taking. I told him he was the key ingredient in efforts to stabilize Guinea-Bissau and put it on the right track. With his effort one day Guinea-Bissau might be governed by politicians who had learned they could not manipulate the armed forces. I asked him what he needed from us to help him in that task.

He replied briefly, requesting technical assistance to develop military policy, and for equipment; for anything that might improve the life of his soldiers – right down to improved living conditions. He explained that the rank and file lived in deplorable barracks, had little to eat and very poor salaries. I took that to mean they were therefore also easily manipulated by any politician that might say 'come with me, do my bidding, and you will live well.'

I promised I would do what I could, but I made it clear that I was not representing a large donor organization with lots of money to hand out, that we were more of a hands-on group of people who specialized in working with local leaders to map out violence prevention actions and plan for peace.

Within weeks, keeping with the theme of reconciliation, I called a meeting of nonpartisan leaders from civil society. The agenda was National Reconciliation. Is it needed? What would it look like? Can we start now?

A dozen people came. One was in an army uniform: Tagme's military liaison.

I put the question to them.

They deliberated in small discussion groups and their reply to the question was – "yes". They said Guinea-Bissau desperately needs national reconciliation. There were many wounds from as many as twenty or more serious acts of political violence. Everyone in the country had been touched by violence. But the timing was wrong. We would never get to a process of national reconciliation if the country did not get through the upcoming presidential election peacefully. Violence was possible. Indeed, it was likely. And it could be widespread.

The group insisted that they needed to work for a free, fair, and peaceful election. And with six weeks to go before the election, they needed to start right away. I seized the moment. I offered immediate financial assistance and we threw our technical support behind them. They took off like a rocket and with our help they succeeded in supporting a non-violent election.

They call themselves the Citizens Good Will Task Force. They were able to get the presidential candidates, except for Kumba Yalla, to sign a code of conduct which we had helped them write. They got the armed forces to commit to staying out of politics and to act as a professional army. They mobilized and financially supported the media so that reporters did not have to succumb to political promises and turn into political hacks. And they placed volunteer peace brigades at election polls, to sort out problems as they arose on election day.

Kumba Yalla proved that he was a loose canon. One night, early into the election campaign, he tried to take possession of the presidential palace. After all, he said, he was the rightful president of Guinea-Bissau. To our great relief General Tagme ordered some soldiers to arrest Yalla and remove him, peacefully, from the palace.

Shortly thereafter I took Milt to meet Tagme and we offered our first concrete form of support; financial assistance to make upgrades to some of the barracks. And I introduced Jeffery, who had been with me at The Carter Center, and retired UK Brigadier General Vere Hayes to work as consultants to General Tagme.

After the incident with Yalla, the election was run peacefully as judged by international observers – thanks in large part to the unbelievably tireless efforts of the Citizens Good Will Task Force. In a run-off vote, Nino prevailed, and took office as the duly elected president.

Then there was another trigger right on the heels of the election. Allegations of political infighting, cronyism, and corruption were producing serious political instability. The World Bank and other international donors began retreating from Guinea-Bissau just when their financial and technical help was so desperately needed. A financial crisis gripped the country. Guinea-Bissau's coffers were empty. Public servants and teachers were going unpaid for weeks, then months.

That turbulence was not easily settled. Elements of it still reverberated two years later. But a degree of stability was achieved. Some international donors, mainly the Portuguese speaking countries, did not abandon Guinea-Bissau. Enough international aid flowed in to just keep the country barely afloat. And the stability came in part because we lobbied for international support, we kept reinforcing the army's professional conduct and we mobilized a national discussion on healing and reconciliation.

This is in a country where local people will be the first to admit that there is blood on nearly everyone's hands. Our efforts to reconstitute and revitalize a credible National Reconciliation Commission provided a climate of conciliation as President Nino faced a crisis of confidence in his government and a new coalition government emerged.

Just as this young government, now allegedly purged of corrupt ministers and senior officials, began to get its feet another crisis has hit: international drug trafficking. The unpatrolled waterways and islands along the country's lush coastline are a stopping place, a safe haven, for cocaine coming from South America en route to continental Europe. Police, military, justice and other senior government officials are now implicated.

What does the new Prime Minister do?

If he presses to arrest and prosecute those involved, he runs the risk of being assassinated. If he doesn't prosecute, his government is compromised. The drug lords will own the country.

When I met the Prime Minister in June, 2007 he was visibly shaken. The drug trafficking story had broken in the *Economist* just weeks earlier. The Prime Minister was certain that a number of key senior officials were implicated. I was meeting him at the request of a senior confidante of mine, to see if we could help.

Now, I am not an expert in drug trafficking. Neither are any of the most active members of my team. My team consisted of my son, Evan, now a political scientist; Philippe Patry, a lawyer trained in conflict resolution; Jeff, my security advisor; and Brigadier Hayes. Expertise on what to do about drug trafficking however is not in their line of work.

Some people thought we should just get out. But I did not think that.

I could not see how our violence prevention efforts should stop because none of my team is expert in that area. Or because it goes beyond the range of peacebuilding activities we might have contemplated at the outset. If drug trafficking is going to lead to the assassination of innocent, well-meaning, duly-elected political leaders when they try to stop it, and if the state is compromised and going to fall into the hands of drug lords if no action is taken, then I saw no alternative but to engage.

In that meeting with the Prime Minister, right on the spot I offered four options to him. I said we could do and say nothing and stick with the program and services we were currently providing in his country; we could go away and sound a loud alarm to the international community; we could go away and sound a quiet alarm to the diplomatic community, to those countries and UN agencies that should be mobilizing now to help Guinea-Bissau; or we could hold a strategy session with a few hand-picked advisors to the Prime Minister, to take place out of the country. No one but those involved would know about the meeting and a strategy for dealing with the drug trafficking threat could be developed.

"Number four," he replied instantly, through my interpreter. And he added, "And quiet diplomacy too."

"How soon?" I asked.

"Now, as soon as you can," and he looked me directly in the eye, adding "I can get shot just leaving this meeting."

Two months later I am back in Guinea-Bissau. Alone this time. I did not want to put any of my team at risk. We had held the strategy session. I had no idea who knew. But I needed to know whether the Prime Minister had taken the initial steps that had been outlined in the strategy. He was to do certain things by certain deadlines. And I didn't know if General Tagme, with whom I had worked closely in the past three years, knew what I was up to. More importantly, I didn't know whether Tagme was one of those implicated. Very regrettably, it was beginning to look like he was. Everyone was talking about the home he had built recently. It was a mansion, well beyond his means on the soldier's salary he received.

I entered the country quietly and deliberately kept a low profile. I had limited my mission to two 'must-dos'. I must meet with the Prime Minister and I must meet with General Tagme. I wanted to look Tagme in the eye. I knew him well enough to trust my face-to-face impression.

I also wanted to meet with a few of the key leaders in civil society, old friends, really; collaborators for peace. We needed to get the Citizens Good Will Task Force, which had run out of steam after the election, re-activated. Other meetings, while important, were not essential.

I stayed at my usual hotel. I took a room on the second story with a balcony that would be hard to reach. I locked my door carefully each time and I tried to secure the door leading to the balcony. I knew that real security was an illusion but I thought I had better do all that I could, within my power.

I laid low.

I began to write this while I waited for my meetings, my faithful interpreter having made contact with the PM and Tagme's chief of staff.

I stayed closer to home at night, visiting the three restaurants in the immediate vicinity of the hotel. I took a flashlight with me as there are no street lights. I drank less alcohol than I might, hoping to keep my wits about me.

I slept poorly.

After two days passed I knew that I would not be meeting Tagme. I have done this kind of thing enough to know when an official is avoiding me. We kept getting evasive responses although my contact kept trying. Somehow Tagme was always busy.

This is not good, I thought. Not good at all.

I thought of all the reasonable reasons why he might not want to meet me. While I had given him moral support in tough times and we had become close enough to embrace upon meeting, I hadn't really been able to deliver much material support. And he needed that. He did not need more visits from international do-gooders or well-intentioned but empty-handed bureaucrats. He needed money, and technical support. He needed equipment and training for his troops. And he needed a real economic project or two that would enable him to de-commission some of the soldiers in his bloated army: they needed jobs that paid and drew them away from a lifelong attachment to the armed forces.

The only substantial thing I had been able to do was provide some financial support to his efforts at reconciling factions within his forces which he had appreciated. And we had tried to help him with a small amount of money that he could use to refurbish the barracks, to show the troops that he could bring in resources that made their lives better, like patching a leaking roof, getting water flowing and the latrines working again. This way the troops might be more prepared to stick with soldiering and not be induced by a political malcontent to join him in yet another coup effort.

These little things had been helpful. And I believe Tagme really appreciated them. But I had not been able to bring any big ticket items into the country. We had tried. Hard. But the international community is not really committed to preventing violence, especially in a little forgotten former Portuguese colony in West Africa. It seems it is almost impossible to attract international resources in these cases until violence breaks out.

So I could see good reason why Tagme might this time simply see no value in meeting with me. In fact, I could see how he deserved to feel fatigued with the likes of me.

But I sensed that it might be more. It might be because he is on the drug lords' payroll.

I then wondered if he might tell the thugs to leave me alone; that I was a small fish.

Day two turned to day three. I only had two days left before my departure.

You have to be ready to wait. That is the way it goes in Africa.

I got a few things done.

I waited. I dozed on the couch.

Then there was a knock at my door.

It was my interpreter saying, "The PM wants to see you, now."

This time I was taken to the Prime Minister's official office. Our meeting would be in the public eye.

The moment I walked into his office I could sense that things had changed.

In June he had been reserved, physically bowed, fearful. This time he rose, dressed in a gold-coloured traditional gown, looking fit and confident.

"Welcome, Dr. Hoffman," he smiled, shaking my hand warmly.

He gestured for me to sit down on a couch at right angles to him, beside another minister in his government, my confidante and initial go-between with the PM. A quiet man by nature, he was smiling warmly too.

"We have heard good things about the strategy session," the PM began, "thank you."

I replied that I was happy it went well, although I wanted to apologize for the length of time it had taken to set it up. I said that I had some difficulty finding the technical experts and I was also hoping to bring some of the donor community along. The Brits, for example, had been interested and helped in the background. But when the session was about to take place, they had backed off. I stated that none of the donors were willing to get out in front of the European Commission. But we were working on that – we were trying to get the donors to put some money in.

He nodded, indicating he understood and shared my frustration with the international community.

"But I have a couple of tough questions for you," I continued. "They are questions that the donors are asking, even if quietly. I think their willingness to help is tied to these."

He nodded patiently, waving his hand for me to continue.

"They have to do with the strategy, and more urgently, with enforcement. Have you taken the first step laid out in the strategy, but more critically, what action have you taken on enforcement. Action against those who you believe are implicated?"

He interrupted me. And with a bravado I could not fathom, he launched into a long diatribe. It sounded like a rehearsed speech that he had given to other visitors from the international community. How he was the Prime Minister. And how he was fighting the drug trafficking. But that he could only set things in motion. The organs of government in a democracy had to take their own action.

Disappointed with this public relations pitch, when I thought we had been building a frank and trusting relationship, I decided to sharpen my questions. I knew what he was saying. That the police and justice officials – the arms of the law – had to do the work they are intended to do. That he as Prime Minister could not arrest people, prosecute and sentence them. But I expected him to be more real with me.

"Excuse me," I interrupted him, "Excuse me, but I understand what you are saying. The problem is the international community, people who do not know you and your trusted colleagues like _____ (I referred to the minister seated beside me) want to know whether you have taken action against the Attorney General, who you said was implicated and most people know it, and what about the two soldiers who had been arrested in the drug bust in the spring? And released. Are they back in custody? Is General Tagme supporting prosecution action against them? And it is an open secret

200

that the Minister of the Interior is implicated. What are you doing on these very specific things? Outsiders who want to help need to know."

He shifted in his seat, but before he could answer there was a knock at his door.

An assistant announced that the Minister of Justice was outside.

"Bring her in," he instructed, looking to me to check that I was comfortable with the invitation. Before I could reply, she was entering the room, being greeted and seated across from me.

The Prime Minster introduced me, briefly. And as we were mid-point in a very delicate exchange, I was reluctant to go on.

The PM and the Minister of Justice exchanged a few words in Portuguese. My interpreter explained she was asking who I was, and what my project was.

"Can I be open here?" I asked the PM, somewhat awkwardly, as the Minister of Justice settled into her chair.

"Yes, go ahead," he replied, "talk freely."

"Does she know about the strategy session?"

"No, she doesn't know about the session."

And I could see that the Minister, a very charming middle-aged woman who radiated professionalism and no nonsense, was now feeling unsettled in her chair. She had understood a bit of our exchange about this strategy session, about which she knew nothing, and she had no idea what my agenda was.

It was an awkward moment but I had heard very good things about her and I decided to be candid.

I briefed her, and told her who I was, and explained our project and how we had felt compelled to assist in some way with fighting drug trafficking. As I spoke I noticed out of the corner of my eye that a relaxed Prime Minster was now sitting comfortably back in his chair. I got the sense that there was no hurry here. That what I was doing was important to him, his government, and the country. He wanted the Minister of Justice to be fully on board.

As we talked I was very pleased to learn from her that General Tagme was working closely with the police to interdict drug shipments. I was happy to hear also that the two soldiers implicated in the drug bust had been transferred from military to civilian jurisdiction as they had committed a criminal act and it was not deemed a military matter. I was also pleased to learn that, having appointed this Minister of Justice as the Head of a new

Anti-Drug Trafficking Commission, the Prime Minister had thereby taken the first step within the time lines that the strategy session called for.

And when the Prime Minster asked me if I was impressed with the practical steps the Minister of Justice told me she planned to take, I answered "Yes, very."

The Minster of Justice and I agreed to work together, a friendly alliance having formed. Most of these meetings with a head of state typically take a half hour, sometimes 45 minutes or an hour at most. We talked and planned for two hours.

I did meet, in passing, with Tagme's chief of staff, someone who I believe is a professional soldier. We talked privately, at length. He assured me of Tagme's integrity. As he had done before, he placed the blame for instability at the feet of the politicians. He insisted that they thrived on stirring things up in an endless struggle for power. He regretted that the international community did not have better insight into Guinea-Bissau, to the motivation and conduct of actors both bad, and good.

We parted on friendly terms and I continued my slow walk, now much more comfortably, in the open daylight. I would be leaving in hours. I started to formulate my assessment of the situation in Guinea-Bissau.

It has become normal to doubt just about everything. I wish it were otherwise.

For all of the Prime Minister's apparent progress, I wondered if some kind of deal has been made.

Have the good guys, the PM and Tagme, cut a deal with the bad guys so that both can carry on? So they can play out the dance of good and evil. The yin and yang of political affairs based on human nature.

On reflection, I recognized that no one is completely without fault. And who has not wanted the Law to show them some discretion? At what point, however, does the centre fail to hold? I was not sure it could hold, in Guinea-Bissau. I developed a rather cryptic notion that Guinea-Bissau was a case of 'nasty pigs at a small trough'. Were the pigs nasty because the trough was so small? Was the trough so small because of the nasty pigs?

Either way, these actors and factors needed to be changed. It seemed unlikely, however, that the elites would stop using violence unless and until the country had enough prosperity in its own right and that was unlikely without a huge infusion of resources. The first priority would be to secure the country, to stabilize it once again. Then old wounds must be addressed. The culture of violence must be transformed to a culture of peace.

A Canadian documentary film crew once accompanied my team and me to Guinea-Bissau to film our work there. They wanted to focus on our healing and reconciliation efforts. We were at the Charles de Gaulle Airport in Paris, en route to Dakar. We would sleep there and the next day be on an aircraft to Guinea-Bissau.

"What is it that you do that is different from other peace workers?" the film director asked.

"Well," I thought, not used to describing my work in a nutshell, "I am a peace guerilla."

"What?" she replied curiously.

"Well, take a war guerilla," I began, "The war guerilla, obsessed with the goal of victory through force, acts strategically; using limited resources to greatest effect. He or she moves quickly to attack targets most likely to weaken the enemy in ways and at points consistent with achieving the long-term goal. A peace guerilla, on the other hand, targets violence."

She kept listening.

"The war guerilla may be invisible, working with collaborators in the general population. The war guerilla must show adaptability, flexibility, and have a sense of urgency when necessary. Be able to react with immediacy."

She nodded.

"The peace guerilla does the same. But for peace.

"And that means we have to get involved with those who use power abusively and transform their behaviour. That means dealing with their values. We have to move them so that they no longer see other people as alien and exploitable. It's not easy. But that's what we do."

"So you are a peace guerilla," she remarked.

"Yes, I am a peace guerilla."

Epilogue

During the very early morning of Monday, March 2, 2009 General Tagme Wai was assassinated by a bomb explosion in his office at the military headquarters. Four hours later President 'Nino' was assassinated, cut to pieces in a machete attack.

Nino's death has been described by some as a 'revenge killing', making it seem that this was a personal matter between the two men. And they had indeed had their differences, but I believe they had resolved those.

Others have said the murders were staged by drug lords.

Whatever the reason, I was devastated by the death of General Tagme.

He had told me that he was committed to reconciliation because he had, as a child, watched in his village as his father was tied to the back of a truck and dragged back and forth behind it until he was dead. Tagme told me that he believed if you take an eye for an eye, everyone ends up blind.

He had also told me that he felt very much alone. I had done what I could. My response was to keep reaching out to him. I tried to bring outside security forces into the country. Just weeks before the murders I had appealed to the Secretary-General of the UN to send a small security force to Guinea-Bissau immediately. And we were also trying to arrange for security experts from the Kofi Annan Centre in Ghana to go to Guinea-Bissau to support General Tagme.

I recall hugging General Tagme the last time I left him and saying how I looked forward to seeing him again. He had replied, "That's if I am still alive."

Following these two horrific murders, we placed calls to several of our contacts both inside and outside the country. We worked to establish more clearly exactly what had happened, and why. As more information became available we were becoming increasingly disappointed to learn that the information and views collected essentially re-affirmed my impressions and the conclusions I had drawn on my first trip to Guinea-Bissau. That is, political violence in Guinea-Bissau is fundamentally the product of elite political actors failing to reconcile differences through dialogue and choosing violence to achieve their objectives, compounded now by the influence of drug trafficking. These problems are exacerbated in a country with little to no capacity to enforce the law, and by an extremely weak economy.

General Tagme and I had been allies. I had gone to bat for him in the corridors of power; with the UN, the British, and other countries interested in Guinea-Bissau. One time we had met in passing at the Bissau airport. Seated at his leisure on a chair under a tree at the tarmac's edge, he was surrounded by a large entourage of senior-ranking military officers and onlookers. He was smoking a pipe and I recognized that it was the pipe Jeff had given him on a prior visit. A token of respect for the great General. And as I approached him he noticed me and rose excitedly. He reached his hand out to me and, looking about to his officers, he remarked, "This is my friend." That was the only time he had ever spoken English and I knew we were friends.

So, while I had formulated a professional opinion of the causes and circumstances and consequences of his death, for weeks I was depressed. And I wondered once again, can violence be prevented? Are the Crimea, Bosnia-Herzegovina, and Sudan better off for the efforts of people like me who devote themselves to peace work?

Will Guinea-Bissau continue to implode, becoming a fully failed state vulnerable to predators like drug lords, or a home for terrorists? Or will it stabilize and prosper one day?

I say violence is the abusive use of power. Those who use power abusively or condone such use do so on the basis of the values they hold. So the peace guerilla really works on the most fundamental of human tasks, transforming values. It is a perennial task, and I believe it is well worth the effort when it allows innocent people to live with a sense of security and with hope for the future.

LaVergne, TN USA
08 July 2010
188838LV00001B/52/P